ASSESSMENT
OF
ORGANIZATIONAL
EFFECTIVENESS

Issues, Analysis,
and Readings

ASSESSMENT OF ORGANIZATIONAL EFFECTIVENESS

Issues, Analysis, and Readings

Jaisingh Ghorpade
San Diego State College

GOODYEAR PUBLISHING COMPANY, INC.
Pacific Palisades, California

39894

© Copyright 1971 by
GOODYEAR PUBLISHING COMPANY, INC.
Pacific Palisades, California

Library of Congress Catalog Card Number: 71-131416

ISBN   0-87620-081-1

Y-0811-3

Current printing (last number):
10   9   8   7   6   5   4   3   2   1

Printed in the United States of America

To Helen

ACKNOWLEDGMENTS

The topic of ORGANIZATIONAL EFFECTIVENESS has occupied my interest for many years. My preliminary attempts to study this field were in the form of graduate research projects at UCLA. Unlike many other projects which I completed at UCLA, and which proved in retrospect to be "hurdles" to get through particular courses, organizational effectiveness turned out to be both a challenging field and a sustaining interest. It opened many vistas and provided a vantage point from which I could approach the broader field of organization and management theory.

This book is an expression of my long-term and on-going interest in the field of organizational effectiveness. I, therefore, have many people to thank for my being able to contribute it. I would like to express my gratitude to the many faculty members of UCLA who stimulated my interest and encouraged me to pursue it. My special thanks in this respect to Professors Robert Tannenbaum, the late Irving Weschler, Fred Massarik, Harold Kassarjian, and William McWhinney of the Graduate School of Business Administration. I am grateful to Professors Melville Dalton (sociology) and William Lessa (anthropology) for introducing and guiding me through the sociological and anthropological literature pertinent to organization and management theory. Professor Dalton is also kind enough to have read and commented upon my contribution on methodology, which is included as the last part of this book. I am grateful to him for his valuable suggestions and criticism.

My writing of this book greatly benefited from discussions and debate with many of my colleagues at San Diego State College. My special thanks to Professors Thomas Atchison, David Belcher and Lynn Peters. Professor Atchison read the preliminary draft of this manuscript and offered many valuable comments which I gratefully acknowledge.

Finally, I would like to thank the various authors and publishers for permitting their materials to be included in this reader.

CONTENTS

II

Criteria
of Organizational
Effectiveness 83

III

Review of Recent
Studies on
Organizational Effectiveness 171

IV

Methodology 207

ASSESSMENT
OF
ORGANIZATIONAL
EFFECTIVENESS

Issues, Analysis,
and Readings

INTRODUCTION

DURING THE PAST FEW YEARS, the topic of organizational effectiveness has received considerable attention from social scientists. This topic has been the subject of at least two Ph.D. dissertations (Yuchtman, 1966; Ghorpade, 1968), a book (Price, 1968), and numerous articles and monographs by scholars from a variety of social science disciplines. (For reviews on major writings pertaining to organizational effectiveness, see Katz and Kahn, 1966: 149–170; Price, 1968; and Ghorpade, 1970.) Additionally, organizational effectiveness has been a focus of investigation of the staffs of three bureaus of research and was the subject of two sessions of The Executive Study Conference published in book form by the Educational Testing Service in 1969. (On-going research on organizational effectiveness is being sponsored by the Foundation for Research on Human Behavior, University of Michigan; Bureau of Business Research, Ohio State University; and Industrial Relations Center, University of Minnesota.)

The current popularity of organizational effectiveness among social scientists can be traced to two main factors. First, interest in this topic has been heightened by a growing appreciation of the vital role played by organizations in the lives of modern man. As things stand, man has become more or less completely dependent upon organizations of various types for the satisfaction of his varied needs (Etzioni, 1964:1). Understanding of the issues involved in the assessment of the effectiveness of organizations, therefore, is of vital importance for society at large. Second, current interest in organizational effectiveness can be traced partly to the central nature of this topic to the field of organization theory. Discussions pertaining to the assessment of effectiveness of organizations invariably lead to head-on confrontations with key definitional, conceptual, and methodological issues pertinent to the analysis and study of organizations. Organizational effectiveness thus provides a valuable focal point for theoretical integration of the emerging but highly diversified field of organizational theory. (For an example of how organizational effectiveness can be used as a focal point for integration of organization theory, see Price, 1968.)

The recent spurt of writings and research pertaining to organizational effectiveness has not as yet resulted in the formulation of a universally acceptable scheme or methodology for the assessment of effectiveness of organizations. In fact, the concept of organizational effectiveness is surrounded by a great deal of controversy and debate. Organization theorists have advocated a perplexing variety of conceptual schemes, analytical points of departure,

1

and models for approaching the study of effectiveness. Furthermore, the literature abounds with discussions about a multitude of criteria of effectiveness
ranging from "hard" productivity and efficiency measures to "soft" behavioral
factors such as morale, organizational flexibility, and internal strain (Katz and
Kahn, 1966:149; Ghorpade, 1970; Seashore, 1965).

The presence of controversy surrounding the concept of organizational
effectiveness presents numerous problems for practitioners as well as scholars
involved in assessing the performance of formal organizations. Due to the lack
of a firm analytical base and unavailability of universally acceptable criteria
of organizational effectiveness, many studies have gotten bogged down or
have arrived at meaningless and even dubious findings (Katz and Kahn,
1966:149–150).

The purpose of this book is to contribute towards the clarification and
resolution of the basic issues involved in the study of organizational effectiveness. Such an attempt at this stage should provide a valuable starting point
for the codification and synthesis of recent research and writings dealing with
this highly important and timely topic.

The Research Task

Research concerned with the assessment of the effectiveness of organizations has to contend with several interrelated issues and problems. A brief
exposition and discussion of these at this point should serve the dual purpose
of providing an overview of the research task while simultaneously assisting
in the delineation of the scope and outline of this book.

At the most general level, a major task facing the researcher in this area
involves the formulation of a conceptual scheme for approaching the study
of organizational effectiveness. The types of questions which need to be
answered in this case are: What exactly is an organization? What is the
composition of its internal structure and its relationships with other organizations? Should the organization as a whole be the focus of the study or should
attention be directed at its component parts? What model should be used in
designing the investigation?

Since the term "effective" implies successful in terms of given standards,
a second task facing the researcher involves choosing meaningful criteria of
organizational effectiveness. The type of questions which need to be answered
in this regard are: What are the goals, if any, of the organization? What part
should organizational goals play in the investigation? Should effectiveness
criteria reflect short-term success or should they measure long-term "health"
and survival potential of the organization? What frame of reference should be
utilized in selecting criteria of effectiveness—owner's, workers', customers',
organizational, society at large, or some other? It may be mentioned that
the task of criteria selection is inextricably related to the underlying conceptualization of organization used by the investigator.

The third major task involved in the study of organizational effectiveness involves the analysis of dynamics underlying organizational functioning—or the study of "process." The types of questions which need to be considered in this respect are: What are the parts of the system? What is the nature of the relationship of the parts to the whole and to the dimensions being investigated? Which parts of the organization are functional and which are dysfunctional in terms of the successful functioning of the organization? What are the forces which influence organizational success or failure in terms of the criteria selected for the investigation? The nature of concern over process variables is determined largely by selected criteria which act as the dependent variables; the research task involves isolating and evaluating the independent and/or intervening variables connected to the chosen criteria of effectiveness. (For a brief discussion of dependent, intervening, and independent variables in social research, see Krech, Crutchfield and Ballachey, 1962:456–458.)

A fourth problem facing the researcher studying organizational effectiveness involves the designing of a methodology for conducting the investigation. This task leads to consideration of the following types of questions: What constitutes data in a study dealing with organizational effectiveness? Should the research be conducted in the form of an experimental or nonexperimental study design? What techniques, tools and methods should be used in gathering and analyzing data pertinent to organizational functioning and effectiveness?

The above discussion has outlined four major issues which comprise the task of studying organizational effectiveness. It needs to be recognized at the outset that none of these issues are mutually exclusive; discussions of any one of these issues invariably get intertwined with discussions about the others. Thus, it is not possible to decide upon a list of criteria of effectiveness without reference to the broad conceptualization about organization which has guided the investigation. In designing a study on organizational effectiveness, the four issues noted above need to be tackled as a whole; they have been separated here purely for the sake of discussion and analysis.

Organization of the Book

This book is divided into four parts. Part I tackles the broad theoretical and conceptual issues involved in approaching a study of organizational effectiveness. Part II is concerned with criteria of organizational effectiveness. Part III discusses some recent studies on organizational effectiveness. Part IV deals with some methodological considerations in studying effectiveness of organizations.

Readings are provided in each of the four parts of this book. The purpose of these readings is largely to elaborate upon and to exemplify the points raised in the discussion pertaining to the issues tackled in these parts.

Lists of additional readings are provided at the end of each of the four parts; in addition, a List of References Cited is included in an appendix at the back of the book. Some of the key works included in the former lists are discussed and commented upon. The references provided in these lists along with the accompanying commentary should prove to be valuable for those desirous of pursuing further the issues discussed in each of the parts. Bibliographical references in the introductory material to the book and each part are to the Appendix, while references in the "Additional Readings" sections are to the immediately following bibliographies.

As is evident from the outline of the book presented above, the study of organizational dynamics or process does not occupy a separate part or concern of this book. This omission is due to the state of the field at this point. A basic requirement for the study of "process" in this context is a firm conceptualization and statement of criteria of organizational effectiveness. Since this is lacking, is was felt that a separate discussion of process would be premature at this stage of development of organization theory. This deficiency is partly remedied, however, by indirect discussion of process issues in the various introductions to each of the parts and by an examination of some key studies on organizational effectiveness in Part III.

THEORETICAL CONSIDERATIONS IN STUDYING ORGANIZATIONAL EFFECTIVENESS

IN EVERY SCIENTIFIC DISCIPLINE, theory and empirical research tend to go hand in hand. A theoretical framework composed of a network of interrelated concepts or body of knowledge can act as a valuable tool for formulation of research designs and for suggesting fruitful lines of investigation. Empirical investigations, on the other hand, provide the basis for crystalizing, modifying, and enlarging the substantive base of theory (Blau and Scott, 1962:8–9).

The researcher undertaking a study of organizational effectiveness is faced with two major hurdles or barriers at the broad theoretical and conceptual level. First, there does not exist a body of substantive knowledge or findings based upon hard scientific evidence about the functioning of organizations. It is a sad but commonly accepted fact that although organizations have existed since the beginning of human history, little is known about their nature and functioning. (Attempts to codify and synthesize available knowledge on organizations have been made by Berelson and Steiner, 1962:363–381; Price, 1968; and J. D. Thompson, 1967.) Second, there does not exist a universally accepted theoretical framework for approaching the study of organizations. As things stand, theory dealing with organizations (or the emerging of knowledge known variously as organization theory, bureaucracy theory, organizational behavior or management theory) is in a very formative stage. The following statement by Robert Merton (1957:9) about the state of sociological theory applies equally well to theory dealing with organizations:

> . . . one must admit that a large part of what is now called sociological theory consists of general orientations toward data, suggesting types of variables which need somehow to be taken into account, rather than clear, verifiable statements of relationships between specified variables. We have many concepts but few confirmed theories; many points of view, but few theorems; many "approaches," but few arrivals.

Numerous attempts have been made in recent years to codify and to synthesize theoretical writings pertaining to organizations. The readings presented in this part are three of the most authoritative statements on this topic. Alvin Gouldner presents an overview of the historical growth and development of organization theory. He states that the field of organization theory has been dominated historically by two models of organizational analysis: the rational system model and the natural system model. Of these two models, the rational system model had a greater impact upon early theorizing and research on organizations. The natural system model is more recent in origin and has developed partly in the course of polemics against the rational system model. While both models have much to offer the student of organizations, neither model in its pure form is complete in itself. The task of the organization theorists is to synthesize these two models and to develop a more powerful model; Gouldner offers some guidelines for synthesizing the two models.

Gouldner's analysis of the historical development of organization theory has been widely accepted. It has been the basis for many commentaries and research on organizations (Burns, 1966; Thompson, J. D., 1967).

Etzioni's article follows the same general theme as that of Gouldner's article discussed above. Etzioni's "goal model" is the result of an underlying conception of organization as a rational instrument or machine. Those using this model tend to rely logically upon organizational goals in assessing effectiveness. Alternately, conception of organization as a social system leads to a consideration of the organization's functional requirements in studying effectiveness. The goal model and the systems model of effectiveness are carefully evaluated by Etzioni. Additionally, Etzioni's article provides a valuable review of some recent literature on organizational analysis, as well as a penetrating analysis of field studies on hospitals and prisons and of the works of Michels, Lipset, Selznick, Georgoplous and others. Also, he introduces two subtypes of the systems model (survival model and effectiveness model) and provides an evaluation of structural-functional analysis as it has evolved and has been applied in organizational studies.

The work by Katz and Kahn is Chapter 6 of their recent book entitled *The Social Psychology of Organizations* (1966). In terms of the aims of this book, this work has several notable features. To begin with, the authors undertake a discussion of the concept of organizational effectiveness from the currently popular "open-systems" model or approach to organizations. Also, they attempt to link in abstract terms the notion of efficiency with organizational effectiveness. Furthermore, the authors raise some important questions about the availability of alternative frames of reference in studying organizational effectiveness.

ORGANIZATIONAL ANALYSIS

Alvin W. Gouldner

For the past several decades, various commentators have viewed with increasing alarm the growth of large-scale organizations, the impending bureaucratization of the world, and the rise of the "organization man." Whether for good or for evil, there is little doubt that the spread of the complex, rational organization is one of the characteristics of modern society, distinguishing it from earlier feudal forms.

Immediately upon the heels of the French Revolution, a few thinkers clearly grasped the significance of the modern organization and gave it a special place in the history of sociology. Both sociology and organizational analysis were early formulated in the work of Henri Saint-Simon.[1] Saint-Simon was probably the first to note the rise of modern organizational patterns, identify some of their distinctive features, and insist upon their prime significance for the emerging society. Saint-Simon argued that, in the society of the future, administrative methods would no longer entail

From Chapter 18 of *Sociology Today,* edited by Robert K. Merton, Leonard Broom, and Leonard S. Cottrell, Jr., © 1959 by Basic Books, Inc., Publishers, New York.

coercion or force, and the administrator's authority would no longer be based upon birth or heredity privilege. The authority of the modern administrator, he held, would rest upon his possession of scientific skills and "positive" knowledge.

Saint-Simon also maintained that there was a close connection between the emergence of modern science, or the professions which grew up around it, and the development of cosmopolitanism. He expected the new professions to be cosmopolitan in their orientation, in that their occupant's loyalties would cut across localistic or national groups. Whatever the extravagances of his plan for social reorganization, Saint-Simon saw with a sure intuition that the ground rules of modern society had been deeply altered and that the deliberately conceived and planned organization was to play a new role in the world.

The transition to Saint-Simon's disciple, August Comte, was a fateful one, both for sociology and for organizational analysis. Comte was much less a relativist than Saint-Simon and lacked his mentor's sensitivity to the novel forms of social organization that were emerging. Consequently, in the program which Comte formulated for modern sociology, the significance of the modern organization was unfortunately obscured. Although Comte believed that planned organization should be used in the event of serious threats to the solidarity of society, his deepest conviction was that the "final order which arises spontaneously is always superior to that which human combination had, by anticipation, constructed."[2] The most eulogistic term in Comte's vocabulary was "spontaneous." In Comte's system, therefore, the "natural" and spontaneous maintenance of social order is counterposed invidiously to planned political, legal, or constitutional organization.

It was not until Max Weber formulated his theory of bureaucracy that the distinctive rational-legal characteristics of the modern organization were systematically explored and Saint-Simon's earlier vision was superseded by scholarly codification. What seems, surprisingly, to have been neglected is the convergence between Saint-Simon and Weber in their views concerning the nature of modern organizations and the basic role in them of rationality, science, and technical experts. Both men stressed the significance of expertise and scientific knowledge for the modern organization, and both also perceived the ways in which these new organizations profoundly affected the character of modern society as a whole.

Despite these similarities, there are nevertheless important differences between Weber's work on bureaucracy and that of his predecessor. Saint-Simon viewed modern organization as a liberating force, emancipating men from the yoke of tradition and heightening productivity and efficiency. Although Weber acknowledged the efficiency of bureaucracy, he feared that it spelled the destruction of individual personality and subjected it to a dehumanizing regimentation.[3] Moreover, Weber saw more clearly than Saint-Simon and the early positivists that authority in the modern organization cannot rest on science and technology alone. He regarded bureaucracy as a Janus-faced organization. He agreed that it was, on the one side, a form of administration based on knowledge and expertise. However, he also insisted that authority in the modern organization is, in some measure, always dependent upon nonrational elements. Weber held that bureaucracies require some degree of obedience as an end in itself; obedience is due a superior, not merely because of his technical knowledge, but also because of the office he occupies.

Weber did not, however, develop both sides of his theory of bureaucracy equally. Because of his concern with the distinctive features of the modern organization (which derives from his use of ideal type concepts), he tended to neglect bureaucratic authority which rests upon nonrational considerations. Thus his work focuses on bureaucracy primarily as a planned and rational form of administration and is consequently discontinuous with Comte's interest in the spontaneous mechanisms in groups.[4]

Although Weber's view of bureaucracy as involving two sources of authority—authority based on sheer incumbence in office and authority based on expertise—was never fully developed theoretically, it is nonetheless an empirically astute observation. For the modern bureaucracy seems indeed to be characterized by this split in its mode of viewing and legitimating authority.

Among the issues to which this line of analysis gives rise is the question of the varying conditions conducive to these different modes of authority. In a recent study,[5] I have taken this problem as my central point of departure, presenting the view that bureaucracy is not a single, homogeneous entity but that there are two types of bureaucracy, the representative bureaucracy and the punishment-centered bureaucracy. The representative bureaucracy is, in part, characterized by authority based upon knowledge and expertise. It also entails collaborative or bilateral initiation of the organizational rules by the parties involved; the rules are justified by the participants on the ground that they are means to desired ends, and persuasion and education are used to obtain compliance with them. The punishment-centered bureaucracy is characterized by authority based on incumbency in office and by the unilateral initiation of organization rules which are enforced through punishments.[6]

The punishment-centered bureaucracy arises "partly because of a dissensus in ends; that is, obedience would tend to be stressed as an end in itself, and authority tends to be legitimated in terms of incumbency in office, when subordinates are ordered to do things divergent from their own ends." This, in effect, expresses a Comteian concern with shared moral beliefs as a basis of group cohesion and solidarity. Moreover, and again in a Comteian manner, this study suggests that one of the latent functions of bureaucratic rules is to provide a managerial indulgency, in the form of withholding application of the rules, which reinforces patterns of informal cooperation and spontaneous reciprocities among those involved. The study notes that "by a strange paradox, formal rules gave supervisors something with which they could 'bargain' in order to secure informal cooperation from workers." This effort to conjoin Comte's focus on spontaneous and informal patterns of organization with Weber's emphasis on rationally planned formal organization was intended primarily to call attention to a major problem of organizational analysis, rather than to provide a definitive solution to it.

The nature of the problem may be summarized as follows: During the historical development of organizational analysis, two distinct approaches to the study of complex organizations have emerged in the work of sociologists. One of these, best exemplified by the work of Max Weber, is a conception of the organization in terms of a "rational" model. The other, which can be termed the "natural-system" model, ultimately derives from Comte, was later reinforced by Robert Michels, and is now best exemplified in the work of Philip Selznick and Talcott Parsons.

One of the central problems of organizational analysis is to reconcile the divergent implications of these two models and to synthesize a new and more powerful model. In the following pages, I shall attempt to clarify some of the advantages and limitations of each of these models. I shall also discuss certain organizational problems for which I believe a synthesized model would provide a more adequate tool of analysis. Before doing so, however, I shall first attempt to state briefly some of the assumptions involved in the rational and natural-system models.

The Rational Model of Organizational Analysis

In the rational model, the organization is conceived as an "instrument" —that is, a rationally conceived means of the realization of expressly announced group goals. Its structures are understood as tools deliberately established for the efficient realization of these group purposes. Organizational behavior is thus viewed as consciously and rationally administered, and changes in organizational patterns are viewed as planned devices to improve the level of efficiency. The rational model assumes that decisions are made on the basis of a rational survey of the situation, utilizing certified knowledge, with a deliberate orientation to an expressly codified legal apparatus. The focus is, therefore, on the legally prescribed structures—i.e., the formally "blueprinted" patterns—since these are more largely subject to deliberate inspection and rational manipulation.

This model takes account of departures from rationality but often tends to assume that these departures derive from random mistakes, due to ignorance or error in calculation. Fundamentally, the rational model implies a "mechanical" model, in that it views the organization as a structure of manipulable parts, each of which is separately modifiable with a view to enhancing the efficiency of the whole. Individual organizational elements are seen as subject to successful and planned modification, enactable by deliberate decision. The long-range development of the organization as a whole is also regarded as subject to planned control and as capable of being brought into increasing conformity with explicitly held plans and goals.

The Natural-System Model of Organizational Analysis

The natural-system model regards the organization as a "natural whole," or system. The realization of the goals of the system as a whole is but one of several important points to which the organization is oriented. Its component structures are seen as emergent institutions, which can be understood only in relation to the diverse needs of the total system. The organization, according to this model, strives to survive and to maintain its equilibrium, and this striving may persist even after its explicitly held goals have been successfully attained. This strain toward survival may even on occasion lead to the neglect or distortion of the organization's goals. Whatever the plans of their creators, organizations, say the natural-system theorists, become ends in themselves and possess their own distinctive needs which have to be satisfied. Once established, organizations tend to generate new ends which constrain subsequent decisions and limit the manner in which the nominal group goals can be pursued.

Organizational structures are viewed as spontaneously and homeostatically maintained. Changes in organizational patterns are considered the results of cumulative, unplanned, adaptive responses to threats to the equilibrium of the system as a whole. Responses to problems are thought of as taking the form of crescively developed defense mechanisms and as being importantly shaped by shared values which are deeply internalized in the members. The empirical focus is thus directed to the spontaneously emergent and normatively sanctioned structures in the organization.

The focus is not on deviations from rationality but, rather, on disruptions of organizational equilibrium, and particularly on the mechanisms by which equilibrium is homeostatically maintained. When deviations from planned purposes are considered, they are viewed not so much as due to ignorance or error but as arising from constraints imposed by the existent social structure. In given situations, the ignorance of certain participants may not be considered injurious but functional to the maintenance of the system's equilibrium.

The natural-system model is typically based upon an underlying "organismic" model which stresses the interdependence of the component parts. Planned changes are therefore expected to have ramifying consequences for the whole organizational system. When, as frequently happens, these consequences are unanticipated, they are usually seen as divergent from, and not as supportive of, the planner's intentions. Natural-system theorists tend to regard the organization as a whole as organically "growing," with a "natural history" of its own which is planfully modifiable only at great peril, if at all. Long-range organizational development is thus regarded as an evolution, conforming to "natural laws" rather than to the planner's designs.

The Two Models Compared

Needless to say, these two models are ideal types in the sense that few modern sociologists studying organizations adopt one to the complete exclusion of the other. Nevertheless, as we have mentioned previously, some sociologists tend to stress one model more than the other.

Each of these models has certain characteristic strengths and weaknesses. The rational model, for example, has the indisputable merit of focusing attention on some of the very patterns which distinguish the modern organization, particularly its rationality. At the same time, however, it tends to neglect the manner in which those patterns which the modern organization shares with "natural" groups may also effect behavior within them. The fact is, of course, that the distinguishing characteristics of a bureaucratic organization are not its only characteristics; systematic attention must also be directed to those features of modern organizations, such as the need for loyalty, which they have in common with other types of groups.

The natural-system model, on the other hand, has the merit of focusing attention on the spontaneous and unplanned (that is, "informal") patterns of belief and interaction that arise even within the rationally planned organization. Often, however, the natural-system model tends to neglect the distinctively rational features of the modern organization.

Sometimes both of these models are used in organizational analysis in an eclectic manner; one part of the organization is analyzed in terms of the rational model and another part in terms of the natural-system model. Studies using this approach tend to present the organization as two distinctive parts, running eternally on parallel tracks; many of them fail to work out the manner in which the rational and informal patterns merge into and influence each other. For example, in the Western Electric studies, Roethlisberger and Dickson distinguished between the logics of cost and efficiency, on the one hand, and the logic of sentiment, on the other. They maintain that the former characterizes managerial elites, whereas the latter is distinctive of employee or worker echelons.[7] Warner and Low's study of industrial conflict in Yankee City[8] makes a similar point. These authors regard the managerial group as dominated by the aim of producing "at the lowest possible cost and highest profit," and maintain that advancement is given primarily to those who contribute more to the "efficiency of production." As a result of this dichotomy between the rational and the natural-system models, the nonrational, traditionalistic orientations of management personnel have been obscured, and informal organization tends to be examined primarily among lower ranking personnel. Conversely, the rationalistic orientations of lower echelons, at least with respect to their own ends, tends to be treated as a façade for their own underlying nonrational needs.

Applied Social Science and Organizational Analysis

The statement that the natural-system model neglects the distinctive features of the modern organization means, above all, that it tends to minimize the significance of rationally organized structures and patterns of planned adaptation. It tends, for example, to overlook the full implications of the fact that the modern organization meets its own peculiar needs, as well as those which it shares with all groups, in certain distinctive ways. To illustrate: Modern organizations systematically evaluate the degree to which their policies are effective; they rationally appraise the relative effectiveness of the various departments within the organization; they conduct market researches and public-opinion studies which keep them in touch with their suppliers and outlets; they select new recruits and evaluate group members through various kinds of psychological tests; they defend policies with the use of research; they wage war against competitors with facts and figures and rationally documented argumentation; and they prepare for unforeseeable contingencies by briefing their administrators with digests of scientifically accumulated "background information." Indeed, these administrators may stake their very authority on what they know or on what knowledge they can purchase. All this is too well known to require further elaboration. There is a question, however, whether its full significance has been appreciated and theoretically assimilated by those using the natural-system model.

One pattern of particular interest to sociologists deserves to be stressed in this connection. In the modern organization, behavioral science has become a kind of working equivalent for, or supplement to, the profit and loss statement; various types of social research have supplanted the book-keeper's ledgers as bases of rational decision in cases in which pecuniary consequences cannot be calculated. The very rationality of the modern organization has made it increasingly dependent upon the kinds of information that can be supplied by operations or market researchers, opinion pollsters, industrial sociologists, morale surveyors, and group dynamicists.

Although these newer patterns require only a small part of the organization's budget, they have substantial theoretical implications for organizational analysis. For applied social science has, in effect, become one of the planned functional substitutes for the spontaneous adaptive mechanisms by means of which the rational organization responds to external threats, reduces internal disruptions, and controls various forms of social deviance. As such, it merits a place in the theoretical models and the empirical researches of organizational analysts. So far, however, organizational analysts have neglected to include in their researches a systematic study of the uses made of applied social science in the modern organization.

The neglect of applied social science within the organization, as an object of analysis and research, is, however, simply a special instance of a larger lacuna in organizational analysis. Modern organizational analysis by sociologists is overpreoccupied with the spontaneous and unplanned responses which organizations make to stress, and too little concerned with patterns of planned and rational administration. Only a few sociologists, notably Peter Blau, whose study of the use of statistical techniques of personnel rating is a trail-blazing research,[9] have investigated the latter area. Nonetheless, many of the current studies guided by the natural-system model are still fixated on the Comteian level.

In general, the natural-system model tends to induce neglect of the rational structures characterizing the modern organization, of the forces contributing to their growth, as well as of the distinctive ways in which they are maintained. It tends to take as given rather than as problematic such distinctive features of the modern organization as its complex division of labor, its legally formalized codes, its reliance upon professional and technical experts, its utilization of systematic bodies of knowledge, and its rationalistic orientation.

Use of the natural-system model tends to focus the analyst's concern on the forces that undermine the organization's impersonal principles and subvert its formal ends to "narrower" interests, rather than on those that sustain these and bolster the distinctively bureaucratic structures. It tends to lead to a focus on the characteristics that all occupations share, rather than on the distinctive features of the modern professional expert, who utilizes a body of systematized information. Nonetheless, the very rationality of the modern organization, as well as its other typical characteristics, varies in degree, and this very variation is itself in need of explanation.

The natural-system model, which developed in the course of polemics against the rational model, tends to minimize the role of rationality in human affairs and to counterstress the way in which organizational behavior is affected by nonrational norms. Theorists who use this model have typically emphasized the inherent vulnerability of rationally planned action, particularly action directed toward what might be termed "liberal" goals. From its Comteian inceptions, the natural-system model has been infused with a conservative and antiliberal metaphysical pathos. In Michels' work this was expressed by an emphasis on the organizational constraints that inherently thwart democratic aspirations. But, characteristically, the natural-system theorists have tended to neglect study of the organizational constraints that conduce to the *realization* of democratic values. It is only recently that this line of analysis has been systematically developed by such organizational analysts as Lipset, Trow, and Coleman.[10]

Manifest and Latent Patterns

There is no doubt, however, that the focus of the natural-system model on the spontaneous mechanisms common to all groups has enabled it to make its most important contribution to the study of organizations. This focus has facilitated the discovery and analysis of the so-called informal organization, which tends to be obscured by the rational model. Yet there is a noteworthy ambiguity in the natural-system model concerning the meaning of "informal organization." In other words, although it is clear that the natural-system model directs attention beyond and away from the formally constituted organizational system, there remains a question concerning what it is that the model directs attention toward.

The notion of informal organization is a residual or cafeteria concept of diverse and sprawling contents. Some informal patterns are organizationally unprescribed culture structures—that is, patterns of belief and sentiment; for example the belief that one should not be a "rate buster." Other informal patterns are organizationally unprescribed social structures; e.g., the cliques that develop among those working near one another. Further, although the term "informal group" is sometimes used to refer to a primary relation, not all informal patterns involve friendly intimacy and closeness. Some may entail personal enmities, feuds, and conflicts.

Informal patterns vary in other significant ways. Some are patterns prescribed by the traditional values in the larger society which are recognized as relevant within the organization; for example, the "no squealing" rules or the special deference which a supervisor may give to an elderly worker. Other informal patterns are prescribed only by the values traditional to a particular organization; for example, the tendency of professors on some campuses to address or refer to one another as "Mr."

Still other informal patterns are not prescribed by any traditional values, either in the larger society or in the particular organization, but largely derive from the competition or conflict for scarce information or goods; for example, the salesman's "personal following," or the congregation of males around their employer's private secretary. It is precisely this last type of informal pattern, which is not normatively prescribed, that characteristically tends to be neglected in the work of the natural-system theorists. Neglect of this pattern accounts in part for the fact that little systematic research has been done on the effects of machinery and office equipment, so characteristic of the modern organization, on social relations within it.

Some of the distinctive characteristics of the modern organization generate peculiar hazards for organizational analysis. In particular, the specialized roles within the organization, having such a high visibility, tend to become a focus of research, and analysis thus tends to become confined to these prescribed and institutionalized roles. This is a hazard to which both the rational and the natural-system models are susceptible, although not equally so. The natural-system theorists, somewhat more astute about this danger, have been concerned about the ways in which the "social" characteristics of personnel may shape organizational policy and behavior. Selznick's study of the TVA is an excellent example of this. Other studies have analyzed the manner in which the ethnic or religious origins of personnel affect their chances of mobility and the allocation of power within the organization.[11] As yet, however, organizational analysts have not incorporated in their theoretical models a systematic concern with the way in which the diverse social identities that people bring into the organization affect organizational behavior.

It is obvious that all people in organizations have a variety of "latent social identities"[12]—that is, identities which are not culturally prescribed as relevant to or within rational organizations—and that these do intrude upon and influence organizational behavior in interesting ways. For example, there is usually something occurring between people of opposite sexes, even though this is prescribed neither by the organization's official rules nor by the societal values deemed appropriate for that setting.[13] Yet many sociologists who study factories, offices, schools, or mental hospitals take little note of the fact that the organizational role-players invariably have a gender around which is built a latent social identity. One does not have to be a Freudian to insist that sex makes a difference, even for organizational behavior. (It should be noted that there is no analytic distinction between giving attention to the ways in which latent ethnic or religious identities affect organizational behavior and examining the implications of latent sexual identities for organizational patterns.)

The point, then, is that there is a need to distinguish systematically between those social identities of organization members which are consensually regarded as relevant or legitimate in that setting, and those identities which are defined as irrelevant or inappropriate to consider in that context. The manner in which both the manifest and the *latent* social identities shape organizational behavior requires more attention. Study of latent identities and roles within organizations promises to be fruitful because, among other reasons, it provides a lever for approaching problems of organizational tension. For the pressure of the latent roles on the manifest or formal roles within organizations is a persistent source of strain on the equilibrium of every organization.

Organizational Tensions

In the following section I want to outline briefly some of the recurrent problems found within the modern organization—particularly those that seem to derive, in part at least, from the interaction of (1) the distinctive traits of the organization as a rational system of administration and (2) the more common needs of the organization as a spontaneously developed social system. My objective is to document the need for a synthesis and reconciliation of the rational and natural-system models. Among these problems are the following:

1. The authority of the modern administrator is characteristically legitimated on the basis of his specialized expertise; that is, administrators are regarded as proper incumbents of office on the basis of what they know about the organization or their professional skills, rather than whom they know. Problems arise, however, when administrators exert control over subordinates whose technical specialties or organizational experience differ from their own. For example, the orders and authority of a plant manager whose experience has been in electronics may be regarded as dubious and may be resisted when it is directed toward subordinates who are expert in chemistry or mechanical engineering. In the modern organization, with its highly specialized division of labor, administrators may know little or nothing of the diverse specializations under their command. How, then, can their authority be legitimated in terms of their specialized knowledge or experience?

There are, of course, various solutions to this problem. One is that, even in highly rational and technically specialized organizations, authority still tends in some measure to be legitimated on strictly legal grounds. That is, those who hold authority are endowed with a measure of imperative control and are authorized to command on the basis of their sheer incumbency in office. Consequently, there are two fundamentally different criteria for the legitimation of authority—authority based on technical knowledge and experience, and authority based on incumbency in office—simultaneously operating in the same organization. One of the deepest tensions in modern organization, often expressed as a conflict between the line and staff groups,[14] derives from the divergence of these two bases of authority.

2. Another solution to the problem of exercising authority over unfamiliar specializations involves a self-imposed limitation on the criteria for inspecting and evaluating the performance of subordinates. The superior relinquishes control over the technical procedures which his subordinate uses, presumably giving the subordinate responsibility for these, and focuses instead on the subordinate's success or failure in realizing organizational goals. In short, it is results that count from the superior's standpoint. From the subordinate's standpoint, however, it is not merely results that count but also conformity with what his professional peers commonly regard as the proper technical procedures. Such conformity is a vital condition of the expert's good standing in his professional community and a significant component of his self-image as a competent professional. Consequently, there is usually some tension in the modern organization between the superior's pressure for results and the subordinate expert's insistence on proper technical procedure. This would seem to be an aspect of what Hughes has referred to as the conflict between "client emergency" and "professional routine."[15]

3. A third solution to the problem of legitimating authority over unfamiliar specializations is to define administration as a distinct field in itself, specializing in problems of "human relations." At this level, however, the problem still remains organizationally taxing, since so many line executives regard themselves as "born" experts in human relations. Pressure is therefore exerted to recruit individuals who have specialized training, and hence legitimate credentials, for human-relations work and administration.

Partly for this reason, new fields of administration and management have developed and acquired a strong infusion of social-science skills and theories. Social science, among other relevant disciplines, tends to serve increasingly as a legitimation for the authority of administrators in the modern organization.[16] To this extent, then, events are confirming the prophecy of Saint-Simon and other early positivists that the social sciences, as well as the physical sciences, would provide a new pillar of authority in the modern world. This tendency, however, brings internal repercussions in the organization, involving conflicts along generational lines, between the new and old organizational elites. It may be that the mounting public criticism of "scientism" is in part a result of the fact that social science has become implicated in the struggle between entrenched and rising elites and provides a basis for the latter's challenge to the former, as well as of the fact that social scientists write stuffy and jargon-laden prose.

4. Also implicated in the strain between authority based on incumbency in office and authority based on technical knowledge are some of the special problems of recruiting, inspecting, and evaluating the performance of technical experts in the modern organization. Often, not only is the expert's immediate superior unqualified to judge him, but there are only one or a few qualified judges in the entire organization. Even if there are a few, they may be close friends or fierce competitors, whose judgments about one another will, in either event, be unreliable. This means that administrative superiors must depend upon persons outside the organization to select experts or to judge the performances of those already employed.

This, in turn, means that the technical expert himself is often dependent on persons outside his organization to validate his position within it. Consequently, his work must manifest a high degree of concern for the maintenance of technical standards. This not only disposes the expert to resist imperative pressures for "results," coming from his superiors, but it also makes him less vulnerable to control from those within and in command of his organization. In short, the expert's cosmopolitanism is in some measure a matter of constraint.

Thus linked with the outside, the expert is less likely to be regarded as an organization or "company" man. This implies that he is likely to be viewed as less than completely reliable or loyal to the organization. Around this focus, a conflict may develop between the organization's need for loyalty and its need for expertise. In industry, this conflict is commonly expressed as a dilemma between promotion on the basis of seniority— commonly used as an informal index of loyalty—and promotion on the basis of demonstrated skills and competence. Similar strains have been noted between "cosmopolitans" and "locals"—that is, between those who are primarily oriented to their professional specialization and those who are primarily committed to their employing organization.[17] When these organizational types become informally organized into cliques, factional conflicts between the "itinerants" and the "home-guard" may result.[18]

As Simon,[19] Barnard,[20] and others have stressed, every organization requires that its members have some degree of loyalty to it as a distinctive group. On the other hand, the modern organization also has a distinctive need for men with specialized skills and expertise. Both the rational-model and the natural-system-model theorists have tended to overlook the tensions which may arise as a result of efforts to satisfy these divergent needs. Weber, for example, tended to assume that the more expert the personnel, the more efficient the organization, and therefore the greater its stability. Suppose, however, as Saint-Simon asserted long ago, that those who are expert are also more cosmopolitan in outlook and, at the same time, less loyal to their employing organization.[21] In these circumstances, organizational survival may be threatened by a recruiting policy that considers only the candidate's expertise as much as by a policy that regards loyalty as more important than "brains."

Much of W. H. Whyte's recent study of the "organization man" is a discussion of current efforts by industry to attach managerial loyalty to the corporation. This attempt to manufacture organization men is, in effect, an effort to produce a new elite of loyal "locals," whose authority will be legitimated in terms of their human relations skills, thus perhaps counterbalancing the great growth of specialized experts, technicians, and engineers who may be more committed to their professions than to the organization.

Tension between the organization's need for loyalty and its need for specialized expertise does not seem to be a peculiarly American phenomenon. It seems likely, for example, to be implicated also in the Russians' periodic outbursts against "cosmopolitanism," in the conflicts between their politically reliable army commissars and their professional military men, as well as in the vagaries of Russian industrial development.[22] In this last connection, it seems noteworthy that some of the earliest Russian purges were directed against engineers and technicians.

There are, in brief, various indications of the existence of tension between an organization's bureaucratic need for expertise and its social-system needs for loyalty; each sets certain limits within which the other may be pursued.

5. Another tension of modern organizations may also be seen as deriving from the relation between its bureaucratic rationality and its social-system imperatives. If the organization is regarded as a natural system, and if its stability, as Parsons contends, depends upon the degree to which the various role players within it conform to one another's expectations, these complementary expectations of the role players will to some degree involve unstated traditional beliefs and values derived during the course of socialization in the larger society.

Often, however, the traditional social values and the distinctively rational bureaucratic values diverge. For example, the bureaucratic premise that organizational authority should be given to those with skill and competence may diverge from traditional values in the environing society which require that authority be vested in older people rather than younger ones, or in males rather than females.[23] Application of the bureaucratic premise in these circumstances may lead to endemic strains in organizations. Here we may note an instance of the tension-inducing pressure which latent social roles can exert on manifest organizational roles.

Furthermore, the primary group, with its traditional values, is usually the first paradigm of group behavior and of "proper" human relations with which the individual becomes familiar. He may then, as Merton[24] has indicated, tend to evaluate secondary groups in terms of primary-group standards and, finding them too impersonal, react with hostility toward the procedures of the organization, criticizing them as "red tape."

The role players in modern organizations must, in some measure, derive their mutual expectations from sources other than the codified rules. Consequently, the stability of their relationship is always to some extent contingent upon the extent to which they conform with one another's informal, traditional, and implicit expectations. However, the very stress in modern organizations upon the formal, legal rules means that the explicit acknowledgment of an expectation frequently becomes the criterion of its legitimacy. Expectations which have not been given explicit acknowledgement, through contractual or other legal enactments, tend to become regarded as liberties which are permissible or even preferred but are not seen as fully obligatory. Consequently, the legitimacy of all merely implied expectations, the traditional supports on which the organization must in part rest, are vulnerable to sudden challenges and disruptions.

This can be stated from a more general perspective. The rationality of the modern organization means that "things can always be made better" that "nothing is sacred," and, consequently, that nothing is unchangeable. Rationality therefore tends to spill over from the administration of inanimate things to the administration of human relations; it invades areas that were hitherto traditionally and informally controlled. This may generate organizational instabilities in several ways: First, the treatment of human beings as instruments may violate cultural norms prescribing that people should be viewed as ends in themselves. It may, therefore, give rise to accusations of manipulation. Secondly, such unceasing drives to rationalize the organization may impair those very spontaneous homeostatic controls that have hitherto contributed to the organization's equilibrium. To the extent that this occurs, the drive toward rational administration creates new problems which then have to be planfully resolved. The drive toward rationality thus becomes self-generative. This process would seem to underlie the tendency toward "increasing rationalization" in modern society of which both Weber and Karl Mannheim spoke.

The Functional Autonomy of Organizational Parts

There is one limitation on the natural-system model which derives largely from certain unexamined assumptions in the notion of a "system." This has to do with its emphasis on the interdependence of the parts within an organization. (In speaking of an organization's "parts," I refer both to its group structures or roles and to the socialized individuals who are its members.) The natural-system model tends to focus on the organization as a whole, to take the "interdependence" of the parts as a given, and therefore fails to explore systematically the significance of variations in the *degrees* of interdependence.[25]

This problem can be stated in terms of the "functional autonomy" of the parts of a system—i.e., the degree to which any one part is dependent on others for the satisfaction of its needs.[26] Systems in which parts have "high" functional autonomy may be regarded as having a "low" degree of system interdependence; conversely, systems in which parts have "low" functional autonomy have a "high" degree" of system interdependence. The concept of functional autonomy directs attention to the fact that *some* parts may survive separation from others, that parts vary in their dependence upon one another, and that their interdependence is not necessarily symmetrical.

It is obvious, for example, that younger children have less functional autonomy than older ones in that they have a lower probability of survival, other things being equal, in the event of their separation from the nuclear family. Within an organizational context, an example of asymmetrical interdependence would be the relation between the production and the public-relations departments of a business firm. If the two are somehow disjoined, the former normally has a higher probability of survival than the latter. That management usually regards the organization as more dependent upon the production department than the public-relations department is evident during times of budgetary crisis, when it is commonly the public-relations rather than the production department that suffers the greatest cutbacks. One crude, rule-of-thumb index of the functional autonomy of an organizational part, at least in a market society, is the extent to which it can obtain independent financing from sources outside of the organization. It would be instructive to examine, within a university, the comparative functional autonomy of, say, its engineering department and its English department from this point of view.

The tendency of the natural-system model, as I have said, is to focus on the system as a whole and to overstate the degree of mutual interdependence and integration among its parts. Conversely, it can be said to neglect the functional autonomy of the parts. One example of this tendency is to be found in Parsons' attempt to define an organization in terms of its orientation to goals.[27] In Parsons' terms, organizations are social systems which are primarily oriented toward the attainment of a specific goal. But an organization as such cannot be said to be oriented toward a goal, except in a merely metaphorical sense, unless it is assumed that its parts possess a much lower degree of functional autonomy than can in fact be observed. The statement that an organization is oriented toward certain goals often means no more than that these are the goals of its top administrators, or that they represent its societal function, which is another matter altogether.

More precise formulation would require specification of the ends of various people, or of the typical ends of different parts or strata, within the organization. Such a specification would indicate that these ends may vary, are not necessarily identical, and may, in fact, be contradictory. The natural-system theorist, however, may tend to neglect this fact because his underemphasis on the functional autonomy of the systems parts and his overemphasis on their mutual interdependence sometimes leads him to treat the organization as if it were a complex organism which, as such, is quite capable of having "ends."

Assuming that the organization's parts, no less than the organization as a whole, operate to maintain their boundaries and to remain in equilibrium, then the parts should be expected to defend their functional autonomy, or at least some measure of it, from encroachment. This suggests that a basic source of organizational tension may derive, on the one hand, from the tendency of the parts to resist encroachments on their functional autonomy and, on the other, from contrary tendencies of the organization's controlling center to limit or reduce the functional autonomy of the parts. The widely noted tensions between field offices and main offices, as well as the common organizational oscillation between centralization and decentralization seem to support this assumption, as do the frequently observed rejection of "close supervision"[28] and the pressure which almost all role players exert to maintain some social distance from and freedom from control by those most crucially concerned with their work.[29]

Mechanisms of Functional Autonomy

Because the natural-system model, as I have mentioned, tends to focus analysis too narrowly on the ways in which parts are integrated into the system as a whole, it neglects systematic analysis of the mechanisms which parts develop to vouchsafe their functional autonomy. One example of these mechanisms is what Goffman has called "rituals of avoidance."[30]

In the modern organization, one of the most common of these is, of course, the "coffee break" (which, needless to say, may involve consumption of other liquids or of none). Only the naive will assume that the sole function of the coffee break is to procure liquid refreshment or will fail to see that its latent function is to get people away from the office.

Mechanisms for the maintenance of functional autonomy may also entail use of various "material props" as devices which both symbolize and constrain a degree of social distance between role players. One case of this occurs in the department-store salesclerk's use of the sales counter as a barrier between herself and the customer.[31] Another interesting example is to be found in W. F. Whyte's analysis of the use of the "spindle" to limit the interaction between waitresses and pantry help in restaurants.[32]

There are many social and culture structures that serve, wittingly or not, to maintain the functional autonomy of the organization's parts; indeed, the point of these remarks is that all major structures can be profitably investigated from this perspective. In the culture structure, for example, norms of privacy, of privileged communication, of confidentiality of information;[33] norms which call for the hoarding of technical knowledge or the guarding of office secrets; norms which deny to "outsiders" the right and competence to judge technical performances—all commonly serve to reinforce the functional autonomy of organizational parts. On the level of social structures, students of "informal" organization have long recognized that cliques function to enable work associates to resist pressures placed upon them by those in formal authority, and that, further, the undertaking of multiple organizational functions often enables a part to resist control from any single quarter. Indeed, one of the basic functions of any system of roles is to limit the control which others may have over a given role player by limiting, either explicitly or implicitly, his obligations to them. Similarly, analysis in terms of "backstage" or "onstage"[34] or in terms of "insulation" often implies a concern for the *ecological* mechanisms[35] by means of which an organizational part maintains its functional autonomy.

The central point here is that current natural-system models tend to lose sight of the autonomy of the system parts, of their autonomy strivings and strategies, as well as of the ways in which such strategies may induce tensions among the other segments or within the system as a whole. This oversight, I suggest, derives primarily from the unqualified assumption which is made about the interdependence of organizational parts.

The natural-system model too readily assumes that the structure of the organization serves only to link parts and to provide avenues for controlling and integrating them. However, the structure of complex organizations also serves to maintain and protect the parts from others within the same system, at least in some degree. Thus organizational structure is shaped by a tension between centrifugal and centripetal pressures, limiting as well as imposing control over parts, separating as well as joining them.

The Reciprocities Multiplier

The natural-system-model theorist commonly assumes that the equilibrium of a group depends very greatly on the conforming behavior of group members. More explicitly, and in Parsons' terms, it is held that group equilibrium is a function of the extent to which group members, Ego and Alter, conform with each other's expectations. Before considering the relevance of this equilibrium model for the analysis of bureaucratic organization, I shall examine one of the general empirical assumptions implicit in it.

This model seems to assume that each of a sequence of identical conforming acts will yield either the same or an increasing degree of appreciation or satisfaction and will thus elicit the same or an increasing amount of reward. This may be regarded as an implicit assumption of Parsons' equilibrium model, for, otherwise it is difficult to understand how he can maintain that "the complementarity of role-expectations, once established, is not problematical. . . . No special mechanisms are required for the explanation of the maintenance of complementary interaction-orientation."[36] So far as I am aware, however, no evidence exists to substantiate the crucial assumption that rewarding responses to a series of identical conforming actions will either remain the same or increase. On the contrary, both impressionistic observations and theoretical considerations would lead one to doubt it. Here, as in the previous discussion of system "interdependence," the crux of the matter is a question of degree.

Ego's conforming acts, it must be assumed, always have some consequences for Alter's expectations; expectations are always modified by prior relevant actions. The question, of course, is, modified in what manner? To state it crudely, we would assume that the longer the sequence of Ego's conforming actions, the more likely is Alter to take Ego's conformity for granted. The more Alter takes Ego's conformity for granted, the less appreciative Alter will feel and the less propensity he will have to reward and reciprocate Ego's conforming actions. For example, we would expect workers to feel less gratified when their employer pays them their regular weekly wage than when he does something for them that they do not take for granted, such as providing an unexpected bonus.

The general theoretical point made here is complementary to the point cogently made by Robert Merton when he holds that *some* measure of anomic or nonconforming behavior may be beneficial to group stability.[37] Approaching the problem from the other side, we have held that at some point repeated acts of conformity may induce a strain toward anomic insatiability and group instability, when, in order to maintain the level of reward previously given him, Ego must conform increasingly with Alter's standards. For our analysis suggests that a sequence of identical conforming actions undergoes an inflationary spiral and that later conforming actions are worth less than earlier ones, in terms of the rewards or propensity to reciprocate which they elicit. We cannot assume, therefore, that identical acts of conformity will yield identical increments in group equilibrium. Consequently, it would seem that, unless Parsons' model is revised to include the "special mechanisms" for which he denies the necessity, his generalized model of a social system contains internally induced tendencies toward entropy or disorder, and the factors now assumed to be involved in it are insufficient to maintain the system in an indefinite state of equilibrium.

Basic to this analysis is the assumption that repeated identical acts of conformity modify—i.e., increase or reinforce—the *expectation* of conformity. Conformity is thus taken for granted, and thereby the propensity to reciprocate is weakened. But other factors in addition to sheer repetition can strengthen the expectation of conformity and thus similarly reduce the appreciation or gratitude felt and undermine the propensity to reward the conformer. Among these other factors, I postulate, is the degree to which Alter feels that Ego's conforming actions are imposed upon him, either by situational constraint or by moral obligation. In other words, if Alter feels that a given conforming act has been imposed upon Ego, we would expect Alter to value and reciprocate it less than if he defined Ego's conformity as "voluntary."[38]

Conversely, the more Ego's conforming action is defined by Alter as voluntary, the greater is Alter's tendency to appreciate and reward it. For example, we would expect a woman to respond to a birthday gift from her husband with less appreciation and less propensity to reciprocate than to the same gift given when there was no special occasion calling for it. Stated generally, the degree of appreciation or propensity to reciprocate is hypothesized to be an inverse (or perhaps a negative exponential) function of the degree to which a desired action is perceived as imposed upon the actor. In other words, reciprocity is a function of the degree to which a given act is desired, multiplied by the degree to which the act is perceived as voluntary.

Since these considerations take a very generalized model as their point of departure, it is clear that they should have application to diverse groups, to family interaction no less than to behavior within a modern bureaucracy. Here, however, we can pursue their implications only with respect to the modern bureaucratic organization. What we mean by "bureaucratization" is, in part, the explication of the group member's rights and obligations through the installation of formal rules and regulations. In other words, the more an organization is bureaucratized (and this is clearly a variable), the more the conforming behavior of people in the oganization will tend to be perceived as imposed upon them by the rules, rather than as voluntary.

This tendency, in turn, may generate a vicious cycle of increasing bureaucratization. That is, the more formal rules there are governing action, the more conforming actions will be devalued in that they will yield smaller increments of appreciation or gratitude which can motivate reciprocity, and the more the rules will be further elaborated and enforced to prevent the decline in motivation from impairing the organization. (It may be that a corollary of this helps to explain the great stability of primary relations: that is, the more vague obligations in primary relations dispose to a greater appreciation of desired and conforming actions.) In the bureaucratic organization, there may, however, be a development of new patterns of "indulgency" based upon the relinquishing of the rules. That is, administrators may voluntarily withhold application of certain formal rules, even though they have a right to apply them. Nonapplication of a rule, when it is not imposed upon or obligatory for the actor, constitutes a "favor" and multiplies the other person's tendency to reciprocate, thus recharging the informal system and making the formal rules less necessary for organizational operation.

To summarize, it has been suggested that a major task confronting organizational analysis is the reconciliation of the rational and natural-system models. What is needed is a single and synthesized model which will at once aid in analyzing the distinctive characteristics of the modern organization as a rational bureaucracy, the characteristics which it shares with other kinds of social systems, and the relationship of these characteristics to one another. I have briefly indicated a number of organizational problems which seem to derive from a conjunction of forces from both these levels. My attention has been focused largely on the natural-system model, because it is the one dominant among sociologists. In effect, this model constitutes a statement of the assumptions which sociologists frequently employ for analysis of diverse kinds of groups, including the modern organization. It becomes apparent, with our discussion of the "reciprocities multiplier," that the further development of organizational analysis is contingent upon the clarification of the basic models of sociological analysis and the verification of the empirical assumptions on which these models rest.

---

1. For an exegesis of Saint-Simon's theories, see Emile Durkheim, *Socialism and Saint-Simon,* ed. A. W. Gouldner (Antioch Press, 1958). A translation of selections from Saint-Simon's work is found in F. M. H. Markham, ed., *Henri Comte de Saint-Simon (1760-1825)* (Oxford: Basil Blackwell, 1952).

2. August Comte, *Early Essays on Social Philosophy,* trans. H. D. Hutton (London: George Routledge and Sons, n.d.), p. 325.

3. The best discussion in English of this aspect of Weber's thinking is in J. P. Mayer, *Max Weber and German Politics* (London: Faber and Faber, 1943). Compare, especially, Weber's polemic against bureaucratization, in his speech of 1909, with William H. Whyte's call to battle against bureaucracy almost a half-century later in *The Organization Man* (New York: Simon and Schuster, 1956). The similarities in their value positions are noteworthy.

4. I have used Comte as a historical marker with the object of emphasizing his intellectual influence rather than his intellectual originality. It is evident that thinkers prior to Comte held some of the ideas here associated with him. My comments, however, are made in the framework of the history of sociology and the actual continuities within it, rather than in terms of a schematic intellectual history. Of course, theorists after Comte have also stressed many of the same ideas, such as the importance of shared moral beliefs as a basis of social solidarity. Among these modern theorists, Durkheim and his school are well enough known not to require comment here.

5. Alvin W. Gouldner, *Patterns of Industrial Bureaucracy* (Antioch Press, 1954), esp. pp. 15-29 and chap. 10.

6. In thus demarcating two types of bureaucracy it is not, of course, my intention to suggest that this is the only way in which concrete organizations may be analyzed or that these are the only two possible types of bureaucracy. Viewed in one way, these comments may be regarded as specifications of two ideal types of bureaucracies, useful for the qualitative comparison of several organizations or in the analysis of different administrative patterns within one organization. Viewed in another light, these comments may be regarded as a "qualitative" factor analysis or as suggestive of hypotheses about dimensions of organizations which might emerge from a factor-analytic research.

7. F. J. Roethlisberger and W. J. Dickson, with the assistance of H. A. Wright, *Management and the Worker* (Cambridge, Mass.: Harvard University Press, 1939), p. 565.

8. W. L. Warner and J. O. Low, *The Social System of the Modern Factory* (New Haven: Yale University Press, 1947), pp. 172-73.

9. Peter Blau, *The Dynamics of Bureaucracy* (Chicago: University of Chicago Press, 1955), chap. 3.

10. S. M. Lipset, M. Trow, and J. Coleman, *Union Democracy* (New York: Free Press, 1956). For an early statement of my own thinking on this problem, see A. W. Gouldner, "Attitudes of 'Progressive' Trade Union Leaders," *Amer. J. Sociol.* 52 (1947): 389-92.

11. See, for example, Orvis Collins, "Ethnic Behavior in Industry," *Amer. J. Sociol.* 51 (1946): 293–98; Melville Dalton, "Informal Factors in Career Achievement," *Amer. J. Sociol.* 56 (1951): 407-15; and E. C. Hughes, "Queries Concerning Industry and Society Growing Out of the Study of Ethnic Relations in Industry," *Amer. Sociol. Rev.* 14 (1949): 211-20.

12. The concepts of latent and manifest organizational identities and roles is discussed in A. W. Gouldner, "Cosmopolitans and Locals: Toward an Analysis of Latent Social Roles—I," *Admin. Sci. Quart.* 2 (1957): 281-306.

13. Among the perhaps esoteric but still theoretically interesting patterns partly structured by latent sexual identities is the "touch system," which regulates interpersonal bodily contacts. See Erving Goffman, "The Nature of Deference and Demeanor," *Amer. Anthrop.* 58 (1956): 486-88.

14. See Melville Dalton, "Conflicts Between Staff and Line Managerial Officers," *Amer. Sociol. Rev.* 15 (1950): 342-51.

15. For some of Hughes' ideas about organizational analysis see E. C. Hughes, "Work and the Self," in *Social Psychology at the Crossroads,* ed. J. H. Rohrer and M. Sherif (New York: Harper & Row, Publishers, 1951).

16. Current efforts of this sort are discussed in Whyte, op. cit. One of the most important stimuli in this direction was the work of Elton Mayo, *The Social Problems of an Industrial Civilization* (Cambridge, Mass.: Harvard University Press, 1945).

17. For more detailed discussion, see Gouldner, "Cosmopolitans and Locals," loc. cit., and W. G. Bennis et al., "Reference Groups and Loyalties in an Out-Patient Department," *Admin. Sci. Quart.* 2 (1958): 481-500.

18. These are analyzed in a study of the nursing profession by Robert W. Habenstein and Edwin A. Christ, *Professionalizer, Traditionalizer, and Utilizer* (Columbia, Mo.: University of Missouri Press, 1955), esp. chap. 6.

19. Herbert Simon, *Administrative Behavior* (New York: Macmillan, 1948).

20. Chester I. Barnard, *Organization and Management* (Cambridge, Mass.: Harvard University Press, 1948).

21. Both Whyte's work and my own seem to have converged independently on this same point. See Whyte, op. cit., p. 232, and Gouldner, "Cosmopolitans and Locals," loc. cit. Bennis's research, op. cit., also seems to support it, although certain seeming divergences from some of my own conclusions have yet to be clarified.

22. Work done by Robert A. Feldmesser at Harvard University would seem to lend substantiation to this.

23. See William F. Whyte, *Human Relations in the Restaurant Industry* (New York: McGraw-Hill Book Co., 1948), esp. p. 75.

24. Robert K. Merton, "Bureaucratic Structure and Personality," *Soc. Forces* 18 (1940): 560-68.

25. Cf. Robert K. Merton, *Social Theory and Social Structure* (New York: Free Press, 1957), pp. 25 ff.

26. For a more detailed discussion of the problem of functional autonomy, see Alvin W. Gouldner, "Reciprocity and Autonomy in Functional Theory," in *Symposium on Social Theory,* ed. L. Z. Gross (Evanston, Ill: Row, Peterson, 1958).

27. Talcott Parsons, "Suggestions for a Sociological Approach to a Theory of Organization—I," *Admin. Sci. Quart.* 1 (1956): 63-85.

28. See Daniel Katz and Robert Kahn, "Human Organization and Worker Motivation," in *Industrial Productivity,* ed. L. Reed Tripp (Industrial Relations Research Association, 1951).

29. Cf. E. C. Hughes, in Rohrer, op. cit. See also Chris Argyris, "The Individual and the Organization: Some Problems of Mutual Adjustment," *Admin. Sci. Quart.* 2 (1957): 1-24. The reader with philosophical interests will detect that I have in part been dealing with a classic problem which has been fruitfully analyzed in terms of the distinction between Apollonian and Dionysian drives in the work of Nietzsche, Cassirer, and, more recently, Charles Morris. I believe that the empirical sociologist can still derive much of value, in connection with the present problem, from a re-examination of their work.

30.   See Goffman, loc. cit., and "Secondary Adjustment in Complex Organizations," a paper presented at the annual meetings of the American Sociological Society, 1957. Compare also the insightful discussion of the mechanisms developed by suburbanites to gain relief from group pressures in W. H. Whyte, Jr., op. cit., p. 390.

31.   See George F. Lombard, *Behavior in a Selling Group* (Cambridge, Mass.: Harvard University Graduate School of Business Administration, 1955), p. 185.

32.   Op. cit., p. 75.

33.   See the discussion of "visibility" in Merton, *Social Theory and Social Structure,* esp. pp. 341 ff.

34.   These concepts are discussed fully in Erving Goffman, *Presentation of Self in Everyday Life* (Edinburgh: University of Edinburgh Press, 1956).

35.   See, for example, Raymond W. Mack, "Ecological Patterns in an Industrial Shop," *Soc. Forces* 32 (1954): 351-56.

36.   Talcott Parsons, *The Social System* (New York: Free Press, 1951), p. 205.

37.   "Bureaucratic Structure and Personality," loc. cit., 182-83.

38.   Research currently being done by Doyle Kent Rice, Richard A. Peterson, and myself is exploring this general problem area, and preliminary indications of our data would seem to substantiate the point made here.

TWO APPROACHES TO ORGANIZATIONAL ANALYSIS: A CRITIQUE AND A SUGGESTION[1]

Amitai Etzioni

Organizational goals serve many functions. They give organizational activity its orientation by depicting the state of affairs which the organization attempts to realize. They serve as sources of legitimation which justify the organization's activities and its very existence, at least in the eyes of some participants and in those of the general public or subpublics. They serve as a source for standards by which actors assess the success of their organization. Finally, they serve as an important starting point for students of organizations who, like some of the actors they observe, use the organizational goals as a yardstick with which to measure the organization's performance. This paper is devoted to a critique of this widespread practice and to a suggestion of an alternative approach.

Goal Model

The literature on organizations is rich in studies in which the criterion for the assessment of effectiveness is derived from organizational goals.

Reprinted from the *Administrative Science Quarterly,* vol. 5 (Sept. 1960), pp. 257-78, by permission of the author and the publishers.

We shall refer to this approach as the goal model. The model is considered an objective and reliable analytical tool because it omits the values of the explorer and applies the values of the subject under study as the criteria of judgment. We suggest, however, that this model has some methodological shortcomings and is not as objective as it seems to be.

One of the major shortcomings of the goal model is that it frequently makes the studies' findings stereotyped as well as dependent on the model's assumptions. Many of these studies show (a) that the organization does not realize its goals effectively, and/or (b) that the organization has different goals from those it claims to have. Both points have been made for political parties,[2] trade unions,[3] voluntary associations,[4] schools,[5] mental hospitals,[6] and other organizations. It is not suggested that these statements are not valid, but it seems they have little empirical value if they can be deduced from the way the study is approached.[7]

Goals, as norms, as sets of meanings depicting target states, are cultural entities. Organizations, as systems of coordinated activities of more than one actor, are social systems.

There is a general tendency for cultural systems to be more consistent than social systems.[8] There are mainly two reasons for this. First of all, cultural images, to be realized, require investment of means. Since the means needed are always larger than the means available, social units are always less perfect than their cultural anticipations. A comparison of actual Utopian settlements with descriptions of such settlements in the books by leaders of Utopian movements is a clear, although a somewhat disheartening, illustration of this point.[9]

The second reason for the invariant discrepancy between goals and social units, which is of special relevance to our discussion, is that all social units, including organizations, are multifunctional units. Therefore, while devoting part of their means directly to goal activities, social units have to devote another part to other functions, such as the creation or recruitment of further means to the goal and the maintenance of units performing goal activities and service activities.

Looking at the same problem from a somewhat different viewpoint, one sees that the mistake committed in comparing objects that are not on the same level of analysis as, for example, when the present state of an organization (a real state) is compared with a goal (an ideal state) as if the goal were also a real state. Some studies of informal organizations commit a similar mistake when they compare the blueprint of an organization with actual organizational practice and suggest that an organizational *change* has taken place. The organization has "developed" an informal structure. Actually, the blueprint organization never existed as a social fact. What is actually compared is a set of symbols on paper with a functioning social unit.[10]

Measured against the Olympic heights of the goal, most organizations scored the same—very low effectiveness. The differences in effectiveness among organizations are of little significance. One who expects a light bulb to turn most of its electrical power into light would not be very interested in the differences between a bulb that utilizes 4.5 per cent of the power as compared with one that utilizes 5.5 per cent. Both are extremely ineffective. A more realistic observer would compare the two bulbs with each other and find one of them relatively good. The same holds for organizational studies that compare actual states of organization to each other, as when the organizational output is measured at different points in time. Some organizations are found gradually to increase their effectiveness by improving their structure and their relations with the environment. In other organizations effectiveness is slowly or rapidly declining. Still others are highly effective at the initial period, when commitments to goals are strong, and less effective when the commitment level declines to what is "normal" for this organization. These few examples suffice to show that the goal model may not supply the best possible frame of reference for effectiveness. It compares the ideal with the real, as a result of which most levels of performance look alike—quite low.[11] Michels, for example, who applied a goal model, did not see any significant differences among the trade unions and parties he examined. All were falling considerably short of their goals.

When a goal model is applied, the same basic mistake is committed, whether the goals an organizaiton claims to pursue (public goals) or the goals it actually follows (private goals) are chosen as a yardstick for evaluation of performance. In both cases cultural entities are compared with social systems as if they were two social systems. Thus the basic methodological error is the same. Still, when the public goals are chosen, as is often done, the bias introduced into the study is even greater.[12] Public goals fail to be realized not because of poor planning, unanticipated consequences, or hostile environment. *They are not meant to be realized.* If an organization were to invest means in public goals to such an extent that it served them effectively, their function, that is, improving the input-output balance, would be greatly diminished, and the organization would discard them.[13] In short, public goals, as criteria, are even more misleading than private ones.

System Model

An alternative model that can be employed for organizational analysis is the system model.[14] The starting point for this approach is not the goal itself but a *working model of a social unit which is capable of achieving a goal.* Unlike a goal, or a set of goal activities, it is a model of a multi-functional unit.[15] It is assumed a priori that some means have to be devoted to such nongoal functions as service and custodial activities, including means employed for the maintenance of the unit itself. From the viewpoint of the system model, such activities are functional and increase the organizational effectiveness. It follows that a social unit that devotes all its efforts to fulfilling one functional requirement, even if it is that of performing goal activities, will undermine the fulfillment of this very functional requirement, because recruitment of means,[16] maintenance of tools, and the social integration of the unit will be neglected.[17]

A measure of effectiveness establishes the degree to which an organization realizes its goals under a given set of conditions. But the central question in the study of effectiveness is not, "How devoted is the organization to its goal?" but rather, "Under the given conditions, *how close does the organizational allocation of resources*[18] *approach an optimum distribution?*" "Optimum" is the key word: what counts is a balanced distribution of resources among the various organizational needs, not maximal satisfaction of any one activity, even of goal activities. We shall illustrate this point by examining two cases; each is rather typical for a group of organizational studies.

Case 1: Function of Custodial Activities

One function each social unit must fulfill is adjusting to its environment. Parsons refers to this as the "adaptive phase" and Homans calls the activities oriented to the fulfillment of this function "the external system." This should not be confused with the environment itself. An organization often attempts to change some limited parts of its environment, but this does mean that adjustment to the environment in general becomes unnecessary. The changes an organization attempts to introduce are usually specific and limited.[19] This means that, with the exception of the elements to be changed, the organization accepts the environment as it is and orients its activities accordingly. Moreover, the organization's orientation to the elements it tries to change is also highly influenced by their existing nature. In short, a study of effectiveness has to include an analysis of the environmental conditions and of the organization's orientation to them.

With this point in mind let us examine the basic assumptions of a large number of studies of mental hospitals and prisons conducted in recent years on the subject "from custodial to therapeutic care" (or, from coercion to rehabilitation). Two points are repeated in many of these studies: (1) The *goals* of mental hospitals, correctional institutions, and prisons are therapeutic. "The basic function of the hospital for the mentally ill is the same as the basic function of general hospitals . . . that function is the utilization of every form of treatment available for restoring the patients to health."[20] (2) Despite large efforts to transform these organizations from custodial to therapeutic institutions, little change has taken place. Custodial patterns of behavior still dominate policy decisions and actions in most of these organizations. "In the very act of trying to operate these institutions their *raison d'être* has often been neglected or forgotten."[21] Robert Vinter and Morris Janowitz stated explicitly:

> Custody and care of delinquent youth continue to be the goals of correctional agencies, but there are growing aspirations for remedial treatment. The public expects juvenile correctional institutions to serve a strategic role in changing the behavior of delinquents. Contrary to expectations, persistent problems have been encountered in attempting to move correctional institutions beyond mere custodialism. . . . Despite strenuous efforts and real innovations, significant advances beyond custody have not been achieved.[22]

The first question the studies raise is: What are the actual organizational goals? The public may change its expectations without necessarily imposing a change in the organization's goals, or it may affect only the public goals. As Vinter and Janowitz suggest, much of the analysis of these organizations actually shows that they are oriented mainly to custodial goals, and with respect to these goals they are effective.[23]

But let us assume that through the introduction of mental health perspectives and personnel—psychiatrists, psychologists, social workers—the organization's goal, as an ideal self-image, changed and became oriented to therapy. We still would expect Vinter's and Janowitz's observation to be valid. Most prisons, correctional institutions, and mental hospitals would not be very effective in serving therapy goals. Two sets of reasons support this statement. The first set consists of internal factors, such as the small amount of professionals available as compared to the large number of inmates, the low effectiveness of the present techniques of therapy, the limitations of knowledge, and so on. These internal factors will not be discussed here, since the purpose of this section is to focus on the second set, that of external factors, which also hinder if not block organizational change.

Organizations have to adapt to the environment in which they function. When the relative power of the various elements in the environment are carefully examined, it becomes clear that, in general, the subpublics (e.g., professionals, universities, well-educated people, some health authorities) which support therapeutic goals are less powerful than those which support the custodial or segregating activities of these organizations. Under such conditions, most mental hospitals and prisons must be more or less custodial. There is evidence to show, for example, that a local community, which is both an important segment of the organizational environment and which in most cases is custodial-minded, can make an organization maintain its bars, fences, and guards or be closed.

> The [prison] camp has overlooked relations with the community. For the sake of the whole program you've got to be custodially minded. . . . The community feeling is a problem. There's been a lot of antagonism. . . . Newpapers will come out and advocate that we close the camp and put a fence around it.[24]

An attempt to change the attitudes of a community to mental illness is reported by Elaine and John Cumming. The degree to which it succeeded is discussed by J. A. Clausen in his foreword to the study. "The Cummings chose a relatively proximate goal: to ascertain whether the community educational program would diminish people's feelings of distance and estrangement from former mental patients and would increase their feelings of social responsibility for problems of mental illness." They found that their program did not achieve these goals.[25] It should be noted that the program attempted by education to change relatively abstract attitudes toward *former* mental patients and to mental illness in general. When the rumor spread that the study was an attempt to prepare the grounds for the opening of a mental hospital in the town, hostility increased sharply. In short, it is quite difficult to change the environment even when the change sought is relatively small and there are special activities oriented toward achieving it.[26]

D. R. Cressey, addressing himself to the same problems, states: "In spite of the many ingenious programs to bring about modification of attitudes or reform, the unseen environment in the prisoner's world, with few exceptions, continues to be charged with ideational content inimical to reform."[27]

This is not to suggest that community orientation cannot be changed. But when the effectiveness of an organization is assessed at a certain point in time, and the organization studied is not one whose goal is to change the environment, the environment has to be treated as given. In contemporary society, this often means that the organization must allocate considerable resources to custodial activities in order to be able to operate at all.[28] Such activities at least limit the means available for therapy. In addition they tend to undermine the therapeutic process, since therapy (or rehabilitation) and security are often at least partially incompatible goals.[29] Under such circumstances low effectiveness in the service of therapeutic goals is to be expected.

This means that, to begin with, one may expect a highly developed custodial subsystem. Hence it seems justifiable to suggest that the focus of research should shift from the problem that, despite some public expectations, institutions fail to become primarily therapeutic to the following problems: To what degree are external and internal[30] organizational conditions responsible for the emphasis on security? Or are these conditions used by those in power largely to justify the elaboration of security measures, while the real cause for that elaboration is to be found in the personal needs or interests (which can be relatively more easily changed and for which the organization is responsible) of part of the personnel, such as guards and administrators? To what degree and in what ways can therapy be developed under the conditions given? Do external conditions allow, and internal conditions encourage, a goal cleavage, i.e., making security the public goal and therapy the private goal of the organization or the other way around?

We have discussed the effect of the two models the researcher uses to study the interaction between the organization and its environment. We shall turn now to examine the impact each model has on the approach to the study of internal structure of the organization.

Case 2: Functions of Oligarchy

The study of authority structure in voluntary associations and political organizations is gradually shifting from a goal model to a system model. Michels' well-known study of socialist parties and trade unions in Europe before World War I was conducted according to a goal model.[31] These parties and unions were found to have two sets of goals: socialism and democracy. Both tended to be undermined: socialism by the weakening of commitments to revolutionary objectives and overdevotion to means activities (developing the organization) and maintenance activities (preserving the organization and its assets); democracy by the development of an oligarchic structure. A number of studies have followed Michels' line and supplied evidence that supports his generalizations.[32]

With regard to socialism, Michels claims that a goal displacement took place in the organizations he studied. This point has been extensively analyzed and need not be discussed here.[33] Of more interest to the present discussion is his argument on democracy. Michels holds that an organization that has *external* democracy as its goal should have an *internal* democratic structure; otherwise, it is not only diverting some of the means from goal to nongoal activities, but is also introducing a state of affairs which is directly opposed to the goal state of the organization. In other words, an internal oligarchy is seen as a dysfunction from the viewpoint of the organizational goals. "Now it is manifest that the concept *dictatorship* is the direct antithesis of the concept *democracy*. The attempt to make dictatorship serve the ends of democracy is tantamount to the endeavour to utilize war as the most efficient means for the defence of peace, or to employ alcohol in the struggle against alcoholism."[34] Michels goes on to spell out the conditions which make for this phenomenon. Some are regarded as unavoidable, some as optional, but all are depicted as distortions undermining the effectiveness of the organization.[35]

Since then it has been suggested that internal oligarchy might be a *functional* requirement for the effective operation of these organizations.[36] It has been suggested both with regard to trade unions and political parties that conflict organizations cannot tolerate internal conflicts. If they do, they become less effective.[37] Political parties that allow internal factions to become organized are setting the scene for splits which often turn powerful political units into weak splinter parties. This may be dysfunctional not only for the political organization but also for the political system. It has also been pointed out that organizations, unlike communities and societies, are segmental associations, which require and recruit only limited commitments of actors and in which, therefore, internal democracy is neither possible nor called for. Developing an internal political structure of democratic nature would necessitate spending more means on recruitment of members' interests than segmental associations can afford. Moreover, a higher involvement on the part of members may well be dysfunctional to the achievement of the organization's goals. It would make compromises with other political parties or of labor unions with management rather difficult. This means that some of the factors Michels saw as dysfunctional are actually functional; some of the factors he regarded as distorting the organizational goals were actually the mechanisms through which the functions were fulfilled, or the conditions which enabled these mechanisms to develop and to operate.

S. M. Lipset, M. A. Trow, and J. S. Coleman's study of democracy in a trade union reflects the change in approach since Michels' day.[38] This study is clearly structured according to the patterns of a system model. It does not confront a social unit with an ideal and then grade it according to its degree of conformity to the ideal. The study sees democracy as a process (mainly as an institutionalized change of the parties in office) and proceeds to determine the external and internal conditions that enable it to function. It views democracy as a characteristic of a given system, sustained by the interrelations among the system's parts. From this, a multifunctional theory of democracy in voluntary organizations emerges. The study describes the various functional requirements necessary for democracy to exist in an organization devoted to economic and social improvement of its members and specifies the conditions that have allowed these requirements to be met in this particular case.[39]

PARADOX OF INEFFECTIVENESS   An advantage of the system model is that it enables us to conceive of a basic form of ineffectiveness which is hard to imagine and impossible to explain from the viewpoint of the goal model. The goal approach sees assignment of means to goal activities as functional. The more means assigned to the goal activities, the more effective the organization is expected to be. In terms of the goal model, the fact that an organization can become more effective by allocating less means to goal activities is a paradox. The system model, on the other hand, leads one to conclude that, just as there may be a dysfunction of underrecruitment, so there may be a dysfunction of overrecruitment to goal activities, which is bound to lead to underrecruitment to other activities and to lack of coordination between the inflated goal activities and the depressed means activities or other nongoal activities.

COST OF SYSTEM MODELS   Up to this point we have tried to point out some of the advantages of the system model. We would now like to point out one drawback of this model: It is more demanding and expensive for the researcher. The goal model requires that the researcher determine the goals the organization is pursuing and no more. If public goals are chosen, they are usually readily available. Private goals are more difficult to establish. In order to find out how the organization is really oriented, it is sometimes necessary not only to gain the confidence of its elite but also to analyze much of the actual organizational structure and processes.

Research conducted on the basis of the system model requires more effort than a study following the goal model, even when private goals are chosen. The system model requires that the analyst determine what he considers a highly effective allocation of means. This often requires considerable knowledge of the way in which an organization of the type studied functions. Acquiring such knowledge is often very demanding, but it should be pointed out that (a) the efforts invested in obtaining the information required for the system model are not wasted since the information collected in the process of developing the system model will be of much value for the study of most organizational problems; and that (b) theoretical considerations may often serve as the bases for constructing a system model. This point requires some elaboration.

A well-developed organizational theory will include statements on the functional requirements various organizational types have to meet. These will guide the researcher who is constructing a system model for the study of a specific organization. In cases where the pressure to economize is great, the theoretical system model of the particular organizational type may be used directly as a standard and a guide for the analysis of a specific organization. But it should be pointed out that in the present state of organizational theory, such a model is often not available. At present, organizational theory is dealing mainly with general propositions which apply equally well but also equally bady to all organizations.[40] The differences among various organizational types are great; therefore any theory of organizations in general must be highly abstract. It can serve as an important frame for specification, that is, for the development of special theories for the various organizational types, but it cannot substitute for such theories by serving in itself as a system model, to be applied directly to the analysis of concrete organizations.

Maybe the best support for the thesis that a system model can be formulated and fruitfully applied is found in a study of organizational effectiveness by B. S. Georgopoulos and A. S. Tannenbaum, one of the few studies that distinguishes explicitly between the goal and system approaches to the study of effectiveness.[41] Instead of using the goals of the delivery service organization, they constructed three indexes, each measuring one basic element of the system. These were: (a) station productivity, (b) intraorganizational strain as indicated by the incidence of tension and conflict among organizational subgroups, and (c) organizational flexibility, defined as the ability to adjust to external or internal change. The total score of effectiveness thus produced was significantly correlated to the ratings on "effectiveness" which various experts and "insiders" gave the thirty-two delivery stations.[42]

Further development of such system-effectiveness indexes will require elaboration of organizational theory along the lines discussed above, because it will be necessary to supply a rationale for measuring certain aspects of the system and not others.[43]

SURVIVAL AND EFFECTIVENESS MODELS   A system model constitutes a statement about relationships which, if actually existing, would allow a given unit to maintain itself and to operate. There are two major subtypes of system models. One depicts a *survival model,* i.e., a set of requirements which, if fulfilled, allows the system to exist. In such a model each relationship specified is a prerequisite for the functioning of the system, i.e., a necessary condition; remove any of them and the system ceases to operate. The second is an *effectiveness model.* It defines a pattern of interrelations among the elements of the system which would make it most effective in the service of a given goal.[44]

The difference between the two submodels is considerable. Sets of functional alternatives which are equally satisfactory from the viewpoint of the survival model have a different value from the viewpoint of the effectiveness model. The survival model gives a "yes" or "no" score when answering the question: Is a specific relationship functional? The effectiveness model tells us that, of several functional alternatives, some are more functional than others in terms of effectiveness. There are first, second, third, and *n* choices. Only rarely are two patterns full-fledged alternatives in this sense, i.e., only rarely do they have the same effectiveness value. Merton discussed this point briefly, using the concepts of functional alternatives and functional equivalents.[45]

The majority of the functionalists have worked with survival models.[46] This has left them open to the criticism that although society or a social unit might change considerably, they would still see it as the same system. Only very rarely, for instance, does a society lose its ability to fulfill the basic functional requirements. This is one of the reasons why it has been claimed that the functional model does not sensitize the researcher to the dynamics of social units.[47]

James G. March and Herbert A. Simon pointed out explicitly in their outstanding analysis of organizational theories that the Barnard-Simon analysis of organization was based on a survival model:

> The Barnard-Simon theory of organizational equilibrium is essentially a theory of motivation—a statement of the conditions under which an organization can induce its members to continue participation, and hence assure organizational *survival.* . . . Hence, an organization is "solvent"—and will continue · in *existence*— only so long as the contributions are sufficient to provide inducements in large enough measure to draw forth these conditions.[48] [All italics supplied.]

If, on the other hand, one accepts the definition that organizations are social units oriented toward the realization of specific goals, the application of the effectiveness model is especially warranted for this type of study.

Models and Normative Biases

The goal model is often considered as an objective way to deal with normative problems. The observer controls his normative preferences by using the normative commitments of the actors to construct a standard for the assessment of effectiveness. We would like to suggest that the goal model is less objective than it appears to be. The system model not only seems to be a better model but also seems to supply a safety measure against a common bias, the Utopian approach to social change.

Value Projection

In some cases the transfer from the values of the observer to those of the observed is performed by a simple projection. The observer decides a priori that the organization, group, or public under study is striving to achieve goals and to realize values he favors. These values are then referred to as the "organizational goals," "public expectations," or "society's values." Actually they are the observer's values projected onto the unit studied. Often no evidence is supplied that would demonstrate that the goals are really those of the organization. C. S. Hyneman pointed to the same problem in political science:

> A like concern about means and ends is apparent in much of the literature that subordinates description of what occurs to a development of the author's ideas and beliefs; the author's ideas and beliefs come out in statements that contemporary institutions and ways of doing things do not yield the results that society of a particular public anticipated.[49]

Renate Mayntz makes this point in her discussion of a study of political parties in Berlin. She points out that the functional requirements which she uses to measure the effectiveness of the party organization are derived from *her* commitments to democratic values. She adds: "It is an empirical question how far a specific political party accepts the functions attributed to it by the committed observer as its proper and maybe noblest goals. From the point of view of the party, the primary organizational goal is to achieve power."[50]

There are two situations where this projection is likely to take place: one, when the organization is publicly, but not otherwise, committed to the same goals to which the observer is committed; the other, when a functional statement is turned from a hypothesis into a postulate.[51] When a functionalist states that mental hospitals have been established in order to cure the mentally ill, he often does not mean this as a statement either about the history of mental hospitals or about the real, observable, organizational goals. He is just suggesting that *if* the mental hospitals pursued the above goal, this *would be* functional for society. The researcher who converts from this "if-then" statement to a factual assertion, "the goal is . . . ," commits a major methodological error.

But let us assume that the observer has determined, with the ordinary techniques of research, that the organization he is observing is indeed committed to the goals which he, too, supports; for instance, culture, health, or democracy. Still, the fact that the observer enters the study of the organization through its goals makes it likely that he will assume the position of a critic or social reformer, rather than that of a social observer and detached analyst. Thus those who use the goal model often combine "understanding" with "criticizing," an approach which was recommended and used by Marx but strongly criticized and rejected by Weber. The critique is built into the study by the fact that the goal is used as the yardstick, a technique which, as was pointed out above, makes organizations in general score low on effectiveness scales.[52]

Effects of Liberalism

The reasons why the goal model is often used and often is accompanied by a critical perspective can be explained partially by the positions of those who apply it. Like many social scientists, students of organizations are often committed to ideas of progress, social reform, humanism, and liberalism.[53] This normative perspective can express itself more readily when a goal model is applied than when a system model is used. In some cases the goal model gives the researcher an opportunity to assume even the indignant style of a social reformer.

Some writers suggested that those who use the system models are conservative by nature. This is not the place to demonstrate that this contention is not true. It suffices to state here that the system model is a prerequisite for understanding and bringing about social change. The goal model leads to unrealistic, Utopian expectations, and hence to disappointments, which are well reflected in the literature of this type. The system model, on the other hand, depicts more realistically the difficulties encountered in introducing change into established systems, which function in a given environment. It leaves less room for the frustrations which must follow Utopian hopes. It is hard to improve on the sharp concluding remark of Gresham M. Sykes on this subject:

> Plans to increase the therapeutic effectiveness of the custodial institutions must be evaluated in terms of the difference between what is done and what might be done—and the difference may be dishearteningly small. . . . But expecting less and demanding less may achieve more, for a chronically disillusioned public is apt to drift into indifference.[54]

Intellectual Pitfall

Weber pointed out in his discussion of responsibility that actors, especially those responsible for a system, such as politicians and managers, have to compromise. They cannot follow a goal or a value consistently, because the various subsystems, which they have to keep functioning as well as integrated, have different and partially incompatible requirements. The unit's activity can be assured only by concessions, including such concessions as might reduce the effectiveness and scope of goal activities (but not necessarily the effectiveness of the whole unit). Barnard made basically the same point in his theory of opportunism.

Although the structural position of politicians and managers leads them to realize the need to compromise, the holders of other positions are less likely to do so. On the contrary, since these others are often responsible for one subsystem in the organization, they tend to identify with the interests and values of their subsystem. From the viewpoint of the system, those constitute merely segmental perspectives. This phenomenon, which is sometimes referred to as the development of department loyalties, is especially widespread among those who represent goal activities. Since their interests and subsystem values come closest to those of the organization as a whole, they find it easiest to justify their bias.

In systems in which the managers are the group most committed to goal activities (e.g., in profit-making organizations), this tendency is at least partially balanced by the managers' other commitments (e.g., to system integration). But in organizations in which another personnel group is the major carrier of goal activities, the ordinary intergroup difference of interests and structural perspectives becomes intensified. In some cases it develops into a conflict between the idealists and the compromisers (if not traitors). In professional organizations such as mental hospitals and universities, the major carriers of goal activities are professionals rather than administrators. The conflict between the supporters of therapeutic values and those of custodial values is one case of this general phenomenon.[55]

So far the effect of various structural positions on the actors' organizational perspectives has been discussed. What view is the observer likely to take? One factor which might affect his perspective is *his* structural position. Frequently, this resembles closely that of the professional in professional organizations. The researcher's background is similar to that of the professionals he studies in terms of education, income, social prestige, age, language, manners, and other characteristics. With regard to these factors he tends to differ from managers and administrators. Often the researcher who studies an organization and the professionals studied have shared years of training at the same or at a similar university and have or had friends in common. Moreover, his position in his organization, whether it is a university or a research organization, is similar to the position of the physician or psychologist in the hospital or prison under study.[56] Like other professionals, the researcher is primarily devoted to the goal activities of his organization and has little experience with, understanding of, or commitment to, nongoal functions. The usual consequence of all this is that the researcher has a natural sympathy for the professional orientation in professional organizations.[57] This holds also, although to a lesser degree, for professionals in other organizations, such as business corporations and governmental agencies.

Since the professional orientation in these organizations is identical with the goal orientation, the goal model not only fails to help in checking the bias introduced by these factors but tends to enhance it. The system model, on the other hand, serves to remind one (a) that social units cannot be as consistent as cultural systems, (b) that goals are serviced by multifunctional units, and hence intersubsystem concessions are a necessary prerequisite for action, (c) that such concessions include concessions to the adaptive subsystem which in particular represents environmental pressures and constraints, and (d) that each group has its structural perspectives, which means that the observer must be constantly aware of the danger of taking over the viewpoint of any single personnel group, including that of a group which carries the bulk of the goal activities. He cannot consider the perspective of any group or elite as a satisfactory view of the organization as a whole, of its effectiveness, needs, and potentialities. In short, it is suggested that the system model supplies not only a more adequate model but also a less biased point of view.

---

1. I am indebted to William Delany, William J. Goode, Terence K. Hopkins, and Renate Mayntz for criticisms of an earlier version of this paper.

2. Robert Michels, *Political Parties* (New York: Free Press, 1949); Moise Ostrogorski, *Democracy and the Organization of Political Parties* (New York: Macmillan Co., 1902).

3. Michels, op. cit.; William Z. Foster, *Misleaders of Labor* (Chicago, 1927); Sylvia Kopald, *Rebellion in Labor Unions* (New York, 1924).

4. John R. Seeley et al., *Community Chest* (Toronto: University of Toronto Press, 1957).

5. A nonscientific discussion of this issue in a vocational school is included in E. Hunter's novel, *Blackboard Jungle* (New York, 1956).

6. Ivan Belknap, *Human Problems of a State Mental Hospital* (New York: McGraw-Hill Book Co., 1956), esp. p. 67.

7. While such studies have little empirical value, they may have some practical value. Many of the evaluation studies have such a focus.

8. Talcott Parsons, *The Social System* (New York: Free Press, 1951).

9. See Martin Buber, *Paths in Utopia* (Boston, 1958).

10. Actually, of course, in order for a blueprint to exist, a group of actors—often a future elite of the organization—had to draw up the blueprint. This future elite presumably itself had "informal relations," and the nature of these relations undoubtedly affected the content of the blueprint as well as the way the organization was staffed and so forth.

11. Paul M. Harrison, *Authority and Power in the Free Church Tradition* (Princeton: Princeton University Press, 1959), p. 6. Harrison avoids this pitfall by comparing the policy of the church he studied (The American Baptist Convention) at different periods, taking into account, but not using as a measuring rod, its belief system and goals.

12. Some researchers take the public goals to be the real goals of the organization. Others choose them because they are easier to determine.

13. Public goals improve the input-output balance by recruiting support (inputs) to the organization from groups which would not support the private goals. This improves the balance as long as this increase in input does not require more than limited changes in output (some front activities). An extreme but revealing example is supplied in Philip Selznick's analysis of the goals of the Communist party. He shows that while the private goal is to gain power and control, there are various layers of public goals presented to the rank and file, sympathizers, and the "masses" [*The Organizational Weapon* (New York: McGraw-Hill Book Co., 1952), pp. 83–84].

14. Compare with a discussion of the relations between a model approach and a system approach in Paul Meadows, "Models, Systems and Science," *Amer. Sociol. Rev.* 22 (1957): 3–9.

15. For an outline of a system model for the analysis of organizations see Talcott Parsons, A Sociological Approach to the Theory of Organizations, *Admin. Sci. Quart.* 1 (1956): 63–85, 225–39.

16. The use of concepts such as goals, means, and conditions does not imply the use of a goal model as defined in the text. These concepts are used as defined on the more abstract level of the action scheme. On this scheme see Talcott Parsons, *The Structure of Social Action* (New York: Free Press, 1937).

17. Gouldner distinguished between a rational model and a natural-system model of organizational analysis. The rational model (Weber's bureaucracy) is a partial model since it does not cover all the basic functional requirements of the organization as a social system—a major shortcoming, which was pointed out by Robert K. Merton in his "Bureaucratic Structure and Personality," *Social Theory and Social Structure*, rev. ed., (New York: Free Press, 1957), pp. 195–206. It differs from the goal model by the type of functions that are included as against those that are neglected. The rational model is concerned almost solely with means activities, while the goal model focuses attention on goal activities. The natural-system model has some similarities to our system model, since it studies the organization as a whole and sees in goal realization just one organizational function. It differs from ours in two ways. First, the natural system is an observable, hence "natural" entity, while ours is a functional model, hence a construct. Second, the natural system model makes several assumptions that ours avoids, as, for example, viewing organizational structure as "spontaneously and homeostatically maintained," etc. See Alvin W. Gouldner, "Organizational Analysis," in *Sociology Today,* ed. Robert K. Merton, Leonard Broom and Leonard S. Cottrel, Jr. (New York: Basic Books, 1959), pp. 404 ff.

18. "Resources" is used here in the widest sense of the term including, for example, time and administration as well as the more ordinary resources.

19. One way in which organizations can change their environment, which is often overlooked, is by ecological mobility, e. g., the textile industry moving to the less unionized South. But this avenue is open to relatively few organizations.

20. Quoted from M. Greenblatt, R. H. York, and E. L. Brown, *From Custodial to Therapeutic Patient Care in Mental Hospitals* (New York: Russell Sage Foundation, 1955), p. 3; see also H. L. Smith and D. J. Levinson, "The Major Aims and Organizational Characteristics of Mental Hospitals," in *The Patient and the Mental Hospital,* ed. M. Greenblatt, D. J. Levinson, and R. H. Williams (New York: Free Press, 1957), pp. 3–8.

21. Greenblatt, York, and Brown, op. cit., p. 3.

22. "Effective Institutions for Juvenile Delinquents: A Research Statement," *Soc. Serv. Rev.* 33 (1959): 118.

23. R. H. McCleery, who studied a prison's change from a custodial to a partially "therapeutic" institution, pointed to the high degree of order and the low rate of escapes and riots in the custodial stage. See his *Policy Change in Prison Management* (East Lansing: Michigan State University, Govt. Res. Bur., 1957). See also Donald R. Cressey, "Contradictory Directives in Complex Organizations: The Case of the Prison," *Admin. Sci. Quart.* 4 (1959): 1–19; and "Achievement of an Unstated Organizational Goal: An Observation on Prisons," *Pacific Sociol. Rev.* 1 (Fall 1958): 43–49.

24. Oscar Grusky, "Role Conflict in Organization: A Study of Prison Camp Officials," *Admin. Sci. Quart.* 3 (1959): 452–72, quoted from p. 457. McCleery shows that changes in a prison he analyzed were possible since the community, through its representatives, was willing to support them, op. cit., pp. 30–31.

25. See Elaine Cumming and John Cumming, *Closed Ranks* (Cambridge, Mass.: Harvard University Press, 1957), p. xiv.

26. Ibid. It is of interest to note that the Cummings started their study with a goal model (how effective is the educational program?). In their analysis they shifted to a system model (p. 8). They asked what functions, manifest and latent, did the traditional attitudes toward mental health play for the community as a social system (ch. vii). This explained both the lack of change and suggested possible avenues to future change (pp. 152–58).

27. "Preface to the 1958 Reissue," in D. Clemmer, *The Prison Community* (New York: Holt, Rinehart & Winston, 1958), p. xiii.

28. Grusky, op. cit.; see also Cressey, "Foreword" to D. Clemmer, op. cit.

29. See Cressey, Contrary Directives.

30. It seems that some security measures fulfill internal functions as well. They include control of inmates till the staff has a chance to build up voluntary compliance and safety of other inmates, of the staff itself, of the inmate in treatment, of the institutional property, as well as others. These internal functions are another illustration of the nongoal activities that a goal approach tends to overlook and that a system approach would call attention to.

31. Michels, op. cit.

32. See Oliver Garceau, *The Political Life of the American Medical Association* (Cambridge, Mass.: Archon Books, 1941); R. T. McKenzie, *British Political Parties* (London: Macmillan Co., 1955). See also note 3.

33. Robert K. Merton, *Social Theory and Social Structure,* rev. ed., (New York: Free Press, 1957), pp. 199–201; Peter M. Blau, *The Dynamics of Bureaucracy* (Chicago: University of Chicago Press, 1955), index; David L. Sills, *The Volunteers* (New York: Free Press, 1957), pp. 62–69.

34. Michels, op. cit., p. 401.

35. The argument over the compatibility of democracy and effectiveness in "private government" is far from settled. The argument draws from value commitments but is also reinforced by the lack of evidence. The dearth of evidence can be explained in part by the fact that almost all voluntary organizations, effective and ineffective ones, are oligarchic. For the most recent and penetrating discussions of the various factors involved, see Seymour M. Lipset, "The Politics of Private Government," in his *The Political Man* (Garden City, N. Y.: Doubleday & Co., 1960), esp. pp. 360 ff. See also Lloyd H. Fisher and Grant McConnell, "Internal Conflict and Labor Union Solidarity," in *Industrial Conflict,* ed. A. Kornhauser, R. Dublin, and A. M. Ross (New York: McGraw-Hill Book Co., 1954), pp. 132–43.

36. For a summary statement of the various viewpoints on the effect of democratic procedures on trade unions, see Clark Kerr, *Unions and Union Leaders of Their Own Choosing* (New York, 1957).

37. Ibid.

38. *Union Democracy* (New York: Free Press, 1956). See also S. M. Lipset, "Democracy in Private Government," *Brit. J. Sociol.* 3 (1952): 47–63; "The Political Process in Trade Unions: A Theoretical Statement," in Morroc Berger et al., *Freedom and Social Control in Modern Society* (New York: Van Nostrand Reinhold Co., 1954), pp. 82–124.

39. Limitations of space do not allow us to discuss a third case of improved understanding with the shift from one model to another. Although apathy among members of voluntary associations as reflecting members' betrayal of their organizational goals and as undermining the functioning of the organization has long been deplored, it is now being realized that partial apathy is a functional requirement for the effective operation of many voluntary associations in the service of their goals as well as a condition of democratic government. See W. H. Morris Jones, "In Defense of Apathy," *Political Stud.* 2 (1954): 25–37.

40. The point has been elaborated and illustrated in Amitai Etzioni, "Authority Structure and Organizational Effectiveness," *Admin. Sci. Quart.* 4 (1959): 43–67.

41. A Study of Organizational Effectiveness, *Amer. Sociol. Rev.* 22 (1957): 534–40.

42. For a brief report of another effort to "dimensionalize" organizational effectiveness, see Robert L. Kahn, Floyd C. Mann, and Stanley Seashore, "Introduction" to a special issue on Human Relations Research in Large Organizations: II, *J. Soc. Issues* 12 (1956): 2.

43. What is needed from a methodological viewpoint is an accounting scheme for social systems like the one Lazarsfeld and Rosenberg outlined for the study of action. See Paul F. Lazarsfeld and Morris Rosenberg, eds., *The Language of Social Research* (New York: Free Press, 1955), pp. 387–491. For an outstanding sample of a formal model for the study of organizations as social systems, see Allen H. Barton and Bo Anderson, "Change in an Organizational System: Formalization of a Qualitative Study," in *Complex Organizations: A Sociological Reader,* ed. Amitai Etzioni (New York: Holt, Rinehart and Winston, 1961).

44. For many purposes, in particular for the study of ascriptive social units, two submodels are required: one that specifies the conditions under which a certain *structure* (pattern or form of a system) is maintained, another which specifies the conditions under which a certain level of activities or *processes* is maintained. A model of effectiveness of organizations has to specify both.

45. Robert K. Merton, *Social Theory and Social Structure,* rev. ed., (New York: Free Press, 1957), p. 52; see last part of E. Nagel's essay, "A Formalization of Functionalism," in *Logic without Metaphysics* (New York: Free Press, 1957).

46. One of the few areas in which sociologists have worked with both models is the study of stratification. Some are concerned with the question: is stratification a necessary condition for the existence of society? This is obviously a question of the survival of societies. Others have asked: which form of stratification will make for the best allocation of talents among the various social positions, will maximize training, and minimize social strains? Those are typical questions of the effectiveness model. Both models have been applied in enlightening debate over the functions of stratification; see Kingsley Davis, "A Conceptual Analysis of Stratification," *Amer. Sociol. Rev.* 7 (1952): 309–21; Kingsley Davis and Wilbert E. Moore, "Some Principles of Stratification," ibid. 10 (1954): 242–49; Melvin W. Tumin, "Some Principles of Stratification:

A Critical Analysis," ibid. 18 (1953): 387–94; Kingsley Davis, "Reply," ibid. 394–97; W. E. Moore, "Comment," ibid. 397. See also Richard D. Schwartz, "Functional Alternatives to Inequality," ibid. 20 (1955): 424–30.

47. For a theorem of dynamic functional analysis see Amitai Etzioni and Paul F. Lazarsfeld, "The Tendency toward Functional Generalization," in *Historical Materials on Innovations in Higher Education,* collected and interpreted by Bernhard J. Stern.

48. *Organizations* (New York: John Wiley & Sons, 1958), p. 84. See also Gouldner, op. cit., p. 405, for a discussion of "organization strain toward survival." Theodore Caplow developed an objective model to determine the survival potential of a social unit. He states: "Whatever may be said of the logical origins of these criteria, it is a reasonable assertion that no organization can continue to exist unless it reaches a minimal level in the performance of its objective functions, reduces spontaneous conflict below the level which is distributive, and provides sufficient satisfaction to individual members so that membership will be continued" ["The Criteria of Organizational Success," *Soc. Forces* 32 (1953): 4].

49. Charles S. Hyneman, "Means/Ends Analysis in Policy Science," *PROD* 2 (March 1959): 19–22.

50. "Party Activity in Postwar Berlin," in *Political Decision Makers,* ed. Dwaine Marvick (New York: Free Press).

51. On this fallacy, see Hans L. Zetterberg, *On Theory and Verification in Sociology* (New York: Tressler Press, 1954), esp. pp. 26 ff.

52. One of the reasons that this fallacy does not stand out in organizational studies is that many are case studies. Thus each researcher discovers that his organization is ineffective. This is not a finding which leads one to doubt the assumptions one made when initiating the study. Only when a large number of goal-model studies are examined 'does the repeated finding of low effectiveness, goal dilution, and so on lead one to the kind of examination which has been attempted here.

53. A recent study of social scientists by P. F. Lazarsfeld and W. Thielens, Jr., demonstrates this point, *The Academic Mind* (New York: Free Press, 1958). Some additional evidence in support of this point is presented in S. M. Lipset and J. Linz, "The Social Bases of Political Diversity in Western Democracies" (in preparation), ch. xi, pp. 70–72.

54. "A postscript for Reformers," in his *The Society of Captives* (Princeton: Princeton University Press, 1958), pp. 133–34.

55. Another important case is the conflict between intellectuals and politicians in many Western societies. For a bibliography and a recent study, see H. L. Wilensky, *Intellectuals in Labor Unions* (New York: Free Press, 1956).

56. These similarities in background make communication and contact of the researcher with the professionals studied easier than with other organizational personnel. This is one of the reasons why the middle level of organizations is often much more vividly described than lower ranking personnel or top management.

57. Arthur L. Stinchcomb pointed out to the author that organizations whose personnel includes a high ratio of professionals are more frequently studied than those which do not.

THE CONCEPT OF
ORGANIZATIONAL EFFECTIVENESS

Daniel Katz and Robert L. Kahn

There is no lack of material on criteria of organizational success. The literature is studded with references to efficiency, productivity, absence, turnover and profitability—all of these offered implicitly or explicitly, separately or in combination, as definitions of organizational effectiveness. Most of what has been written on the meaning of these criteria and on their interrelatedness, however, is judgmental and open to question. What is worse, it is filled with advice that seems sagacious but is tautological and contradictory.

In recent years the research evidence of this unsatisfactory state of affairs has begun to accumulate. For example, an attempt to make comparisons in rate of growth among 40 organizations performing similar functions (selling and servicing automobiles) encountered difficulties with the use of growth rate as a criterion of effectiveness. It appeared that the

Reprinted from Daniel Katz and Robert L. Kahn, *The Social Psychology of Organizations* (New York: John Wiley & Sons, Inc., 1966), pp. 149–70, by permission of the publisher.

meaning of growth for the health, survival, and overall effectiveness of an organization was very different at different stages of the organizational life cycle.[1]

A study using expert rankings to determine the effectiveness of 20 successful and 20 unsuccessful insurance agencies developed signs of internal contradiction in the course of analysis. These resulted from the fact that the concept of organizational effectiveness was understood as multidimensional by the expert raters who were in some disagreement with respect to the weighting of the various dimensions. Moreover, they were unaware of their disagreements. A factor analysis of 70 measures of performance obtained from these agencies (independent of the ratings) demonstrated that the effectiveness concept utilized in the research contained no fewer than seven independent factors, and that the expert judgments of effectiveness corresponded very badly to any of them.

A study of 32 operating units of a nationwide service organization was designed to evaluate leadership practices in relation to unit effectiveness, the latter based on managerial rankings. The data for five criteria of effectiveness (overall ratings, productivity as measured by time study, chargeable accidents, unexcused absences, and observed errors) were analyzed separately, after an attempt to predict according to the overall rankings showed an overlarge unexplained variance. The correlations among the five criteria of effectiveness were generally low, with fewer than half of them reaching significant levels. Even more disturbing was the fact that the magnitude of the intercorrelations varied greatly within the 32 organizational units. For example, the relationship between productivity and effectiveness varied from $-.56$ to $+.83$, and the relationships among the other criteria were no less erratic.[2]

The existence of the problem of developing satisfactory criteria of organizational performance is clear enough; its solution is much less obvious. Our working assumption is that the difficulty is essentially theoretical and conceptual, and that the remedies must begin with conceptual clarification. Organizational effectiveness has become one of those handy but treacherous pseudo concepts, connoting a sort of totality of organizational goodness—a sum of such elements as productivity, cost performance, turnover, quality of output and the like. This rudimentary model, as Seashore[3] states, "is false to most of the data we have examined so far, and more complex models needs to be invoked." In earlier chapters we have proposed that open-system theory supplies the elements of such a model for human organization, and we have attempted an elaboration of that theory to fit the phenomena of large-scale human organizations. With this model in mind, let us consider the meaning of organizational effectiveness, beginning with one of its major components, efficiency.

The Efficiency of Organizations

As open systems, organizations survive only so long as they are able to maintain *negentropy,* that is, import in all forms greater amounts of energy than they return to the environment as product. The reason for this is obvious. The energic input into an organization is in part invested directly and objectified as organizational output. But some of the input is absorbed or consumed by the organization. In order to do the work of transformation, the organization itself must be created, energized, and maintained, and these requirements are reflected in an inevitable energic loss between input and output. The electric transformer is a relatively efficient machine, but it extracts an energic price (recognizable as heat) in the process of changing alternating current to direct. The vacuum tube must be heated before it can do its work; even the transistor passes on less energy than it receives.

For all open systems, it is appropriate to question the amount of the cost. How much of the energic input from the outside into the system emerges as product, and how much is absorbed by the system? In other words, what is the net energic cost of the transformation? The ideal answer to this question would be provided by a system which exported as intended output 100 per cent of the energy which it received. For such a system the efficiency ratio of output/input would be 1.00 or 100 per cent.

There is a convenient simplicity to examples like that of the electric motor or transformer. They are systems for which the input is a single energic form—electricity—and the output is a single but different energic form—the kinetic energy of a rotating shaft in the case of the motor, and an altered electric current in the case of the transformer. In such cases the efficiency concept (ratio) is relatively obvious in meaning and easy in computation. In all human organizations, however, there are many additional complications, and in private industry there is the special complication of profit and its relation to efficiency.

One of the major and characteristic complications of human organizations lies in the multiple forms in which energy is imported. Almost all organizations take in energy in at least two forms: *people,* as energy sources; and *materials,* which already contain the energic investment of procurement, extraction, or partial manufacture. Many organizations also import energy in other forms such as steam, electricity, or the movement of water.

Rough distinctions are often made among these energic sources and among the uses to which each may be put. For example, it is customary to refer to the energic input of people as *direct* or *indirect,* according to its closeness to the basic transformation in which the organization is engaged. In general, direct labor refers to all energy which acts directly on the materials being put through the organization. (Forming metal, grinding corn, and selling groceries are direct labor.) Energy which acts directly on other members of the organization (supervision or staff services), or on materials not part of the organizational through-put (accounting, running time studies, or planning future requirements), we are accustomed to call indirect labor. It is a long-standing convention of industry, although one which we predict will be shattered by the combined demands of labor unions and automated procedures, to pay for direct labor by the hour and indirect labor by periods of time ranging from a week to a year.

A distinction in some ways similar to that between direct and indirect labor is made with respect to materials. Reflecting primarily their directness of use in the organizational through-put (that is, the rapidity with which they are consumed in the productive process), they are classified as *supplies* or *equipment*. The ideal supply is completely consumed in the process of organizational transformation; it emerges transformed and without waste as product or output. The ideal equipment, on the other hand, is eternal and indestructible; it facilitates the organizational through-put but is not transformed. In practice, of course, the distinction blurs; the electric utility uses up its generators and steam turbines no less than the coal which feeds them—but more slowly.

A further complication in studying the efficiency of human organizations stems from the inadequacy of our methods of accounting and reckoning. The measurement of organizational input and output is not often done in energic terms, nor in any other common denominator which might be translated readily into some energic measure. We speak in tons, board feet, hours, or gallons, according to the material or commodity in question. The nearest we come to a common measure of these diverse units is the dollar (cost), which is not necessarily commensurate with energic input and output. It is interesting, perhaps even ironic, that economists have long recognized the disadvantage of using money as a unit of measure in circumstances that really require measures of energic investment and psychic return. Most economists have nevertheless become so convinced of the elusiveness of such concepts that they have given up trying to make operational their psychic concept of utility and have preferred to be guided by its distant and distorted fiscal echo.

To regard the cycles of organizational life in energic terms does not solve all the conceptual problems of organizational effectiveness. Miller[4] has proposed that organizations must be regarded both as information-processing and energy-processing systems, and in subsequent chapters on communication and policy-making we will be concerned more with informational than with simple energic processes. Nevertheless, in conceptual terms, if not in terms yet convenient for measurement, we can speak of the efficiency of an organization in a fashion analogous to that of the motor: How much output do we get for a given input? How much input must we invest to assure a given output? And where an absolute answer to such questions may be difficult or impossible, approximations thereto or relative efficiencies of two or more similar organizations are often quite feasible.

Imagine two modest establishments engaged in the manufacture of baseball bats, one producing the bats entirely by hand, and the other making use of a lathe, power saw, and power sander. One immediate measure of the relative efficiency of these two establishments could be had by comparing the energic input required by each to produce a finished bat. It is likely, however, that these quantities would not be readily available, and we might therefore make use of an approximation: the number of man-hours of input required to produce a bat, assuming for the moment that the energic input of the hand-worker during an hour was equal to that of the tool-worker. (We assume, in other words, that the lathe-hand is working as "hard" as the worker using a spoke shave.) If we found that the lathe-hand made one bat during each hour of an eight-hour day, while the hand-worker made only one bat during an entire day, we would conclude that the lathe system was eight times as efficient as the hand system for the manufacture of baseball bats.

The example would have to be elaborated in many respects before it would begin to do justice to the complexities of our subject. The two manufacturing operations do not permit such simple comparisons. They both make direct use of human labor and of wood. But the lathe system uses lathes, and the hand system does not. True, the lathe system does not use up the lathe very fast; it may last, let us say, for the manufacture of 100,000 bats. Nevertheless, it is part of the input, and 1/100,000 part of the energic cost of creating a lathe must be included in the energic cost of each bat. The advantage will still lie with the lathe system over the hand system. But an important principle is involved: our first comparison disregarded entirely the cost of the physical plant; our second comparison at least raised the problem of computing and including such costs. Obviously a complete energic accounting, like a complete cost accounting, would include all inputs—labor, electricity, plant, equipment, and the rest.

The system theorist is not rigid about such matters, however; for him the inclusion or exclusion of any input is a problem of frame of reference. It is permissible (and it is sometimes very useful) to compare the efficiency of two systems with each in a prime ongoing state, without regard to the cost of achieving and maintaining that state. If you do not want to accept the physical equipment of a system as given, or if (which amounts to the same thing) you want to measure efficiency over a period of time longer than the life of the equipment, then the energic cost of replacement must be included in your calculations. Efficiency becomes a matter not only of labor input and materials (direct costs) but also of plant and equipment (indirect costs). For most purpose, any statement regarding efficiency must include both direct and indirect costs, especially in light of the increasing rate at which industrial equipment becomes obsolete.

The problem of defining spatial boundaries for some purpose of organizational analysis is much like the temporal problem. How much space (what activities) are we to include in the system under analysis? The nature of this problem can be readily illustrated by means of the previous example, if we bring into the manufacture of baseball bats the additional issue of wood supply and procurement. Suppose that the Lathe Bat Company is located in New York City and imports its wood from an average distance of 500 miles. The Hand Bat Company is located next to a mature ash grove and brings its wood an average distance of 500 yards. If our comparison of efficiencies is defined solely in terms of the manufacturing process, the facts of location are irrelevant. If we are interested in a larger organizational space of procurement-plus-production, then nearness to source of materials is important. In this example, the relative efficiency of the Lathe Bat Company as compared to its competitor is less because of its location. Analogous arguments with respect to location could be made for any other needed resource and for any other environmental transaction including marketing.

The spatial and temporal boundaries to system analysis are characteristically interdependent. Suppose we specify that our analysis of bat manufacture is to apply in perpetuity, or at least for a time period of great and indefinite length. To guarantee a permanent supply of the appropriate wood, the bat company may find it necessary (as some large lumber companies do) to extend its boundaries to include operations which will guarantee renewal of major supplies at a rate which balances their consumption in manufacture. Thus the bat company must grow ash trees as fast as it cuts them down and uses them, and a subsystem of reforestation becomes part of the total energic cost of bat manufacture and part of the system for manufacture.

Which frame of reference, or definition of system boundaries in space and time, is appropriate depends on what we want to do. If we want to make an overall comparison between two companies or predict their profitability, the legal boundaries of the establishment may be appropriate for our purpose. But suppose that our efficiency study is intended to determine whether or not the Hand Bat Company should install lathes. For this purpose the comparison of manufacturing operations per se is most appropriate. Similarly, a decision about plant location would involve efficiency comparisons with respect to procurement and marketing with manufacturing procedures as such largely irrelevant. Empirical studies of industrial mobility have documented the considerations which are dominant in determining the location and relocation of companies.[5]

There is no limit to the extension of time-space boundaries in the study of human systems, since all seemingly independent and separate human systems are linked together into the total system of human life. The human enterprise as a whole, moreover, represents a system of great negative entropy. It persists only by means of massive importation of energy—first of all from the sun, on a continuing basis, and second from other natural processes—some of time long past, like the formation of coal and oil, and some continuing, like the power of rivers and waterfalls.

Potential and Actual Efficiency

The efficiency ratio tells us how well the organization utilizes the energy at its disposal, how much energic investment in all forms (labor, supplies, power, and the like) is required for each unit of output. This concept of efficiency, in turn, can be resolved into two distinct components: the potential efficiency of the system design, and the extent to which that potential is realized in practice.

Suppose that two plants identical in technology are set up with different organizational structures, one plan calling for a supervisor for each ten workers and the other calling for a supervisor (putting forth equivalent effort) for each twenty workers. If both plants operate as designed, let us say to produce 1000 television sets in an eight-hour shift, clearly the more efficient system is the organization with fewer supervisory positions. It is achieving the same output with less energic input. Furthermore, its superior efficiency is intrinsic in the organizational *design*. Each system is operating as designed, but one design is more efficient than the other.

The example might not work out this way, of course. If the thinness of supervision in the "20:1" plant were reflected in higher scrap loss and lower production, so that this plant produced only 800 working television sets per day, the efficiency comparison between the two plants would be different. One plant would have the more economical (efficient) organizational plan, but would be unable to fulfill in practice the production which the plan called for; the other organization would have a more costly (less efficient) plan, but its operation would meet fully the specifications of the plan. Which of the two plants was more efficient overall would be an empirical question.

This kind of distinction between components of efficiency is common enough. Every automobile enthusiast will assure us that an engine like that of the Jaguar, with its double overhead camshafts and hemispherical combustion chambers, is inherently more efficient than a flathead, side-valve engine of the same displacement. If both engines are in prime condition and properly tuned, the facts of this comparison can be readily demonstrated in terms of speed, developed horsepower, and other criteria of performance and efficiency. One engine is simply a better, more elegant design than the other; it is a superior system of transforming gasoline into transportation. But what if the superior automobile has been badly driven, let out of adjustment, or otherwise abused, so that its actual performance falls far short of its potential efficiency? It may realize so little of its potential that it will in practice be less efficient than its plebeian competitor. There are, in short, two quite separate aspects of the efficiency of any functioning system: the potential or abstract efficiency in the system design and the extent to which that efficiency is realized in the concrete instance.

The two aspects are not wholly independent, of course. Some organizational designs are more capable of actualization than others, some more fragile or more accident-prone than others. The concept of the socio-technical system as proposed by Trist and his colleagues[6] and to some extent the concept of man-machine systems represent attempts to bring into the same framework both aspects of efficiency—the ideal efficiency of the system and the practicability of attaining that ideal with human beings and realistic conditions of work. Herman Wouk (1951) offered a more colorful comment on the same general issue when he observed in *The Caine Mutiny* that the Navy was an organization designed by geniuses to be run by idiots.[7]

Profit and Efficiency

Let us turn to the special but extensive case of the profit-making organization. We said that the efficiency of an organizational system is given by the ratio of its energic output (or product) to its energic input (or cost). We stipulated also that total cost per unit of production includes procurement, marketing, maintenance, depreciation of plant, and the like. Will this efficiency ratio also define precisely the profitability of the plant? No.

An increase in efficiency will tend to make a plant more profitable, since the greater efficiency means a lesser cost per unit of product and implies no immediate reduction in selling price. Prices tend to be set by what consumers will pay and correspond roughly to the production costs of the least efficient producers. In 1963, for example, the General Motors Corporation reported profits of approximately 20 per cent on sales; its competitors reported profit rates of about half that magnitude. No doubt many factors entered into the profit advantage of General Motors, the efficiencies of size and volume prominent among them. A gain in the efficiency of a particular company, then, is likely to mean an increase in profit.

But other considerations must be introduced even into an elementary discussion of profit, considerations which have little to do with system efficiency. Suppose that a manufacturer of television sets has two plants in different parts of the country, and that the plants are technologically identical. The dollar investment in plant and equipment is identical, and the costs of procuring supplies and marketing the finished product are the same. In Plant A, however, the employees work 25 per cent harder than in Plant B, and they produce 25 per cent more sets. As a result, Plant A is certainly more profitable than Plant B, and there is a presumption that it is better managed. Is it also 25 per cent more efficient as a system?

In the energic terms of reference we have employed, it is not. Plant A uses the same number of energy units per product unit as does Plant B. Plant A is simply getting a greater energic input from each worker. Suppose that employees in Plant A worked ten hours each day instead of eight (an alternative way of obtaining a 25 per cent increase in energic input from each worker). Would this increase in hours of work make Plant A more efficient than Plant B as a producing system? Of course not—at least not in the terms in which we have defined efficiency. Efficiency has to do with the ratio of energic output to input; increasing the output by running the system longer or by increasing the rate of energic input does not per se alter the efficiency ratio.

Only in certain limited respects would such changes in operation tend to affect efficiency. The plant in which workers are suddenly motivated to work 25 per cent harder and produce 25 per cent more has not had a 25 per cent change in the efficiency ratio of output/input, since both numerator and denominator have increased. There will have been some genuine gain in efficiency, however, insofar as the greater output is obtained from the same plant and equipment without a corresponding increase in its rate of depreciation. If the gross increase in product is not cancelled out by the more rapid using-up of plant and equipment, there will be some resultant gain in efficiency. There will be greater differences between these two plants in profitability, however. The company which has induced its employees to increase output by 25 per cent has probably realized a profit increase of much greater magnitude, unless the production increase has been motivated by or rewarded with a corresponding increase in the wage bill. In any case, the important point is that profitability and efficiency are not synonymous, as energic and dollar accounting are not synonymous, although they are certainly related.

Efficiency and Survival

The discussion of efficiency has so far made little reference to the dimension of time. The definition of efficiency as an energic ratio can be applied at any instant of time; the cost of the organizational transformation of inputs into product can be computed for any span of time. Short-term analyses are, as is often the case, easier and more obvious. The previous examples of organizations differing in efficiency have stipulated some of the major short-term advantages of the more efficient organization in comparison to its competitors. The more efficient organization can lower prices and thus gain a larger share of the market. Or it can, at a given market price, make more gross profit than its competitors. It can, as a result, increase the return to the members of any or all of its subsystems—managers, stockholders, and wage-earners. The more efficient organization, in short, is in the process of acquiring an energic surplus, because the terms of its input and output transactions are set by its less efficient competitors.

This operating advantage has long-term implications of importance, beginning with the storage of energy. Efficiency gives a margin over the organizational hand-to-mouth condition in which the return from product is barely sufficient to purchase the inputs needed to repeat the productive cycle. This margin can be immediately distributed as wage payments, bonuses, or dividends. In American industry executive bonuses and dividend payments vary sharply with changes in relative efficiency and gross profits; wage payments are more likely to be set by industry-wide standards of collective bargaining, although they, too, respond to increases or decreases in the margin between organizational income and outgo.

It is most unlikely that an organization will distribute all of the surplus of income over cost of production. Some of it is characteristically retained—as reserve funds, as capital funds for expansion, as funds for replacement of equipment and for various kinds of emergencies. All these funds represent the storage of energy by the organization, and the storage process can take other forms than money. The organization can stockpile materials, as manufacturers who can do so stockpile steel and coal under the threat of a strike. Some part of a surplus over immediate operating needs is typically used for expansion of the enterprise, for additions to plant or for still more efficient equipment, or for extension of organizational activity into new fields or product lines.

The major long-range outcomes of efficiency-generated surpluses are therefore organizational *growth* and an increment in the *survival power* of the organization. The storage of energy permits the organization to survive its own mistakes and the exigencies of its environment. For the organization without such storage, every untoward event, internal or external, is in some degree incapacitating, and mishaps of size can be deadly.

The contribution of efficiency to growth is not a one-way or a one-time organizational event; it is a cycle which continues over a wide span of time and a wide range of organizational circumstances, sizes, and structures. Efficiency begets growth, but growth brings new gains in efficiency. There are limits, of course; for any organization and technology there is some optimum size. But the optimum for technical purposes is apparently very large and the relationship of production costs to size can for many purposes be regarded as a linear function. The auto industry, for example, operates on the basis of substantial annual alterations in style or mechanical specifications, with annual costs of retooling running to the tens and hundreds of millions. The more units produced during the year by a given company, the lower the cost of that retooling which must be borne by each unit. This is an elementary kind of arithmetic, but inexorable. There is, of course, that theoretical point at which size becomes a handicap, and there are environmental changes which can make efficiency irrelevant. In general, however, the long-range effects of efficiency are growth and survival, and the effect of growth is likely to be increased efficiency.

Efficiency in Nonprofit Organizations

The foregoing analysis developed in the course of exploring the relationship of two common measures of organizational effectiveness, efficiency and profitability. To what extent is the analysis applicable to other human organizations, organizations which do not sell products and accumulate profits or losses? We can answer this question by posing another: What does profit signify? It means merely that people "want" the organizational product enough to forego other things and choose it, that is, buy it at a price which covers the costs of production, including profit. This is one way by which the larger social environment permits an organization to import energy—that is, hire people, build plants, and buy materials. If there is an overwhelming preference for other organizational products, or if people lack the economic means to signify their wants by buying, then in effect the organization is denied the means to import energy and it must reduce its operations or go out of business.

Business organizations differ, of course, in the advantageousness of their environmental transactions. As they become more efficient, they require less energic return in order to maintain their operations. There are also the many forms of special advantage bestowed by location, by exclusive production of certain goods, or by reserves built up from past efficiencies. The basic equation remains, however; in the long run the organization must receive its necessary quantum of energy from outside or it must cease to be, and a business receives this input only by selling its product.

For other kinds of organizations, the life-giving or death-dealing energic decisions are made in quite different fashion. A community college does not typically operate at a profit. In a sense, perhaps, the students "buy" its product but they do not pay a tuition high enough to permit the organization to hold its faculty and maintain its plant. The real sale of the college product is to the public, and the decision that the organization shall continue is given by the city council or other legislative body which appropriates the funds for operating the college. The legislature has, in effect, "chosen" the product of the community college in preference to other products which might have been had for the same appropriation. In so doing, the legislature makes it possible for the college to import the energy it requires.

The environmental decision to support the college differs in many respects from the decision to support the business establishment. The decision about the college is made formally and explicitly by a legislative body which has the legitimate power to appropriate funds or refuse them, power which in turn has been given to the legislature by the body politic and which can be withdrawn (at least from specific legislators) at the next election. In the case of a business, no purchaser of goods makes the decision to sustain the establishment or commit it to organizational ruin, and yet the sum of individual consumer decisions adds up to that determination.

For some other kinds of nonbusiness organizations, the picture is still more complicated. The military, for example, is sustained in part as is the college; it is awarded tax funds by legislative act. But it imports human energy in a more direct fashion by conscription. This, too, in our society requires legislative sanction, but it takes the form of a direct awarding of human energies to the military organization, rather than an awarding of money which enables the organization to attract people. Other inputs are acquired by the military, as by other organizations, through negotiation and purchase.

For some voluntary organizations, the process which determines organizational input is both individually decided and direct. A student weighs the decision to join the Chess Club, wondering whether the psychological return will be sufficiently great and its probability sufficiently high to make it "worth his while" to join and invest some part of his energies in the activities of the club. If he and a sufficient number of other students decide in favor of the club, it will have an organizational existence. If it fails to return enough psychic satisfaction to its members to motivate their continuing investment of energy, it will go out of existence. The "efficiency" of the club and its prospects for survival are given by the amount of such return to members in relation to the demands made on their time and energy.

The concept of efficiency does not have meaning only for business organizations, and the survival benefits of efficiency are not limited to profit-making organizations. These notions are inherent in the characteristics of human organizations as open systems. They remind us that the ultimate decision to give or withhold the needed organizational inputs lies in the environment, and that the larger social environment in this way holds the power of life and death over every organization.

Effectiveness: Maximizing Return to The Organization

We have seen that efficiency in business organizations produces immediate increases in profits, creates the possibility for energy storage, and is conducive to long-run growth and survival. Certainly the organization which increases its efficiency also increases its effectiveness as a viable system. Nevertheless, the efficiency criterion is insufficient for purposes of a complete organizational analysis; it is only an aspect of organizational effectiveness.

Efficiency is primarily a criterion of the internal life of the organization, and it is concerned with economic and technical aspects of the organization. By itself, it takes inadequate notice of the openness of human organizations. (Especially is this true when the efficiency concept is applied at a single moment of time.) Yet we have defined organizations as open systems, dependent on outside agencies in the environment for making available required energic inputs (labor, materials, and others) and for absorbing the organizational product. This means that the organization is constantly engaged in several kinds of environmental transactions—disposal or marketing, procurement or recruiting, information-getting, and the exertion of influence to accomplish organizational goals. The profitability of a business organization and the survival prospects of all human organizations are not given solely by considerations of efficiency in internal system design and actualization; they are determined also by the advantageousness of the organization-environment transactions.

In our society, as in other industrialized cultures, these transactions are usually carried on by means of money. Profit-making organizations sell their products for money and use the money to buy materials, pay wages, and thus renew the productive cycle. For charitable organizations, educational institutions, and agencies of government, the "sale" of the product may be less obvious but, as we have seen, there is still the problem of persuading some appropriate source in the environment to make operating funds available.

Regardless of the exact forms of the environmental transactions, they are of major significance for the organization. In industry, margin of profit and therefore security and survival are determined in part by such transactions, quite independently of the internal systemic efficiency of the organization. In the discussion of efficiency and profit, we have already considered two of the more obvious examples of such transactional advantage—nearness to supplies and nearness to markets. The location of an organization in relation to agencies in its environment with which it must relate is a clear source of economic advantage or disadvantage. This is true in the absolute reckoning of total costs of production and distribution; it is even more significant in terms of relative costs or the state of the organization in relation to its competitors.

Such advantages of location may be accidental, arising from causes wholly outside the organization and unforeseen within it. They may also come about because of successful planning within the organization. In the latter case, persisting advantage has accrued to the organization because of better information-getting (another form of transaction), or because of superior processing of and inferring from information within the organization.

Location is only one source of advantage in organizational input and output. The getting and sending of information across organizational boundaries are other important sources. Indeed, a key measure of efficiency for a procurement department is the thoroughness with which it scans the potential sources of supply and chooses the source with least organizational cost.

For sales and marketing departments, the analogous function is the discovery of customers who offer greatest organizational advantage. Such transactions, however, are not merely informational; they involve persuasion and exercise of influence. The terms of purchase or sale must be negotiated. We can generalize this point by stating that environmental transactions are in some degree *political*; they involve the making and engineering of choices on grounds other than economics and efficiency in an open market.

The pursuit of organizational goals by political means is most prevalent and a most natural outcome of the dynamics of organization. The very achievement of internal organizational efficiency promotes growth and, if continued, dominance with some degree of monopolistic control over the terms of procurement and marketing. But even where that degree of internal efficiency has not been attained, a company has much to gain in overall effectiveness by using political tactics. Some of these tactics have been outlawed for almost a century (although the simultaneous existence of anti-trust and "fair-trade" legislation suggests confusion and ambivalence in these matters). Conspiracy in restraint of trade, monopolistic dominance of an industrial field, price fixing among major producers, and the like are illegal. They are nevertheless live legal issues, and few years pass without trials and suits of substantial scope. Political advantages in sale and purchase are pressed, and the number of corporations (and corporate executives) that choose to live dangerously near the legal margin gives testimony to the rewards of doing so.

Many forms of political influence in the service of organizational goals are judged legitimate by the larger society. We are indignant at "payola," and prosecute some forms of bribery. It is considered appropriate, however, for an organization to attempt to bring about advantageous environmental relationships by persuasion of influential people, by lobbying, or even by donations to election funds. These advantages may take the form of subsidies, as in the case of airlines and the merchant marine, or special tax arrangements, as in the case of oil and gas producers. They may take the form of tariffs and duties or even of attacks on unions and legislation to weaken union influence on the conditions under which business is conducted. It is no less an example of political means in the service of organizational effectiveness, of course, when labor unions create their own legislative programs and political campaigns.

Political and economic transactions merge in some instances. A company which has sufficient resources to afford the maneuver may reduce prices below the cost of production for a time, in order to eliminate or make more tractable a competitor who lacks the cushion of stored resources to survive such a program. This is essentially a political tactic, although the immediate means involve economic manipulation.

It is not necessary for our present purposes to attempt a catalogue of political extensions of organizational control over the environment. It is important to recognize such extensions as inevitable outcomes of the organizational dynamic for survival, growth, security, and return to members. The textbook path to organizational survival is internal efficiency: build the better mousetrap or build the old trap less expensively. There is, however, a whole class of alternative or supplementary solutions—the political devices which maximize organizational return at some cost to other organizations or individuals. These alternatives we have called political, in contrast to the economic or technical alternatives.

Economic-technical solutions are reflected as increases in organizational efficiency. They make the organization a more efficient system for the transformation of energy and thereby contribute to its growth and survival. They do not necessarily make the organization more efficient in the acquisition of inputs and the disposal of outputs, although they may contribute to the advantageousness of such transactions by improving the organizational ability to scan the environment broadly and accurately for sources of supply or for markets. Political solutions complement economic ones by dealing with problems of input and disposal in other ways, usually involving direct manipulation of the environment. Both economic and political means contribute to profitability and to organizational effectiveness. We can define organizational effectiveness, then, as the maximization of return to the organization, by economic and technical means (efficiency), and by political means.

The examples of political effectiveness we have offered have dealt entirely with external transactions—with arrangements to maintain price levels, to get subsidies or other preferments, to eliminate or restrict competition, or to get some commitment to obtain inputs on advantageous terms. The use of political means to obtain organizational advantage need not always be directed outside the organization, however, although outside efforts are more conspicuously political. We would also define as political rather than technical most devices for getting more energic investment from the worker for each wage dollar. Extreme cases make the point obvious: slavery is a political institution, a set of political means for guaranteeing labor input to organizations concerned with agriculture and construction. The institution of indenture provides another example.

We would argue also that, if one firm pays lower wages than another, or induces its workers to work longer hours, or to work harder, all these would constitute political increments to organizational effectiveness. And the opposition to such attempts by management takes political forms— in terms of the demand for collective bargaining, for a minimum wage, for a contractual agreement about hours of work and speed of work.

There is admittedly a certain arbitrariness in deciding where to draw the line between efficiency and political effectiveness, and it is tempting to draw it at the organizational boundary. This would have the effect, however, of defining as efficiency all internal arrangements which increased the organizational return—whether by improvements in the energic ratio of input required to create a given amount of product, or by devices for inducing increased energic input from organizational members. We prefer to distinguish between these two kinds of increments to effectiveness, keeping the term efficiency to describe the former and including the latter with other, externally oriented political approaches.

There is in this distinction no implication that to increase organizational return by means of efficiency gains is virtuous and to do so by political means is reprehensible. The value issues involved require separate argument and justification. The neutrality of the political classification can perhaps be illustrated by those programs which are designed to induce greater energic input from organizational members by means which enhance the return to those members. Many human relations programs are frankly intended to increase both energic investment and psychological return to the worker; to the extent that they involve no systemic or structural changes within the organization, they contribute to organizational effectiveness by political means rather than by increasing the efficiency ratio.

Political effectiveness, then, consists, in the short run, of maximizing the return to the organization by means of advantageous transactions with various outside agencies and groups, and with the members of the organization as well. Like efficiency, political effectiveness contributes to the immediate profitability of the enterprise and to its growth and survival power for the longer term. It leads also to increased control over the organizational environment, as short-term advantages in external transactions are reinforced and made permanent by precedent and legal recognition.

The preceding exposition of efficiency and political effectiveness in the short term and the longer run is summarized in the figure below.

Frame of Reference and The Supersystem

We have defined organizational effectiveness as the extent to which all forms of energic return to the organization are maximized. This is determined by a combination of the efficiency of the organization as a system and its success in obtaining on advantageous terms the inputs it requires. We have also distinguished between effectiveness in the short-term and in the long-term sense. The marks of long-term effectiveness we

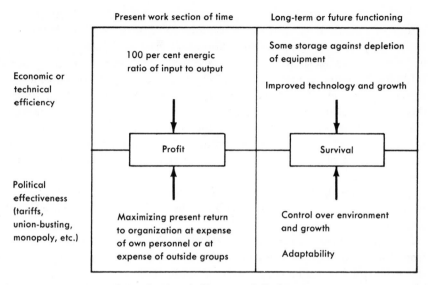

Organizational Frame of Reference

have identified as storage, growth, survival, and control over the environment. This discussion has taken place within the organizational frame of reference—effectiveness from the point of view of the organization.

All frames of reference are arbitrary, however, and there are advantages and disadvantages to the one we have used. In a book on organizations as systems, it is perhaps unnecessary to justify the use of the organizational frame of reference, but we should not leave the issue of organizational effectiveness without reminding ourselves that the single organization is an intermediate level of discourse, and that either a lesser or loftier frame is appropriate for some purposes. We can discuss organizational effectiveness from the point of view of the individual member, defining as most effective that organization which offers the greatest aggregate return to the member. We can also consider organizational effectiveness in terms of the supersystem, the society of which the organization is a part.

At this level, the effectiveness of the organization would be assessed in terms of its contribution to the efficiency, survival power, and environmental control of the entire societal system. The transactions between the organization and other agencies in the society would be judged effective to the degree that the organization provided maximal return to the society for the energic demands which it made on the society. The test of effectiveness, in other words, would be little changed, but would be applied at the next higher level of social organization. In doing so, the prosperity and survival of the organization become secondary.

For example, consider an organization established to discover the causes of cancer. It is most successful and contributes most to the larger society by completing its mission promptly, even if in doing so it terminates its own existence. The agonies of the National Foundation for Infantile Paralysis to convert its March of Dimes and its organizational mission from the cure of polio to the cure of other diseases illustrates this contradiction between organizational survival and societal needs. During wartime, when the needs of the larger society are prominent in the minds of all citizens, the distinction between the organizational and societal frames of reference is obvious and frequently invoked. Organizations are expected to concentrate on meeting the societal need of maximum production and they are criticized if they do "business as usual," that is, operate in such a way as to maximize the gains and survival of the organization as such.

Ordinarily, however, we expect the managers of organizations to act from the organizational frame of reference, and we do not impose on them the strain of acting consistently in the interests of the larger community. We know that what is good for the country may not always be good for the organization, and we expect the concern for the larger society to be concentrated in those roles which are organization-free. Indeed, we are suspicious of conflict of interest on the part of individuals who show themselves to be carrying some of the old impediments into the new role.

Perhaps monopoly is the most obvious example of an organizational form which constitutes high effectiveness in terms of the organizational frame of reference, and reduced effectiveness in terms of the societal or supersystem frame of reference. Monopoly implies extensive control of the environment by the organization; competitors have been eliminated and potential competitors are discouraged by various means. The terms (price, amount of supply) on which the organizational product will be made available to the larger society are determined largely from within the organization. There is typically a restriction of product below the potential levels of output. Monopoly is, in short, a relationship of organization to society characterized by a peculiar degree of political control and effectiveness by the organization. (That effectiveness may have been facilitated by economic efficiency, but it has gone beyond efficiency.)

From the societal view, the political effectiveness of the monopoly is experienced as additional costs in the sense of restricted supply of goods and disadvantageous terms of exchange with the organization (higher prices than are required for organizational sustenance). To risk a generalization which is much more hypothetical than demonstrated, we could say that gains in organizational effectiveness which come about through improved organizational efficiency are likely to be gains also from the societal frame of reference. Gains in overall organizational effectiveness which come about through gains in the political component of effectiveness are more variable in their implications for the larger system. They may be, as in the monopolistic examples, losses to the society as a whole.

Examples of discontinuity between the requirements of different systemic levels do not all consist of organizational gains at societal costs. There are times when societal needs, especially in the short term, impose inefficiencies on organizations: the society asks the organization to become less effective in its own terms in order to become more effective in meeting the needs of the supersystem. The sharpest examples can be found in the wartime operation of industry. The short-term demand of the larger society for maximizing gross product takes precedence over all the usual criteria of organizational efficiency. Production costs become almost irrelevant; criteria of employee selection are rewritten. The cost-plus contract is not merely a pressing of organizational advantage for the purpose of profit; it symbolizes the abandonment of one set of criteria and frame of reference for another.

We can imagine a similar imposition of supersystem criteria with respect to any goal of great social importance. The identification of such goals is essentially a problem in values rather than organizational theory as such. We might decide, for example, that the importance of discovering causes and cures for cancer in the least possible time is far more important than making such discoveries at the least possible cost, or in ways that conform to the usual signs of organizational efficiency. The indications of such a decision would be the availability of massive inputs for cancer-related research, willingness to support conflicting approaches simultaneously instead of in some sequence of learning, tolerance of duplication, and many other violations of the etiquette of efficiency. It is interesting that the word *war* (war on disease, war on poverty) is in general use to indicate the abandonment of the organizational frame of reference and the launching of a major effort in which the societal frame of reference defines effectiveness.

The conflict between the organizational and societal frames of reference is essentially spatial; it has to do with the number of organizations, roles, and individuals to be considered in applying criteria of effectiveness. An analogous problem arises in connection with issues of time; short-term and long-term frames of reference are no less different than organizational and societal. Like spatial differences, temporal differences may or may not create differences in the criteria and definition of organizational effectiveness. A business may, for example, come into a situation where it must get a product on the market during a certain season or lose the market entirely, get a plant into production during a certain year or lose major initiative to a competitor. In the extreme case, an organization may be faced with attaining some short-run goal for the sake of long-run survival. Under such circumstances, the usual criteria of efficiency and effectiveness are violated in the short run for the sake of long-term success. The contract is accepted even though the organization will lose money on it; supplies are bought on terms which would otherwise be rejected. Overtime wages are paid; premiums are offered for completion of work ahead of schedule. The short-term criteria of effectiveness, including profit, are sacrificed for that ultimate long-term criterion—survival.

The foregoing section has been a discussion of frames of reference, and the ways in which criteria and judgments of effectiveness are transmuted by changing spatial and temporal frames of reference. It is perhaps appropriate to conclude by considering a frame of reference which has pervaded the entire chapter, which pervades no less the thinking of most people about organizational life, and which is in process of being upset by the changing technology of our time. This frame of reference has as its central assumption the scarcity of energy. It follows that efficiency or energy-conserving modes of production are preferred, that time and energy must be bought, that leisure (time free from outside ·energic demands) is scarce and precious. The proposition of energic scarcity and its various corollaries probably provide a good and perhaps necessary basis for working toward an affluent, leisure-based society. But do they offer an appropriate basis for maintaining and living in such a society, and especially for understanding the problems and opportunities posed by such a society?

To state in extreme form the argument for a new set of assumptions, we would say that the achievement of real affluence by means of technical success and automated means of production inverts the old assumption of energic scarcity. Real affluence creates a situation in which meaningful outlets for human energy are scarce, while available energy abounds. Under such circumstances, new criteria of organizational effectiveness may be evolved. Organizations of size less than that indicated for maximal efficiency may be chosen for the satisfactions of the social relations they provide. Processes of production less than maximally efficient may be chosen for the intrinsic satisfaction they offer the worker or the aesthetic satisfaction their variability of product offers to the consumer. These speculations are offered without substantiation or elaboration here, because their accuracy is unimportant for the point of this chapter; they are relevant here only to remind us that virtually every definition and research effort in the area of organizational effectiveness is involved with the unspoken and now shaky assumption of energic scarcity.

Summary

Organizational effectiveness is introduced as a term which has been subject to numerous and conflicting uses. An attempt is made to resolve such conflicts by distinguishing among several components of organizational effectiveness.

Organizational efficiency is the first such component, and is defined as the ratio of energic output to energic input. Efficiency thus tells us how much of the input of an organization emerges as product and how much is absorbed by the system. Further distinctions are made between human energy and materials as organizational inputs, between direct and indirect uses of human energy in organizations, and between the use of materials as supplies and as equipment. The computation of organizational efficiency is shown to be dependent upon the spatial and temporal definitions of organization.

A further distinction is introduced between the potential efficiency of an organization and its actual efficiency. This distinction contrasts the elegance of a given organizational design with the degree to which a given design is realized in organizational practice.

Efficiency is also distinguished from profit, although the two are asserted to be strongly related. The contribution of efficiency to survival is discussed in terms of the storage of energy which efficiency permits and the consequent margin for error which it provides.

The chapter concludes with an explication of organizational effectiveness as the maximization of return to the organization by all means. Such maximization by economic and technical means has to do with efficiency; maximization by noneconomic or political means increases effectiveness without adding to efficiency. Increases in effectiveness by both means are typically observable as storage of energy, organizational growth, organizational endurance and survival, and as organizational control of the surrounding environment. All definitions of effectiveness involve some assumptions with respect to frame of reference. Two such frames are considered, that of the organization as a system in its own right, and that of the larger society or system of which the organization is a subsystem.

---

1. S. E. Seashore, *The Assessement of Organizational Performance* (Ann Arbor, Mich.: Survey Research Center, 1962).

2. S. E. Seashore, B. P. Indik, and B. S. Georgopolous, "Relationship Among Criteria of Job Performance," *J. Appl. Psych.* 44 (1960): 195–202.

3. Seashore, op. cit., 1962.

4. D. R. Miller, "The Study of Social Relations: Situation, Identity, and Social Interaction," in *Psychology: A Study of a Science,* vol. 5, ed. S. Koch (New York: McGraw-Hill Book Co., 1963), pp. 639–737.

5. E. M. Hoover, *The Location of Economic Activity* (New York: McGraw-Hill Book Co., 1948); G. Katona and J. Morgan, *Industrial Mobility in Michigan* (Ann Arbor, Mich.: Institute for Social Research, 1950); E. Mueller and J. Morgan, "Location Decisions of Manufacturers," *Amer. Econ. Rev.* (May 1952): 204–17.

6. F. E. Emery and E. L. Trist, "Socio-Technical Systems," in *Management Sciences, Models and Techniques,* ed. C. W. Churchman and M. Verhulst (London: Pergamon Press, 1960).

7. H. Wouk, *The Caine Mutiny* (Garden City, N.Y.: Doubleday, 1951).

ADDITIONAL READINGS

The three readings included in this part provide valuable insights into the broad theoretical and conceptual issues involved in analyzing organizations and in approaching the study of organizational effectiveness. The bibliography provided at the end of this part is intended to be a guide for further readings and study of theoretical foundations of modern theory dealing with organizations. The bibliography is divided into four sections. The first section presents a list of some major books and monographs pertinent to the field of organization theory.

The second section provides a list of some major critiques and discussions about the historical roots, growth, and present state of organization and bureaucracy theory. Broad critiques and overviews of this field are provided in the works of Burns, 1966; Mayntz, 1964; W. G. Scott, 1961; W. R. Scott, 1964; Stodgill, 1966; and Wolin, 1969. Kaufman, 1964, undertakes an interesting comparison between organization theory and political theory; students of organization should find this article a useful pathway into the rich field of political theory which appears to have been neglected by modern organization theorists. Landsberger, 1961, and Whyte, 1961, provide a critical review of the relevance of Talcott Parsons' writings to organization theory and analysis. As Parsons' works have had a notable impact on modern organization theory, these two critiques of his works should be particularly helpful to students of organizations. Bakke, 1959; Barnard, 1938; and Bettner, 1965, provide analytical discussions of the concept of organization. Bennis, 1966, and Crozier, 1964, undertake discussions of the role of bureaucratic organizations in modern society.

The third section of the bibliography lists some major theoretical works dealing with the emergent field of management or administrative theory. The distinguishing feature of this field is its focus upon analysis of the job of the administrator or manager of complex organizations. Its roots lie in diverse disciplines such as organization and bureaucracy theory, human engineering, industrial psychology and "behavioral science." Critiques and overviews of this field are provided by: Alton, 1969; Basi, 1969; Massie, 1965; and Zaleznik, 1967.

The fourth section provides a list of some conceptual schemes, models and frameworks for organizational analysis and research. These have their primary roots in bureaucracy and organization theories discussed in the works listed in section one of this list; they are influenced also by general research in the social and behavioral sciences. Review and application to organizational analysis of the comparative method, which has figured prominently in social research, is provided by Blau, 1965; Burns, 1967; Perrow, 1967; and Udy, 1965. Exposition and application of general systems theory to organizational analysis is undertaken by Boulding, 1956; Chin, 1961; and Mesarovic, 1964. The socio-technical systems approach is discussed by Trist, 1959.

Selected Books on Organizational Theory

Bennis, Warren G. 1966. *Changing organizations.* New York: McGraw-Hill Book Co.

_____. 1968. *The temporary society.* New York: Harper and Row.

Berrien, F. Kenneth. 1968. *General and social systems.* New Brunswick, N.J.: Rutgers University Press.

Bowers, Raymond V. 1966. *Studies on behavior in organizations.* Athens, Ga.: University of Georgia Press.

Buckley, Walter. 1967. *Sociology and modern systems theory.* Englewood Cliffs, N.J.: Prentice-Hall.

_____. 1968. *Modern systems research for the behavioral sciences.* Chicago: Aldine Publishing Co.

Churchman, C. West. 1968. *The systems approach.* New York: Delacorte Press.

Cooper, W. W., Leavitt, H. J., and Shelley, M. W., eds. 1964. *New perspectives in organization research.* New York: John Wiley & Sons.

Crozier, Michael. 1964. *The bureaucratic phenomenon.* Chicago: University of Chicago Press.

Etzioni, Amitai. 1969. *A sociological reader on complex organizations.* 2nd ed. New York: Holt, Rinehart & Winston.

Kahn, R. L., and Boulding, Elise. 1964. *Power and conflict in organizations.* New York: Basic Books.

Katz, Daniel, and Kahn, Robert L. 1966. *The social psychology of organizations.* New York: John Wiley & Sons.

Lawrence, J. R., ed. 1966. *Operational research and the social sciences.* London: Tavistock Publications.

Lawrence, Paul R., and Lorsch, Jay W. 1967. *Organization and environment: Managing differentiation and integration.* Boston: Division of Research; Graduate School of Business Administration, Harvard University.

Leavitt, Harold J. 1967. *The social science of organizations.* Englewood Cliffs, N.J.: Prentice-Hall.

Likert, Rensis. 1967. *The human organization: its management and values.* New York: McGraw-Hill Book Co.

March, James G. 1965. *Handbook of organizations.* Skokie, Ill.: Rand McNally & Co.

Miller, E. J., and Rice, A. K. 1968. *Systems of organization: The control of task and sentient boundaries.* London: Tavistock Publications.

Monane, Joseph H. 1967. *A sociology of human systems.* New York: Appleton-Century-Crofts.

Mouzelis, Nicos P. 1968. *Organization and bureaucracy.* Chicago: Aldine Publishing Co.

Schein, Edgar H. 1965. *Organizational psychology.* Englewood Cliffs, N.J.: Prentice-Hall.

Scott, William G. 1967. *Organization theory: A behavioral analysis for management.* Homewood, Ill.: Richard D. Irwin.

Seiler, John A. 1967. *Systems analysis in organizational behavior.* Homewood, Ill.: Richard D. Irwin.

Thompson, James D., ed. 1966. *Approaches to organizational design.* Pittsburgh: University of Pittsburgh Press.

Thompson, James D. 1967. *Organizations in action.* New York: McGraw-Hill Book Co.

Von Bertalanffy, L. 1968. *General systems theory.* New York: George Braziller.

Warner, W. Lloyd. 1967. *The emergent organizational society: Large scale organizations. vol. 1.* New Haven, Conn.: Yale University Press.

Woodward, Joan. 1965. *Industrial organization: Theory and practice.* London: Oxford University Press.

Critiques of Organization and Bureaucracy Theory

Allen, V. L. 1967. "Conceptual foundations of the theory of organizations." *L'Homme et la Societe* 4: 79–96.

Bakke, E. Wight. 1959. "Concept of the social organization." In *Modern organization theory,* ed. Mason Haire, pp. 16–75. New York: John Wiley & Sons.

Barnard, Chester I. 1938. "Organizations as systems of cooperation." In Chester I. Barnard, *The functions of the executive,* pp. 65–74. Cambridge, Mass.: Harvard University Press.

Bennis, W. G. 1966. "Organizational developments and the fate of bureaucracy." *Ind. Manage. Rev.* 7: 41-55.

Bettner, E. 1965. "The concept of organization." *Soc. Res.* 32: 239–55.

Blau, Peter M. 1962. "Studies on formal organizations: An editorial forward." *Am. J. Sociol.* 68 (Nov.): 289–90.

_____. 1966. "The structure of small bureaucracies." *Am. Sociol. Rev.* 31: 179–91.

Burns, Tom. 1966. "On the plurality of social systems." In J. R. Lawrence, *Operational research and the social sciences,* pp. 165–77. London: Tavistock Publications.

Chapman, R. A. 1964. "The real cause of bureaucracy." *Admin.* (Dublin) 12: 55–60.

Crozier, Michel. 1961. "Concerning bureaucracy as a system of organization." *Eur. J. Sociol.* 2(1): 18–52.

_____. 1964. "Bureaucratic organizations and the evolution of industrial society." In *A sociological reader on complex organizations,* 2d ed., ed. Amitai Etzioni, pp. 357–74. New York: Holt, Rinehart & Winston.

Eisenstadt, S. N. 1949. "Bureaucracy, bureaucratization and debureaucratization." *Admin. Sci. Quart.* 4: 302–20.

Graham, George. 1968. "The theory of organization." *Public Admin.* 46: 191–201.

Hall, Richard H., Haas, J. Eugene, and Johnson, Norman J. 1967. "An examination of the Blau-Scott and Etzioni typologies." *Admin. Sci. Quart.* 12: 118–39.

Heydebrand, W. V. 1967. "The study of organizations." *Soc. Sci. Information* 6: 59–86.

Hickson, J. D. 1966. "A convergence in organization theory." *Admin. Sci. Quart.* 11: 224–37.

Kaplan, B. H. 1968. "Notes on a non-Weberian model of bureaucracy: The case of development bureaucracy." *Admin. Sci. Quart.* 13: 471–83.

Kaufman, Herbert. 1964. "Organization theory and political theory." *Am. Political Sci. Rev.* 58: 514–23.

Landsberger, Henry A. 1961. "Parsons' theory of organizations." In *The social theories of Talcott Parsons,* ed. Max Black, pp. 214–49. Englewood Cliffs, N.J.: Prentice-Hall.

Laski, Harold J. 1930. *Bureaucracy encyclopedia of the social sciences.* vol. 3, pp. 70–73. New York: Macmillan Co.

Mayntz, Renate. 1964. "The study of organizations." *Current Sociol.* 13: 95–156.

_____. 1965. "Max Weber's ideal type bureaucracy and the sociology of organizations." *Koelner Z. Soziol. Soz. Psychol.* 7: 493–502.

Meadows, Paul. 1967. "The metaphors of order: Toward a taxonomy of organization theory." In L. Gross, *Sociological theory: Inquiries and paradigms,* pp. 77–103. New York: Harper and Row.

Scott, William G. 1961. "Organization theory: An overview and an appraisal." *J. Academy Manage.* 4: 7–26.

Scott, W. Richard. 1964. "Theory of organizations." In *Handbook of modern sociology,* ed. R. E. L. Farris, pp. 485–529. Skokie, Ill.: Rand McNally & Co.

Selznick, Phillip. 1948. "Foundations of the theory of organizations." *Am. Sociol. Rev.* 13: 25–35.

Spann, R. N. 1962. "The study of organizations." *Public Admin.* 40: 387–405.

Strother, G. B. 1963. "Problems in the development of a social science of organizations." In *The social science of organizations,* ed. H. J. Leavitt, pp. 2–37. Englewood Cliffs, N.J.: Prentice-Hall.

Stogdill, Ralph M. 1966. "Dimensions of organization theory." In *Approaches to organizational design,* ed. James D. Thompson, pp. 3–56. Pittsburgh: University of Pittsburgh Press.

Thompson, J. D., and McEwen, W. J. 1958. "Organizational goals and environment: Goal-setting as an interaction process." *Am. Sociol. Rev.* 23: 23–31.

White, Orion F. 1969. "The dialectinal organization: An alternative to bureaucracy." *Public Admin. Rev.* 29: 32–42.

Whyte, William Foote. 1961. "Parsonian theory applied to organizations." In *The social theories of Talcott Parsons,* ed. Max Black, pp. 250–67. Englewood Cliffs, N. J.: Prentice Hall.

Wolin, S. A. 1969. "A critique of organizational theories." In *A sociological reader on complex organizations,* 2d ed., ed. Amitai Etzioni, pp. 133–49. New York: Holt, Rinehart & Winston.

Management and Administrative Theory

Alton, A. J. 1969. "Comparative management theory." *Manage. Int. Rev.* 9: 3–11.

Basi, R. S. 1969. "The study of management: A critique and a suggestion." *Manage. Int. Rev.* 9: 113–19.

Carlisle, Howard M. 1968. "Measuring the situational nature of management." *Calif. Manage. Rev.* 11: 45–52.

Carlisle, H. M. 1969. "Are functional organizations becoming obsolete?" *Manage. Rev.* 58: 2–9.

Davis, Ralph C. 1958. "A philosophy of management." *J. Acad. Manage.* (Dec.): 37–40.

Duce, Leonard A. 1968. "The administrator: Today and tomorrow." *Hosp. Admin.* 13: 7–24.

Epstein, J. H., and Warren, R. H. 1968. "The role of behavioral sciences in organizations." *Personnel J.* 47: 716–24.

Gordon, P. J. 1963. "Transcend the current debate on administrative theory." *J. Acad. Manage.* (Dec.) : 290–303.

Halff, John F. 1960. "Applying the scientific method to the study of organization and management." *J. Acad. Manage.* (Dec.) : 193–96.

Hoaglund, John H. 1955. "Management before Frederick Taylor." *Proc. Acad. Manage.* (Dec.) : 15–24.

Johnson, R. A., Kast, F. E., and Rosenzweig, J. E. 1964. "Systems theory and management," *Manage. Sci.* (Jan.) : 367–84.

Koontz, Harold. 1961. "The management theory jungle." *J. Acad. Manage.* 4: 174–88.

Lawrence, Paul R., and Lorsch, Jay W. 1967. "New management job: The Integrator." *Harvard Bus. Rev.* 45: 142–51.

Leavitt, H. J., and Whisler, T. L. 1964. "Management in the 1980's." In *Readings in managerial psychology,* ed. H. J. Leavitt and L. R. Pondy, pp. 578–91. Chicago: University of Chicago Press.

Lilienthal, David. 1968. "The goal of management is to get things done." *Columbia J. World Bus.* 3: 55–60.

Litchfield, E. H. 1956. "Notes on a general theory of administration." *Admin. Sci. Quart.* 1: 3–29.

Massie, Joseph L. 1965. "Management theory." In *Handbook of organizations,* ed. James G. March, pp. 382–422. Skokie, Ill.: Rand McNally & Co.

Megginson, Leon C. 1958. "The pressure for principles: A challenge to management professors." *J. Acad. Manage.* (Aug.) : 7–12.

Nairne, P. D. 1964. "Management and the administrative class." *Public Admin.* 42: 113–32.

Roethlisberger, F. J. 1964. "Contributions of the behavioral sciences to a general theory of management." In *Readings in managerial psychology,* ed. H. J. Leavitt and C. R. Pondy, pp. 518–41. Chicago: University of Chicago Press.

Scheuplein, H. 1968. "Towards the unification of management theory." *Manage. Int. Rev.* 8: 95–96.

Scott, W. G. 1959. "The early record of a modern administrative dilemma." *J. Acad. Manage.* (Aug.) : 97–110.

Simon, H. A. 1969. "The proverbs of administration." In *Readings on modern organizations,* ed. Amitai Etzioni, pp. 32–49. Englewood Cliffs, N.J.: Prentice Hall.

Siroyezhin, I. M. 1968. "Measuring management responsibility." *Admin. Manage.* 29: 52–55.

Stephenson, T. E. 1968. "The longevity of classical theory." *Manage. Int. Rev.* 8: 77–83.

Tilles, Seymour. 1963. "The manager's job: A systems approach." *Harvard Bus. Rev.* 41: 73–81.

Zaleznik, Abraham, and Jardin, Anne. 1967. "Management." in *The uses of sociology,* ed. P. F. Lazarsfeld, W. H. Sewell, and H. L. Wilensky, pp. 193–233. New York: Basic Books.

Models, Conceptual Schemes, Frameworks
for Organizational Analysis

Becker, S. W., and Gordon, G. 1966. "An entrepreneurial theory of formal organizations." *Admin. Sci. Quart.* 11: 315–44.

Blalock, H. M., and Blalock, Ann B. 1959. "Toward a clarification of system analysis in the social sciences." *Phil. Sci.* 26: 84–92.

Blau, Peter M. 1957. "Formal organization: Dimensions of analysis." *Am. J. Soc.* 63: 58–69.

_____. 1965. "The comparative study of organizations." *Ind. Labor Rel. Rev.* 18: 323–38.

Boulding, Kenneth E. 1956. "General systems theory: The skeleton of a science." *Manage. Sci.* (Apr.): 200–202.

Briggs, G. E. 1964. "Engineering systems approaches to organizations." In *New perspectives in organization research,* ed. W. W. Cooper, H. J. Leavitt, and M. W. Shelly, pp. 479–92. New York: John Wiley & Sons.

Burns, Tom. 1967. "The comparative study of organizations." In *Methods of organizational research,* ed. V. H. Vroom, pp. 113–70. Pittsburgh: University of Pittsburgh Press.

Caruth, Donald L. 1968. "The total systems concept." *Bus. Stud.* (Fall): 67–72.

Caplow, Theodore. 1963. "Trends in corporate organizations." *Rev. Mex. Sociol.* 25: 695–703.

Chin, Robert. 1961. "The utility of systems models and developmental models for practitioners." In *The planning of change,* ed. W. G. Bennis, K. D. Benne, and R. Chin, pp. 201–14. New York: Holt, Rinehart & Winston.

Cyert, R. M., and March, J. G. 1964. "The behavioral theory of the firm: A behavioral science-economics amalgam." In *New perspectives in organization research,* ed. W. W. Cooper, H. J. Leavitt, and M. W. Shelly, pp. 289–304. New York: John Wiley & Sons.

Dill, William R. 1965. "Busines organizations." In *Handbook of organizations,* ed. James G. March, pp. 1071–1114. Skokie, Ill.: Rand McNally & Co.

Etzioni, Amitai. 1968. "A basis for comparative analysis of complex organizations." In *A sociological reader in complex organizations,* 2d. ed., ed. Amitai Etzioni, pp. 59–76. New York: Holt, Rinehart & Winston.

Haas, J. E., Hall, R. H., and Johnson, N. J. 1966. "Towards an empirically derived taxonomy of organizations." In *Studies on behavior in organizations,* ed. R. V. Bowers, pp. 157–80. Athens, Ga.: University of Georgia Press.

Haberstroh, Chadwick J. 1965. "Organization design and systems analysis." In *Handbook of organizations,* ed. James G. March, pp. 1171–1212. Skokie, Ill.: Rand McNally & Co.

Hage, Jerald. 1965. "An axiomatic theory of organizations." *Admin. Sci. Quart.* 10: 289–320.

Haire, Mason. 1959. "Biological models and empirical histories of the growth of organizations." In *Modern organization theory,* ed. Mason Haire, pp. 272–306. New York: John Wiley & Sons.

Hinings, C. R., Pugh, D. S., Hickson, D. J., and Turner, C. 1967. "An approach to the study of bureaucracy." *Sociol.* 1: 61–72.

Howland, Daniel. 1964. "Approaches to the systems model." *Gen. Syst.* 9: 283–85.

Krech, D., Crutchfield, R. S., and Ballachy, E. L. 1962. "A framework for the study of group effectiveness." In *Individual in society,* ed. D. Krech, R. S. Crutchfield, and E. L. Ballachy, pp. 456–58. New York: McGraw-Hill Book Co.

Mesarovic, M. D., Sanders, J. L., and Sprague, C. F. 1964. "An axiomatic approach to organizations from a general systems viewpoint." In *New perspectives in organization research,* ed. W. W. Cooper, H. J. Leavitt, and M. W. Shelly, pp. 493–512. New York: John Wiley & Sons.

Parsons, Talcott. 1956a. "Suggestions for a sociological approach to the theory of organizations—I." *Admin. Sci. Quart.* 1: 63–85.

――――. 1956b. "Suggestions for a sociological approach to the theory of organizations—II." *Admin. Sci. Quart.* 1: 225–39.

――――. 1958. "Some ingredients of a general theory of formal organizations." In *Administrative theory in education,* ed. Andrew W. Halpin, pp. 40–72. New York: Macmillan Co.

――――. 1960. "The analysis of formal organizations." In *Structure and process in modern societies,* ed. Talcott Parsons, pp. 16–96. New York: Free Press.

Perrow, Charles. 1967. "A framework for the comparative analysis of organizations." *Am. Sociol. Rev.* 32: 194–208.

Pugh, D. S. et al. "A conceptual scheme for organizational analysis." *Admin. Sci. Quart.* 8: 289–315.

Rice, C. E. 1961. "A model for the empirical study of a large social organization." *Gen. Sys. Yearbook* 6: 101–06.

Sells, S. B. 1964. "Toward a taxonomy of organizations." In *New perspectives in organization research,* ed. W. W. Cooper, H. J. Leavitt, and M. W. Shelly, pp. 515–32. New York: John Wiley & Sons.

Sells, S. B. 1968. "General theoretical problems related to organizational taxonomy: A model solution." In *People, groups and organizations,* ed. Bernard P. Indik and F. Kenneth Berrien, pp. 27–46. New York: Teachers College Press.

Trist, E. L. 1959. "Socio-technical systems." Lecture delivered at University of Cambridge. Mimeographed.

Udy, Stanley H. 1965. "The comparative analysis of organizations." In *Handbook of organizations,* ed. James G. March, pp. 678–709. Skokie, Ill.: Rand McNally & Co.

Vollmer, Howard M. 1966. "Structural-functional analysis as a method." In *Studies on behavior in organizations,* ed. Raymond V. Bowers, pp. 45–63. Athens, Ga.: University of Georgia Press.

Weiss, Robert S., and Jacobson, Eugene. 1955. "A method for the analysis of the structure of complex organization." *Am. Sociol. Rev.* 20: 661–68.

CRITERIA
OF ORGANIZATIONAL
EFFECTIVENESS

A CONSIDERABLE AMOUNT has been written in recent years about criteria of organizational effectiveness. Contributions on this topic have been made by scholars from a variety of social science disciplines. There is thus a wide variety of viewpoints and positions on criteria of organizational effectiveness. In spite of the diversity of writings on this subject, however, theoretical statements on criteria found in the literature fall roughly into two types: "goalistic" and "systemic."

Goalistic Criteria of Organizational Effectiveness

Goalistic criteria are derived from some conceptualizations of goals which the organization is expected to attain. Conceptualizations of goals take varied forms. One common practice is to use statements of organizational goals as criteria of effectiveness. These organizational goals may be the formal goals found in charters, company manuals, and other formal documents. They may also be informal or operative goals which may not be formally stated or emphasized, but in fact are the goals to which the organization is actually dedicated. (For discussions of use of various types of organizational goals as criteria, see Thompson and McEwen, 1958; Perrow, 1961; and Price, 1968: 1–14.)

Statements of goals may also be derived from conceptualizations of societal missions or functions with which the organization is identified in a social context. Organizational functions, in this context, refer to contributions made by the organization in the form of tangible or intangible outputs to the society in which it is located, and/or to its members, customers, and other groups related to it in some manner. Goals thus take the form of usable outputs which are consumed as inputs by some other system. Such goals may be derived from notions about characteristic roles or missions of various types of organization, from theoretical, ethical, or value considerations or a combination of all of these. (For elaborations on this point, see Parsons, 1960: 16–96; Etzioni, 1964: 1–19; and A. K. Rice, 1963: 179–202.)

The articles by Charles E. Rice and Bernard Bass printed in this part are intended to exemplify the rationale of "goalistic" criteria of organizational effectiveness. In the case of Rice, the effectiveness of the organization under consideration is to be measured in terms of criteria derived from goals commonly sought by organizations within a class or type of social organization. Since the organization studied was a public psychiatric hospital, statements of goals commonly sought by such organizations were derived from discussions with hospital personnel such as nurses, psychologists, psychiatrists, and social workers and from community members and surveys of literature relating to hospitals. In studying organizational effectiveness, these goals are to serve as output variables and are to be correlated with input and systems variables.

Bernard Bass approaches the problem of criteria selection from multiple frames of reference, i.e., organizational, members, and society at large. The worth of the organization is to be judged in terms of criteria which simultaneously measure the organization's productivity, profitability and self-maintenance as well as its contributions to its members and the society in which it is located. Bass's rationale for his schema for studying organizational effectiveness is worthy of note. He states frankly that his schema is based upon the value framework of democratic societies and traces its widespread acceptance in the fields of law, armed forces, and labor relations. This is in marked contrast to many social scientists who seek consciously to develop "value-free" frameworks and who defend their particular models or schemas in terms of theoretical or "scientific" considerations.

Systemic Criteria of Organizational Effectiveness

Systemic criteria of organizational effectiveness are derived from conceptualizations of "needs" experienced by the organization as a living social system. In this context, needs refer to the requirements which organizations have to meet in order to survive and/or to work effectively within a given situation. The effectiveness of organizations is to be studied in terms of their ability to meet the requirements arising from their situations. Conceptualization of organizational needs, and the resultant criteria of effectiveness, take many forms. Illustrations of such criteria are provided in the articles by Warren Bennis and Ephraim Yuchtman and Stanley Seashore printed in this part. (For other examples of criteria of organizational effectiveness derived from conceptualization of needs, see Schein, 1965: 97.)

Bennis approaches the task of studying organizational effectiveness from the point of view of mental health. He views the major need experienced by organizations to be that of adapting to a changing and turbulent environment. Bennis's criteria of organizational effectiveness parallel those advocated by psychologists concerned with the development of healthy human personalities: (1) adaptability—the ability to solve problems and to react with flexibility to changing environmental demands, (2) a sense of identity—knowledge and insight on the part of the organization of what it is, what its goals are, and what it is to do, and (3) capacity to test reality—the ability to search out, accurately perceive, and correctly interpret the real properties of the environment, particularly those which have relevance for the functioning of the organization. (This summary of Bennis's criteria is provided by Schein, 1965: 97.)

Yuchtman and Seashore propose a system resource approach to organizational effectiveness based upon the currently popular open-system model of organization. (For more elaborate discussions of the open-system model, see Katz and Kahn, 1966: 1–148; A. K. Rice, 1963: 179–277; Von Bertalanffy, 1950; and Berrien, 1968.) As a point of departure, the organization is perceived as being interdependent with its environment, that is, it is involved in constant transactions with other organizations and entities outside its boundaries. The organization imports various types of scarce and valued resources, converts these into outputs which are exported to the environment. The organization's success over a period of time hinges upon its ability to maintain a favorable input-output ratio. The system resource approach to organizational effectiveness proposes that the relative success attained by a particular organization in retaining a favorable bargaining position be taken as the expression of its overall effectiveness.

Concluding Remarks

The above discussion has presented an overview of two major types of criteria of organizational effectiveness found in the literature. It needs to be recognized that the classification of criteria provided here is somewhat arbitrary; it does not take into account the major variations and overlaps found in the proposals of criteria advanced by numerous scholars. For example, from the classification presented in this part and earlier discussions by Gouldner and Etzioni, it may be presumed there is a broad coherence between the underlying model used by the researcher and the types of criteria suggested. Thus, one would expect that those who rely upon the rational model would advocate the use of goals as criteria of effectiveness, while those who utilize the natural or systems model would advocate "systemic" criteria of effectiveness. (For an extensive discussion of this point, see Ghorpade, 1970.) But yet we find that Parsons and Etzioni, two of the most ardent advocates of the social systems model, insist upon linking effectiveness with goal attainment (Parsons, 1956; Etzioni, 1964: 8). At first glance this would seem inconsistent and contradictory. The position of these scholars, however, makes sense if one takes into account the system-within-system logic of the structural-functional theorists. As a point of departure, the organization is viewed as a subsystem of a larger social system or society. Organizational goals are thus synonymous with the primary societal missions or functions performed by the organization which give it its legitimacy and uniqueness.

Viewed from the external frame of reference, organizational goals emerge as outputs provided by the organization for the system which contains it. Judgments of organizational worth or effectiveness are to be made in terms of the quality and relevance of the organization's outputs towards assuring the survival, stability and growth of some other system, usually the larger system or society. Viewed from the organizational frame of reference, organizational goals or outputs emerge as one of the functional requirements which the organization has to meet in order to assure its own survival, stability, and growth. Thus, what appears at first glance as an overt contradiction is really a logical extension of the underlying model.

There are many other inconsistencies and overlaps in the writings of scholars regarding criteria of organizational effectiveness. The systematic isolation and resolution of these, however, is beyond the scope of this book. The classification presented here should be used merely as a starting point for further discussion and synthesis of varying viewpoints on organizational effectiveness.

Another problem which needs mention before concluding this discussion is that of operationalization of criteria of effectiveness. A vast number of studies in the past have restricted themselves to using "hard" criteria of effectiveness such as productivity and profitability. These measures had the merit of being easy to measure in terms of conventional, statistical, accounting, and other methods of measurement. Their utility as criteria of effectiveness, however, was marred by their static nature and their dependence upon other variables. (For a discussion of the limitations of such hard criteria, see Seashore, 1965: 27.) In recent years, organization theorists have emphasized the need for the development of more dynamic criteria which reflect the overall "health" and effectiveness of organizations. The references and readings provided in this part are examples of the types of criteria of effectiveness currently under consideration by modern organization theorists. While these criteria have the merit of widening the concept of organizational effectiveness and making it more dynamic, they raise some serious methodological problems and questions. For example, how are these criteria operationalized in formulating research designs? What types of techniques and methods should be used for gathering and analysing data pertinent to such criteria? What, if any, is the relationship of these criteria to each other and to more conventional measures such as productivity, profitability, and so on? Solutions to such methodological problems are not easy to provide; they are certainly not evident in the writings of the proponents of these criteria of effectiveness. Some progress, however, has been made in this respect by a few empirical studies which have been conducted in recent years. Some of these are listed in the bibliography provided at the end of this part and Part III.

A MODEL FOR
THE EMPIRICAL STUDY
OF A LARGE
SOCIAL ORGANIZATION

Charles E. Rice

In recent years, the administrators and personnel in some of our larger social organizations (such as schools, hospitals, and prisons), have been appealing to social scientists for help concerning the following problems:

1. How can these organizations' contributions to society be specified? More especially, that is, how can such an organization effectively evaluate its performance, when its accomplishments seem intangible when compared with industrial or military organizations?

2. How can such organizations determine what kinds of policies, facilities, and personnel to employ?

The purposes of this paper are to show that advances in the area of the first problem have implications for a concerted attack on the second, and to describe a research strategy being developed to study these problems in public psychiatric hospitals. It is believed that the model described

Reprinted from *General Systems Yearbook*. Yearbook of the Society for General Systems Research, vol. 6, pp. 101–106, by permission of the publishers.

in this paper might prove useful in studying the function of many large social organizations.

The research project, Medical Audit Plan for Psychiatric Hospitals[1], has been organized to develop a methodology which can be used by the staffs of hospitals in evaluation of performance and in the assessment of policies and resources. The term "medical audit" refers to procedures for obtaining information about hospitals often used as a basis for decision on whether or not a hospital meets specific standards for accreditation. Medical audit data has thus been used both to set up standards and to detect deviations from these standards.

Application of typical medical audit to a psychiatric hospital meets with some difficulty in that medical audits have no specified external criteria for evaluating the performance of an entire hospital. The validity of accreditation standards therefore remains untested. For example, one might feel that a given ratio of physicians per patient is optimal, but unless it can be empirically demonstrated that this ratio is related in some measure to hospital performance we cannot be certain that the ratio actually represents optimum function. The use of this ratio as a standard for evaluation of hospitals is consequently seen to be of dubious value.

What seems to be needed here is a research model which involves: (1) the development of criterion measures for psychiatric hospital performance, (2) the development of measures for hospital resources, programs, and policies, and (3) the determination of possible relationships between these two sets of measures. Data pointing to the existence of such relationships might then be used to guide the hospital administrator in deciding what policies or procedures to adopt in order to achieve a certain kind of hospital performance.

The Research Model

A "research model," as we use the term, is simply a strategy which helps in the selection and measurement of the system variables and relationships we wish to study. (The term is not necessarily synonymous with the term "explanatory model.") It has proven convenient to structure our research model in terms of general systems concepts.

One such strategy may be called the "classical model," and its application to the above problems in a single large social organization might proceed in the following steps:

1. Certain variables of the system would be designated as dependent variables whose measures would be designed to reflect various aspects of an organization's performance or behavior.

2. Specific independent variables would be selected and appropriate measures devised.

3. The independent variables would be systematically manipulated or allowed to vary with time, and their effects on the performance variables noted.

There would, however, be several difficulties in this approach. One, imposing variation on the system's independent variables would be impractical except in the cases of very limited problems. Direct manipulation by an investigator might disturb the system's routine functioning, while variation over time, for many variables, would take an inordinately long period of observation. Another, the results derived from a limited study of one organization might be of such a nature that to generalize the findings to other similar organizations would be unfeasible. Solutions to some restricted problems of one organization would not necessarily benefit administrators of other similar institutions having their own unique problems and settings.

What we would want, therefore, is a broad-scale approach which would provide data to aid administrative decision-making for all social organizations of a given type. The research model we have been developing, which might be called a "multiple systems" model, has the following features:

1. The initial step in our thinking about the problem involved the conceptualization of a class of social organizations. One might attempt to sort organizations into classes by comparing sizes or internal structures, but our approach was limited to generalized concepts of the goals of organizational functioning. The term "organizations of a given type" then means organizations sharing common purposes or goals. In other words, if we consider some of the behavior of social organizations to be "goal-seeking," then public psychiatric hospitals differ from other organizations in that their goals are different. The first step involves the specifications of these common goals along with the selection of variables whose measurement would reflect the performance of any such organization with respect to these goals. These variables are designated as *output* variables.

2. Having conceptualized the organization as a system with output, the next step concerned the specification of *input* variables and *system* variables. The distinction between these two classes of variables has not been rigorously defined in our thinking because it is difficult to specify the boundaries of the system in regard to input variables. However, it should be pointed out that we are not making use of a black box model since many aspects of the "inner" structure and functioning of the system would seem to be amenable to observation and measurement.

3. Variation in the three classes of variables is observed by measuring

these variables in many organizations of the given type over the same time interval. All variables are represented by a single measure considered a sample of that variable's values during the given time interval. Then, using each organization as an experimental unit, input and system measures will be related to output measures by means of statistical correlation methods. In addition, input measures might be related to system measures in order to study the effects of input variation upon changes in the system variables.

This approach, which is an extension of the field-study or correlational model widely used in psychology and sociology, will now be described with more detail in its proposed application to the study of public psychiatric hospitals.

Output Variables

The first step in our strategy was selecting those aspects of a psychiatric hospital's behavior to serve as output variables. One means of selecting output variables for social organization study is to ask, "For what purposes was this system created and for what purposes is it being maintained?" These organizational purposes, or *goals,* usually represent the conceptualization of organizational members and of the community as to what contributions the system is and should be making to society. We wanted a list of goals that would be an abstraction in that it would not represent exactly the goal structures of any single psychiatric hospital, but would be a generalization from all such hospitals.

Discussion with mental hospital personnel and a survey of the literature resulted in the following list of public psychiatric hospital goals:

Care of patients is defined as encompassing those hospital activities which involve the "daily maintenance" of patients, i.e., keeping them alive, physically healthy, and as comfortable as possible within the hospital.

Protection includes preventing the occurrence of harm or injury to patients, hospital staff, hospital property, or to the surrounding community.

Social restoration includes those hospital activities aimed principally at releasing patients into the community so that they are able to remain there with an improved degree of adjustment.

Training and education involves the training of professional people and hospital employees as well as the dissemination of information to the community.

Research encompasses the scientific study of hospital and mental health problems.

The final goal, for want of a better name, has been termed *"adminis-tration."* It includes those hospital activities aimed at controlling and coordinating the operations of various sub-units of the system, as well as the relationship of the hospital to other organizations of society.

It should be noted that these concepts are neither mutually exclusive nor do they constitute the *only* list that could be formulated. We wanted a list that represented a parsimonious abstraction of hospital purposes while simultaneously comprehensive.

The comprehensiveness of our list resulted from a nation-wide survey of over a thousand psychiatrists, psychologists, psychiatric nurses, psychiatric social workers, and board members of the National Association of Mental Health. These people were asked to supply their own lists of mental hospital goals. We are able to define our list so that well over 90 per cent of the items received in the survey could be classified reliably under one or another of the goals mentioned above.

It should further be noted that the six goals are not themselves variables, but rather classes of variables. These groups constitute the set of hospital behaviors designating the output variables of our design. The survey aided us in deciding which variables, or hospital behaviors, to include in each goal category.

Having proceeded to the point where we had conceptualized classes of output variables, it was then necessary to examine these classes in order to determine which of the variables in each category seemed amenable to operational definition and thereby to measurement. We examined those hospital behaviors subsumed in order to see which of them appeared promising in terms of feasible measurement procedures. The measures of the variables thus selected were to represent estimates of a hospital's performance with respect to care, protection, etc.

In addition to measurability, we have also been guided in our selection of output variables by the notion that we wanted our measures to represent characteristics of "products" of the system's functioning. This criterion is admittedly vague, but it may be illuminating to note that many of our output measures are expressed in terms of things that "happened" to groups of patients *after* they had been exposed to the hospital environment. In a sense, for some of our output measures, we have been thinking of patients as being "processed" by the hospital.

At this point, it may be enlightening to briefly describe our measures of hospital performance with respect to one of the goals, social restoration. Consideration of hospital behavior subsumed under this goal resulted in our focusing on the "returning patients to the community" concept.

Basically, we have three variables here. The first of these is measured by the probability that a patient, admitted to hospital A in time interval

T_1, will be released to the community during a subsequent interval T_2, following a hospital decision that he is "ready" for release. This is called the release rate of hospital A and it measures, you might say, the social restoration performance of hospital A insofar as *quantity* of output is concerned.

The second measure is given by the probability that a patient admitted to hospital A in T_1, and released from A in T_2, will return to institutional status (in A or other psychiatric hospital, prison, home for the aged, etc.) during subsequent interval T_3. This is the *return rate* of Hospital A and, continuing the analogy, represents a first approximation for the measurement of the *quality* of Hospital A's social restoration output.

The third measure represents the probability that a patient who was admitted to Hospital A in T_1, released in T_2, and remained in the community throughout T_3, will show a prehospital-posthospital improvement in adjusting to the community's expectations. If one considers the helping of patients to resume or improve their status as socially-acceptable community residents to be the essence of social restoration, then this measure is seen to be critical for representing a hospital's social restoration performance.

Procedures for collecting the necessary information for these measures have been worked out in some detail, but I will not attempt to describe them in this paper. The reader who is interested in a detailed account of these measures and of the data-collection procedures underlying them is referred to another publication by the author.[2]

We have no guarantee, of course, that our output measures will prove workable, for we have no generally accepted and reliable measures. We are working in new territory. All that can be done at this stage is to devise measures which appear relevant to the general goal definitions, free of contradictions and opportunity for bias and distortion, sensitive enough to detect interhospital differences, and which involve information, comparable from hospital to hospital, we can reasonably hope to gather.

The Input and System Variables

Turning to a discussion of the input and system variables, we are faced again with the task of selecting which variables to include in the design. There is no solid notion of which input and system variables have relevance for any given output variable simply because there has been very little research in this area. Selection has been guided by choosing those variables which seem to embody issues and problems of relevance to hospital administrators and mental health personnel. A few have been suggested in consulting the literature in the fields of administrative science, social psychology, and psychiatry.

With respect to the study of hospital output in the area of social restoration the following types of input and system variables are included in our design:

INPUT VARIABLES   By input is usually meant "those parameters of the system's environment whose variability affects the system's functioning." This definition includes the notion of something entering the system or impinging upon its boundaries. Although it is difficult to decide, in the case of social organizations, what is system and what is environment, we have achieved at least a preliminary specification of the input variables.

One class of input parameters involves specification of the type of community in which the hospital is located. This includes such things as rural vs. urban location, as well as various characteristics of the larger mental health organization (state mental health department) to which the hospital is subordinate. This class of parameters may be looked upon as providing some real constraints to the variation in the remaining classes of input variables.

A second, and very basic, class of input variables involves certain measurable features in the patient population entering the hospital through-out a given time interval. These variables include the size of this population and measures of central tendency with respect to age, socio-economic level, education, and prehospital level of social adjustment.

A third class of input parameters comprises the various aspects of direct community participation in the hospital's functioning, such as amount of professional consultation afforded to the hospital during a given interval of time.

A final class of input variables encompasses basic resources which the hospital receives during a given time period, such as financial allocations, food, and medical supplies, etc.

SYSTEM VARIABLES   Herein are included variables which we feel characterize the "internal" structure and functioning of the system. The system variables also fall into various categories.

The first class of system variables contains physical characteristics of the hospital such as measures of size and capacity, measures of treatment, maintenance, and recreation facilities.

The second class of system parameters includes variables reflecting the hospital's staffing pattern, such as size of staff, formal and informal patterns of authority, and attitudes of the staff toward mental illness and mental patients.

A third and final class of system variables might be termed "policies and procedures." The parameters in this class may be said to reflect the hospital's internal functioning rather than its structure. Included here are a great many variables such as characteristics of interdepartmental contact and communication and measures of the "operating characteristics" of the various hospital services and departments. In short, this class contains variables which reflect "what goes on" inside the system.

Having gained a general idea of what the input and system variables were to be, the next task is devising measures for these variables. Here again, one finds quite often there are no "ready-made" measures whose usefulness as operational definitions have been demonstrated.

Some of the variables present little difficulty because their measurements result more or less directly from the level of simple observation, e.g., the total number of buildings, or the total number of physicians employed fulltime by the hospital, or the sex of the director of nursing. These are measures of what we call "low-level" variables.

Constructs and measures of a higher order may be defined by combining "low-level" constructs. For example, one could consider the variable "physical size of hospital" whose measure could be defined in terms of the number of buildings in conjunction with the area of the grounds and the average amount of floor space per building. Or, one might define the construct "degree of dignity with which patients are treated" as, a great number of variables of lower order such as, amount of hospital censorship of patient mail, degree of privacy of patient's bathing facilities, and amount of time allotted for patients to eat in hospital dining halls. It becomes obvious that there are many possibilities for constructing higher order variables and each of their measures could be constructed from a great many different combinations of lower order variables.

We have been striving to specify some of these variables to have as high an order as possible and yet be meaningful in the light of our knowledge of hospital operations. One reason we are doing this is to reduce the number of variables considered. This *a priori* construction of parameters has its pitfalls, however. If we have measures x, y, and z, and combine these to derive higher order measure A, which we then relate to a given output measure, we may fail to demonstrate a relationship simply because we specified an "incorrect functional relationship between A and variables x, y, and z, or because variable w was omitted from the construction of A. All is not lost, however, because we will, after data collection, have measurements for w, x, y, and z, and we are free to try other functional relationships which might be suggested by the data. It is anticipated that there will be a considerable amount of empirical construction in higher order variables.

It is possible, of course, to construct higher order variables by using the empirical method only. A factor or principal components analysis of the intercorrelations of all input or system variables might seem to be indicated here so that "clusters" of variables could be elicited from the data and used as the basis for higher order parameters. This would represent an attempt to discover the basic dimensions underlying the measures.

At the present time, however, it is felt that the rational, *a priori* approach should definitely accompany the empirical in the construction of higher order input and system measures. Our aim is to provide the staff of a mental hospital with some tools for manipulating very real and palpable features of the hospital so as to enhance a specific output. This aim has guided us in the construction of these measures. Should a higher order construct appear to be of little predictive value, one of its constituent lower level measures may still be quite useful in being highly correlated with a given output.

The collection of data relevant to the input and system measures will consist largely of structured interviews and systematic observations on visits to public psychiatric hospitals throughout the country. At present, we anticipate data collection relevant to several hundred such variables. This "broad" approach is pragmatically necessary if entire hospitals are to be used as the experimental units. It is much more efficient to gather a great deal of information at one time from a hospital than to return again and again for additional data.

Input-Output Relationships

Our research design is a correlational one, in which input and system measures (predictors) are to be statistically correlated with output measures (criterion measures), both sets of measures resulting from the observation of many hospitals. For each hospital we will have several hundred measures of input and system variables and an anticipated two or three dozen measures of output. Our task will then consist of trying to detect relationships between the two sets of variables, input and system variables on the one hand and output variables on the other. Many problems confront us here, some of which have already been suggested, and I can do no more than to outline our thinking as to how we should proceed.

First, some of the input and system measures may fail to reflect any interhospital variation. These variables will then be dropped from further consideration because, insofar as our measuring techniques could detect, they would not be variables at all. This points up a difficulty in our "multiple systems" approach. The lack of variation displayed by an input or system variable could result from the "single-value" nature of our measure. It would not be legitimate to infer, in this case, that such a variable has no relationship to a given output. We can only report that the variable's lack of interhospital variance precludes any inferences about its relationships to output and that its further consideration should be shelved, but not discarded altogether.

Our next step will be working with each class of output variables, one at a time. Each input and system variable will be related to each of the output measures in the given class. As a first approximation, this would be accomplished by the use of product-moment correlation. (Should a higher order variable, of *a priori* construction, fail to be correlated with any output, its lower level constituents would then be tried.)

For any given input-output or system-output pair we would then begin to "partial out" other variables one at a time in order to gain a truer picture of the relationship. This "partialing-out" process will be limited by pragmatic considerations, and guided by the realization that psychiatric hospital people have some specific questions and problems about which we desire to supply some information. Should the use of multivariate statistical methods, such as principal components analysis, point up some underlying dimensions of the input of system measures, these too might be exploited by relating them to output measures.

I might remark that input-output and system-output relationships are not the only ones that might be considered. Relationships between output variables might be of vital importance to administrators if high performance with respect to one goal, say protection, tended to be accompanied by low (or high) performance in another goal area, say social restoration. Should such relationships be found it could prove helpful to the management of hospitals in deciding which objectives should receive emphasis in the planning of long-range policies.

Another aspect of our model is that it lends itself to the determination of input-system relationships. It would be of particular interest, not only to a hospital administrator, but also the social scientist, to learn how changes in input affect the structure and functioning of the system.

Our design represents an attempt to predict various hospital outputs from a knowledge of various input variables, but it would also be meaningful to attempt to predict input by using output variables as predictors and, in those cases where temporal priority could be established, we would speak of "feedback." Thus, a hospital with high performance in training and education might attract better professional personnel.

Our research strategy will not enable us to derive a determinate system of variables; causal relationships will not be deduced. For this, the "classical" strategy, involving more restricted sets of variables, would be necessary. Data from our research, pointing up the possibility of useful relationships, would be a guide in such efforts.

We realize, of course, that we are dealing with extremely complex systems of variables. However, it is felt that this "broad-scale" research strategy is a necessary first step in establishing an empirical base for further investigation in the area of research in organization theory and in psychopathology. Even if all of the data is not put to immediate use, it is felt that this broad approach will provide mental hospital personnel with some new ways of looking at the operations of their hospitals. Our preliminary work in several state hospitals has already resulted in a stimulating interchange of ideas between our staff and the personnel of these institutions.

A Summary of the Model

The research model described in this paper provides an approach to the study of a given class of social organizations, especially where it is desirable to evaluate the effectiveness of the organization's functioning and thereby determining which aspects of the organization's environment, structure, and "inner functioning" are related to the effectiveness of the organization's performance.

The first step in such an approach requires defining a class of social organizations in terms of a generalized set of organizational goals. These organizations are viewed as systems having input and output.

Output is defined by total system performance with respect to the achievement of organization goals and indices thereby devised to measure this performance. Input and system variables are defined and measures are designed to reflect these variables. The input variables represent those features of the environment which are seen as impinging upon the system or serving as constraints to system behavior. The system parameters represent various structural and operating characteristics of the organization.

We then wish to relate the input and system parameters to the output variables by observing the covariation of their measures. Because it may be difficult or impractical to impose variation on the system's variables in any direct fashion our research strategy involves the measurement of these variables in a great many of the organizations, comprising the given class, within the same time interval. Relations between the measures will be ascertained by means of statistical correlation methods.

Input-output and system-output relationships furnish information which can be used by organization members as a basis for policy decisions aimed at achieving a given level of output. Input-system relationships can be used to understand how organizational structure and functioning are affected by changes in environmental conditions. This "multiple-systems" model can be used as a basis for studying and evaluating the effectiveness of many types of social organizations and agencies such as schools, prisons, libraries, and hospitals.

It may be instructive, in closing, to note how the above research strategy differs from typical operations research procedures whose aims are very similar.

The first difference can be seen by comparing the scope of the two approaches. Operations research methodology focuses typically on the functioning of a single organization, the aim being to provide information relating to the optimum performance of the system with regard to the achievement of objectives which are more or less unique to that organization. Our approach, on the other hand, involves the simultaneous study of many organizations of a given class, and measures performance in terms of the achievement of generalized goals which typify the entire class of organizations.

Secondly, operations research usually involves the development of an *a priori model* (that is, the model is developed prior to data collection) to represent system functioning. This model and its solutions are then tested by employing empirical data. Our approach does not involve this type of model construction, but calls for the collection of data which can then be used as a basis for constructing models of system functioning.

---

1. Jointly supported by the Veterans Administration and the National Institute of Mental Health, and sponsored by Johns Hopkins University.

2. C. E. Rice, D. G. Berger, L. G. Sewall, and P. V. Lemkau, "Measuring Social Restoration Performance of Public Psychiatric Hospitals," *Public Health Reports* 76 (May 1961): 437–46.

ULTIMATE CRITERIA
OF ORGANIZATIONAL
WORTH[1]

Bernard M. Bass

The purpose of this article is to suggest that the ultimate criteria of organization worth be expanded.

Instead of evaluating the success of programs for improving selection, placement, training, job methods, and human relations in an industrial organization solely in terms of the extent to which they serve to increase the company's productivity, profits, and efficiency, it has been proposed that they also be evaluated on the extent to which they increase the worth of the organization to its members and society as a whole. It is felt that this proposal is consonant with the philosophical principles underlying certain aspects of labor legislation, labor relations, military organization, and industrial organization. It is probably much more acceptable to the trade unionist than the present approach to evaluation and may have more support from management than might be apparent at first—although the verification of this last hypothesis will have to await research on the subject.

Reprinted from *Personnel Psychology*, vol. 5, 1952. pp. 157–173 by permission of the author and publisher.

Discussion

Fiske[2] in a recent article suggested that the need to judge the worth of individual workers within an organization could be minimized by developing general principles concerning the relationships between the worth of the organization to the individual worker interacting with others and the success with which the organization attained its goals. If such relationships were known, then value judgments would have to be made only about the success of the organization as a whole; criteria of success or worth of individual employees would be empirical functions of organizational success.

The concept of organization success or goal attainment is a valuable one, and the uses Fiske proposes to make of it appear most fruitful. However, a thorough examination of the meaning of organizational success appears in order.

Upon What Ultimate Criteria
Should Organizational Success Be Evaluated?

The criterion question may be expanded further by considering the bases upon which organizational success or degree of goal attainment should be evaluated. The present tendency of personnel psychologists is to accept as ultimate criteria[3] of organizational success organizational productivity, net profits, success with which the organization maintains or expands itself, and the degree to which the organization accomplishes its missions as assigned by higher authority.

Following Fiske's suggestions, one would evaluate the individual employee in terms of the degree to which his performance increases the worth of the organization as estimated by the above indices. Likewise, the adequacy or success of new personnel programs of selection, training, counseling, and so forth would be evaluated in terms of these same indices.

The purpose of this article is to try to broaden the bases for evaluating the success of an organization and also, therefore, the success of the individual employee and the individual personnel program. It is felt that two additional indices of value should be introduced formally into the final evaluations of organizations and their dependent employees and programs. The proposal is that in addition to the previously cited indices of organizational success there be included as measures of organizational value *the worth of the organization to the individual members and the worth of both individual members and the organization to society*. It is suggested, therefore, that an organization be evaluated in terms of: (1) the degree to which it is productive, profitable, self-maintaining, and so forth; (2) the degree to which it is of value to its members; and (3) the degree to which it and its members are of value to society. Since there will be little quarrel with ultimate criterion 1, we shall concentrate our efforts on supporting the introduction of criteria 2 and 3 into the formal evaluation of organizational success.

Nothing really new has been suggested. Rather, what has been suggested is that the goals and objectives which the industrial psychologist has recognized informally be integrated formally into his methods of evaluating the success of his own work.

Two Alternatives

The nature of the argument necessary to support the introduction of criteria 2 and 3 will depend on the extent of the correlation between (1) the "material" criteria of profits, productivity and self-maintenance and, (2) the "social" criteria of worth of the organization to the individual members and, (3) the worth of both to society. In the absence of systematic quantitative evidence, the amount of correlation is a matter for conjecture. At least two hypotheses concerning this correlation appear tenable. The first hypothesis is that the three criteria are so highly interrelated that a company which scores highly on any one always tends to score highly on the others. The second hypothesis that the three criteria may tend to be related either to a small extent or not at all, or may be highly related only if a number of other conditions are present. For the sake of argument, these two possibilities have been labeled Hypothesis A —a high positive correlation always exists among the three criteria—and Hypothesis B—a high positive correlation does not always exist among the three criteria.

Hypothesis A—The Ultimate Criteria Are Always Highly Correlated

A number of personnel psychologists have suggested this hypothesis. Thus, Blum introduces the student to the purpose of industrial psychology by declaring: "(The) goal of (industrial psychology) should be the satisfaction of man, not of any one man to the disadvantage of others, or of one group over the other. Men must be free to express their feelings, to reach goals, to produce, and to develop as secure individuals. These and other freedoms are possible . . . in an industrial system operating in a democracy." But, he finds it necessary to add: "Efficiency then follows as a necessary accompaniment."[4]

Similarly Ghiselli and Brown[5] point out that whenever management —whatever the motive—introduces programs to increase worker comfort, safety, and satisfaction, such programs in the long run lead to higher profits. In other words, they suggest that a high correlation exists among the ultimate criteria 1, 2, and 3 formulated in this article. This same view is expressed by V. J. Bentz, of Sears, Roebuck & Company, who asks the question, "Can an organization survive and perpetuate itself solely on profit and productivity?" Again, W. V. Bingham observes in a letter to the author:

> "To my mind, one of the outstanding characteristics of the American enterprise system is that, by and large, two spectacularly dissimilar goals of organizational success namely (a) corporate profits in the long run and (b) worth of the enterprise to the community and to the individual worker, lie so nearly in the same general direction that steady advance toward either goal commonly means progress toward the other.
>
> I do not happen to be acquainted with *any* wise, able, successful employer who defines his business goals solely in economic terms, namely profits . . . nor (anyone) whose goal of organizational success is defined in such very broad social terms that it fails to include the financial interests of . . . the . . . investors who have saved and supplied the indispensable capital requirements."

Bingham goes on to cite the attitude toward this issue of two European industrial psychologists, Walther and Poppelreuter. Walther insisted that he was completely disinterested in profits or anything concerned with money. Poppelreuter declared, "I touch nothing that does not mean profit for the employer." Both used the immediate criterion of more productivity with less expenditure of energy; both introduced into various industrial concerns almost the same identical programs of job analysis, work simplification, selection, and training!

To sum up his opinion concerning the correlation between the material and social organization goals, Dr. Bingham concludes: "Standing between two enormous cauldrons of chocolate, I had bluntly asked the President of Suchards's, 'Why do you have in your staff a psychologist like Dr. Walther?' His prompt reply was 'I find that it pays.' "

If Hypothesis A is tenable, then psychologists can feel free to expand the ultimate criteria of organizational success as suggested in this article and to use the three criteria interchangeably. Criteria 2 and 3 could be used where more easily obtainable than criterion 1, and where it was pertinent to demonstrate to the public, to legislatures, to employees, or to other interest groups the value of the company to society. In a certain sense, the validity or reliability of any one of the measures could be checked by obtaining any one of the others. It is difficult to see any particular objections or disadvantages to expanding the ultimate criteria of organization worth if Hypothesis A is tenable.

Hypothesis B—The Ultimate Criteria Are Not Always Highly Correlated

It is the writer's conviction that Hypothesis B is far more tenable. The validity of Hypothesis B is suggested by the following:

1. MacGregor[6] has pointed out that supervisors can motivate workers to perform well in two ways. Supervisors can serve as potential aids to the workers' attainment of material and psychological rewards or they can serve as potential barriers or threats to the workers' attainment of such rewards. The positive or "augmentation" approach is favored over the negative one because although the supervisor can energize the workers by means of threats, there is no guarantee that the worker will be motivated in the direction desired by the supervisor. It is possible to use the negative or punishment approach only where rigid controls and restrictions can be exerted on the workers' behavior. Thus, if a rider whips a horse, it will run, but not necessarily in the direction desired by the rider. However, the horse *will* run in the direction desired by the rider if the reins are held tightly while the horse is being whipped. In other words, where most of the possible behavior of the workers can be controlled—such as in Nazi, Soviet, or other slave-worker situations—high productivity may be maintained by force and threat, despite ensuing low morale and job dissatisfaction.

2. High productivity appears to occur along with low morale in many work situations in the United States. The reverse is also true. For example, 156 respondents each were able to describe at least one efficient but unpleasant work group. Similarly 344 each were able to describe at least one inefficient but pleasant work group.[7]

From the above considerations it is inferred that although satisfied and secure workers will tend to be more productive, there are many situations where such is not the case.

If Hypothesis B is tenable—and the writer would be inclined to accept this alternative—then a series of arguments must be marshalled to justify the inclusion of criteria 2 and 3 as ultimate objectives of business and industrial organizations.

The Thesis

It is proposed that the worth of the organization to the individual worker and the worth of both individual and organization to society should be used as ultimate criteria of organizational success apart from any consideration of the effect these two criteria may or may not have on the ultimate criterion of profits, productivity, and self-maintenance. This proposition is presented as an axiom. It cannot be proved or disproved. The acceptance by industrial psychology of the proposition as axiomatic will depend on whether it can be demonstrated: (1) that the proposition is self-evident; or (2) that it is an established principle, which although unverified and unverifiable is accepted widely especially by those disciplines whose areas of study overlap in content with those of industrial psychology. Since the writer knows of no way of demonstrating the self-evident nature of the axiom, he will be content to emphasize the established nature of the axiom. If it can be shown that the proposition is accepted as an axiom by fields close to industrial psychology, then acceptance of this axiom by industrial psychologists will be profitable. It will enable the derived principles of industrial psychology to be consistent with and to be integrated with a larger framework of consistent knowledge.

A series of briefs follow to show that the proposed axiom has been accepted as fundamental in the fields of jurisprudence, military management, industrial management, and labor relations. The briefs are intended to be illustrative rather than expository.

Organizational Worth and the Law

The worth of the organization to the individual and the worth of both organization and individual to society have been recognized matters requiring control by both federal and state legislation. This legislation has tended to regard labor as a natural resource to be protected and conserved —and more recently, as a group of human beings with certain absolute rights. Legislative control of organizational worth to the individual has been covered by state legislation concerning the "mental and moral" health of women workers since 1842, by Congressional action concerning hours of work since 1869, by state legislation concerning industrial safety since 1903, and by many other city, state, and national legislative enactments, court decisions, and executive orders.[8] Anti-trust legislation illustrates the kind of legislative attempts which have been made to control the worth of the organization to society.

Organizational Worth and the Armed Forces

In the military organizations of democracies today, organizational worth to the individual is considered of basic importance. For example, the Armed Forces medical programs are not evaluated solely against such ultimate criteria as the degree to which they raise morale and indirectly help to win battles but also in terms of the deaths and disabling handicaps they can help to avoid among members of the Armed Forces in the course of the member's training and combat activities. Saving lives wherever possible is regarded by those that justify the expense and effort of the medical programs as an important, if not most important, value of the programs. Maintaining a maximum of combat effectiveness, preventing disease, lowering loss of trained veterans, and keeping morale high are all important indications of the worth of the medical corps, but it is probable that the degree to which the medical programs aid the Armed Forces to be of maximum help to their wounded, injured, and diseased members is regarded by a nation which values the life of the individual highly, as an extremely important index of the success of the Armed Forces and their medical programs.

Witness the following two excerpts from *The Senior R.O.T.C. Manual,* prepared in 1948 under the direction of the Army Field Forces, United States Army:

> Our current democratic ideals shun all concepts which tend to cheapen human life. These ideals are reflected in our military principles and operations to the extent that during World War II, our leaders often revised strategic plans to save lives.
>
> The public (during World War II) expected that every effort would be made to keep the American soldier in perfect health; that safety devices would be devised for his benefit or convenience.[9]

While the primary objective of the American Armed Forces is to win wars, other objectives more closely related to criteria 2 and 3 are present which may or may not necessarily be related to the primary objective. In fact, the attainment of these "social" objectives may actually, at times, be detrimental to the attainment of the primary objective.

Organizational Worth and Principles of Industrial Organizations and Labor Relations

The essence of the thesis advanced in this article suggesting the expansion of the ultimate criteria of organizational worth is manifest in Davis' *Industrial Organization and Management,* which probably can be considered a representative text in this area. Davis states:

> Business objectives . . . those values which a company must preserve, acquire, create or distribute to justify its right to exist

. . . include the broad social values which it must contribute to society, the economic values with which it must serve the public, and the personnel values that it must supply its own personnel.

In a more detailed statement of the business organization's social objectives—defined as broad, general values necessary to the well-being of society that are affected by business activity—Davis points out that a business organization cannot employ child labor in a manner detrimental to the child's well-being and development, since the public interest is more important than the interests of any group. Social security for employees is another social objective of a business organization.

> Any intelligent employer has a direct and immediate interest in the economic security of his employees, and within the limits of his ability and his understanding of his obligations, he attempts to provide this security to a reasonable degree. On the other hand, employers are not in the general business of providing economic security. Nevertheless, our society has decided to attempt this, and the Social Security Act has been passed. The Act requires a business organization to maintain extensive and expensive records, and to pay taxes to the state and federal government for the purposes of the Act. The values growing out of social security also have become collateral social objectives of business. Business organizations stand in the position of an agency of the government, in that they collect money from the public in the form of taxes to be used for various social purposes. The collateral social objectives of business are closely related to fair-practice standards and business ethics, and today are given careful consideration by executive leaders.[11]

Scott, Clothier, et al. echo similar sentiments in more emphatic form:

> But the tenet of this new doctrine (the human conception of labor) that left many of the old school executives gasping for breath, was that *the workers had certain "inalienable" rights as human beings, that these rights were as important as the rights of other persons with whom they had dealings, and that it was industry's duty to recognize these rights. . . .* In short, *this doctrine stated brazenly that industrial concerns have three obligations—to their stockholders, to their customers and the public, and to their employees.*
>
> Whereas some years ago the employers who entertained such enlightened views were in the great minority, it is now true that industry generally is adopting their beliefs.[12]

Writing similarly of labor relations, Yoder emphasizes the widespread interest and concern of the public in social problems that arise from industrial relations.

> Among the problems that are of the greatest importance to our society in the United States are those of industrial unrest, notably strikes and lockouts, economic insecurity, unemployment, old age and disability dependency, sub-standard wages, long hours, discrimination on the basis of race, color, nationality, or religion, health hazards in industry; the under-utilization of skills and monopolistic tendencies inherent in over-zealous or unscrupulous combinations of employers and unions.[13]

Numerous other authorities in this area of personnel and industrial management could be cited to illustrate similar viewpoints.[14]

Where Does the Personnel Psychologist Fit In?

If a personnel psychologist comes along and is able to mitigate some of the above ills, should this work not be judged a worthwhile contribution? If an industry creates these problems, should not, as Davis suggests, one of its objectives be to solve the problems or reduce their effects as much as possible? If an industry, in attaining its production goals contaminates the air surrounding the plant, society can act quickly to force the industry to correct this difficulty. The engineer who prevents further contamination is regarded by the company as a serviceable individual who is helping the company to attain one of its objectives—namely, keeping the air clean around it. If a personnel worker reduces psychological contamination in the area surrounding a plant, should not that likewise be considered a service which is helping the company to attain its social objectives?

Advantages of Accepting the Proposed Axiom

In addition to increasing the consistency and integration of the principles of industrial psychology with available knowledge gathered by other disciplines interested in business, industrial and military personnel, three other advantages should accrue from accepting the axiom that the worth of the organization to the individual worker and the worth of both to society are as relevant ultimate criteria as organization productivity, profits, and self-maintenance.

First, much of the work of the industrial psychologist is most directly concerned with improving the job situation for the employee although the psychologist attempts to justify this professional activity mainly by trying to demonstrate how it will ultimately increase organizational productivity and profits. The immediate criteria of morale, job satisfaction, fatigue, safety, health, and energy required for the worker become much more relevant or valid as indices of the value of personnel and industrial procedures and innovations if they are related to ultimate criteria such as the worth of the organization to the individual, of both to society as well as to ultimate criteria such as organizational productivity and profits. For example, the success with which a psychologist matches employees to jobs may not be gauged merely by the serviceability of the employees to the organization while performing these jobs, but also on the basis of the satisfaction that accrues to the employees by being placed on the given jobs—not because this increased satisfaction necessarily will lead to increased productivity and lower turnover within the organization, but because worker satisfaction is considered an intrinsic value—desirable in its own right.

Suppose a marginal coal mine, where job satisfaction has been low because of the accident hazards and the instability of employment, improves its safety and employment security. The change in conditions may not only be evaluated ultimately in terms of the degree to which profits and productivity are increased but also in terms of the degree to which worker dissatisfaction is decreased; the degree to which less widows and orphans are created; and the degree to which the more contented workers become better heads of families and better citizens. In addition, account can be taken of the fact that hazardous conditions which lead to accidental deaths and injuries, besides being inherently and intrinsically undesirable, represent economic losses to society as a whole.

A second advantage to the broadened approach to evaluation of personnel innovations is that it should provide an additional argument for enabling the personnel technician to enlist the very essential support of labor in studying and making the changes he wishes to evaluate or introduce. The past history of the "speed up" system, the feelings of the workers and organized labor that what benefits management does *not* necessarily benefit them, and the personal reticence to be a human guinea pig make it often difficult if not impossible for industrial psychologists to collect satisfactory immediate criteria of worker performance. If the viewpoint suggested by this article were accepted and followed, it seems reasonable that the cooperation of organized labor and the individual worker would be easier to secure.[15]

A third advantage of adopting the value judgment proposed is that it may help to merge the role played by the psychologist in industry with his stated ethics concerning his roles in industry and elsewhere.[16] For the psychologist, as a scientist, has professed objectivity and impartiality towards management and worker and yet worked mainly for the benefit of the former, assuming that what was good for management was good for the worker—even when he was not financed by management—*because the problems have been defined for him in a way which forced him to do so.*

It is not meant to suggest that the personnel psychologist has not heretofore been interested in improving the employee's working situation; but what is being suggested is that too often these improvements have been justified or evaluated on the basis of their ability to increase indirectly the worth of the employee to the company. The argument is that personnel practices leading to improved working conditions should also be evaluated against a measure of the extent to which the conditions benefit the worker —and this measure should be considered as ultimate a criterion as any measure of increased worth of the individual to the organization.

Although the point of view expressed is in itself a value judgment, subject to arbitrary acceptance or rejection, it is consonant with the legal and philosophical attitude which has enabled capitalism to survive as a productive, progessive economic system in this country. It is also consonant with the humanistic and moral attitudes toward the individual which prevail here. Thus, acceptance of the proposed axiom will enable the industrial psychologists formally to adopt some of the values about the individual the great majority of the nation holds—which the psychologist as a private citizen does consider, but which he has not incorporated into his evaluation of his own professional services.

What is Management's Attitude Towards Ultimate Criteria of Organizational Success?

The reader may well agree with what has been said. Yet, he may raise a very fair question, "This is all very well and good in theory but in practice will management be interested in financing a personnel research program which at its outset does not have as its ultimate goal the increase of company profits or productivity?"

Before an adequate answer to this question can be obtained it will be necessary to poll a representative sample of top management throughout the country. No doubt, wide variations in management's responses are to be expected. It is probable that some of these variations will be accounted for by the size of the company concerned, its past history of relations with labor, and whether the company is a relatively new, expanding concern, or an old well-established institution. It is also probable that the final answer will have to be in terms of the extent to which management accepts its obligations to workers and society rather than whether or not it recognizes these obligations.

However, there are some indications available as to what some management representatives' attitudes may be. For example, one answer is suggested by Browne[17] when he reports the goals which twenty-three executives perceived in the planning of top management of a tire manufacturing concern. A summary of these seventeen types of goals enumerated included "to develop a better community and to help the general prosperity of the city" (Rank 15); To promote good labor relations and have satisfied workers" (Rank 4), and "To provide good working conditions and good living standards for employees" (Rank 8). By way of contrast, the goal "To make as much money as possible for the stockholders" was ranked thirteenth!

An answer is also suggested by the program of the Esso Standard Oil Company for preparing employees for retirement. In its approach to the problem of retirement, the company appears motivated by the three ultimate goals we have suggested. In the case of Esso, *these* three goals appear as follows: (1) increasing industrial efficiency, prestige, worker satisfaction, reducing costs, and increasing public good-will; (2) aiding the nation and community to solve problems of the aged; (3) helping the worker to be well adjusted in retirement.

> Industry has accepted its share of the responsibility for finding the economic solution to this problem by providing retirement income for employees that is in most cases based on the productivity of the person's working career. Our government's Social Security program has the same basis. This type of retirement income, in the form of an earned annuity, is an approach toward the problem that recognizes the dignity and independence of the individual. It is not a handout.
>
> In the sociological field, the same type of approach is needed in stimulating and helping retired employees to seek a retirement that will be active, fruitful, and constructive, one that will combat frustration. Here again, industry must not be guilty of paternalism, the sociological equivalent of a handout. Rather it should strive to give real help and counsel to the individual in thinking through his problem. By such action, industry can contribute to the solution of the national and community problems in addition to deriving obvious direct benefits.[18]

An answer is also suggested by a cursory examination of a few recent issues of *Advanced Management,* the official publication of the Society for the Advancement of Management which revealed numerous illustrations of where representatives of management showed recognition of industrial objectives other than profits and productivity alone. For example:

> The motivating factors which caused the businessmen of Worcester (Mass.) to catapult their Chamber of Commerce into the field of industrial management are basic to any community. In 1945, a local committee for economic development decided that Worcester's economic progress would be thwarted by a post-war recession. The best approach to offset resulting unemployment would be the development of new and existing Worcester companies. . . . The committee not only recommended, but sold a program to hire four consultants working at this community level under the auspices of the Worcester Chamber of Commerce. . . .
>
> Since the program is financially supported by the larger businesses . . . (it) demonstrates greatly that the Worcester business community recognizes its spiritual as well as economic responsibilities.[19]

In this same journal, a company president writes:

> Business leaders today who are outstanding in their field are making their decision on a far broader basis than at any time in the past.
>
> They are realizing that they have a responsibility, not merely to their stockholders, but to their employees and to the public and to their community and to their nation.
>
> Unless his decisions can stand up under these tests, a true business leader is failing in his responsibilities.[20]

Although writing to oppose present management attitudes towards personnel programs, the criticisms of the following author incidentally expose the bases upon which personnel work has been accepted in many organizations.

> . . . Too many personnel departments . . . seem to be engaged with activities on the periphery of operating realities . . . (Personnel executives)—and their presidents, too—act as if they do not understand the profit-making nature of the personnel function. . . . The (personnel executive) can no longer be thought of as the "professional do-gooder," dealing only in a colorful array of fancy "programs" which in themselves don't contribute to the profitability of the enterprise.[21]

Ghiselli and Brown describe what they believe to be a trend in management thinking towards the concept of efficiency. This trend is also suggestive of management attitudes toward proposed ultimate criteria 2 and 3.

> In the beginning, with narrowed vision, management evaluated most (efforts to streamline production) in terms of the profit motive. In recent years, with wider vision, interests have broadened to include the . . . criterion of workers' comfort and safety in conjunction with that of profits. . . .
> . . . changes (have been) introduced solely on the criterion of the worker's improvement. At the present time there is a further broadening of management's perspective, which is leading it to include other kinds of worker adjustments as necessary criteria to be used in the evaluation of industrial work.[22]

Of course, one reason management may evidence interest in the value of the organization to its workers or to the community is that they accept Hypothesis A—namely that the attainment of social objectives will lead in the long run to increased profits, productivity, and company security, as suggested earlier by Blum, Ghiselli and Brown, Bentz, and Bingham. However, it is difficult to determine to what extent management recognizes or is aware of this correlation when it subscribes to the non-material or social ultimate criteria of organizational success.

1. The writer is indebted to the many persons who read and criticized this manuscript in its various stages of development. These include: C. L. Shartle, V. J. Bentz, R. R. Canter, W. V. Bingham, L. W. Ferguson, E. E. Ghiselli, R. N. Hobbs, D. W. Fiske, C. G. Browne, J. E. Moore, A. Glickman, P. A. Carmichael, F. M. du Mas, N. Lawrence, and M. Lawrence.

2. D. W. Fiske, "Values, Theory and the Criterion Problem," *Personnel Psychol.* 4 (1951): 93–98.

3. For a discussion of the distinction between immediate, intermediate, and ultimate criteria, the reader is referred to R. L. Thorndike, *Personnel Selection: Test and Measurement Techniques* (New York: John Wiley & Sons, 1949), pp. 121–24.

4. M. L. Blum, *Industrial Psychology and Its Social Foundations* (New York: Harper & Row, Publishers, 1949).

5. E. E. Ghiselli and C. W. Brown, *Personnel and Industrial Psychology* (New York: McGraw-Hill Book Co., 1948).

6. D. MacGregor, "The Staff Function in Human Relations," *J. Soc. Issues* 4 (1948): 10–13.

7. B. M. Bass, "Feelings of Pleasantness and Work Group Efficiency," *Personnel Psychology.*

8. P. Taft, *Economics and Problems of Labor* (Harrisburg, Pa.: Stackpole Books, 1942).

9. Office of the Chief, Army Field Forces, U.S. Army, *The Senior R.O.T.C. Manual, Vol. II* (Washington, D. C.: U.S.G.P.O., 1948), pp. 484–85, 487.

10. R. C. Davis, *Industrial Organization and Management* (New York: Harper & Row, Publishers, 1940), p. 20.

11. Ibid., p. 27.

12. W. D. Scott et al., *Personnel Management* (New York: McGraw-Hill Book Co., 1941), pp. 5–6.

13. D. Yoder, *Personnel Management and Industrial Relations* (Englewood Cliffs, N.J.: Prentice-Hall, 1948), p. 67.

14. For further illustrations the reader is referred to E. Peterson and E. G. Plowman, *Business Organization and Management* (Homewood, Ill.: Richard D. Irwin, 1949), pp. 40–41; C. C. Balderston et al., *Management of Enterprise* (Englewood Cliffs, N.J.: Prentice-Hall, 1949), pp. 3, 4, 8, 9; B. E. Goetz, *Management Planning and Control: A Managerial Approach to Industrial Accounting* (New York: McGraw-Hill Book Co., 1949), pp. 21, 25; P. Pigors, L. C. McKenney, and T. O. Armstrong, *Social Problems in Labor Relations* (New York: McGraw-Hill Book Co., 1939), pp. v-xi (Foreword written by P. Cabot); H. P. Dutton, *Business Organization and Management* (New York: McGraw-Hill Book Co., 1935), pp. 18–21.

15. For a discussion of the trade unionist's attitude towards management personnel philosophy, the reader is referred to S. A. Barkin, "A Trade Unionist Appraises Management Personnel Philosophy," *Harvard Bus. Rev.* 28 (1950): 59–64.

16. A tentative formulation by the Committee on Ethical Standards for Psychology of the American Psychological Association of ethical standards with reference to the public responsibility includes Principle 1.12-1, which reads as follows: "The psychologist's ultimate allegiance is to society, and his professional behavior should demonstrate an awareness of his social responsibilities. . . ." Committee on Ethical Standards for Psychology, "Ethical Standards and Public Responsibility," *Amer. Psychol.* 6 (1951): 626–49.

17. C. G. Browne, "Study of Executive Leadership in Business," *J. Appl. Psychol.* 4 (1951): 93–98.

18. Esso Standard Oil Company, *Preparation for Retirement: A Study of Post-Employment Adjustment* (New York: Esso, 1951).

19. J. P. Cleaver, "The Worcester Story," *Adv. Mgmt.* 16 (1951): 2–5.

20. R. H. Rich, "Management and the Community–the Human Factors of Management," *Adv. Mgmt.* 16 (1951): 5–6.

21. A. V. MacCullough, "Off the Fringe and Onto the First Team," *Adv. Mgmt.* 16 (1951): 20–21.

22. Ghiselli and Brown, op. cit., pp. 219–20.

TOWARDS A "TRULY" SCIENTIFIC MANAGEMENT: THE CONCEPT OF ORGANIZATION HEALTH

Warren G. Bennis

Muggeridge: Now, Charles, you, because you're a scientist . . . you have this idea, as I understand from your writings, that one of the failings of our sort of society, is that the people who excercise authority, we'll say Parliament and so on, are singularly unversed in scientific matters.

Snow: Yes, I think this is a terrible weakness of the whole of Western society, and one that we're not going to get out of without immense trouble and pain.

Muggeridge: Do you mean by that that, for instance, an M. P. would be a better M. P. if he knew a bit about science?

Snow: I think some M. P.'s ought to know a bit about science. They'd be better M. P.'s in the area where scientific insight becomes important. And there are quite a number of such areas.[1]

From *Changing Organizations* by W. G. Bennis. Copyright © 1966 by McGraw-Hill, Inc. Used with permission of McGraw-Hill Book Company. Also appeared in the *General Systems Yearbook,* vol. 7, pp. 269-82; reprinted by permission of the author and the Society for General Systems Yearbook.

Extolling Science has become something of a national and international pastime which typically stops short of the truly radical reforms in social organization the scientific revolution implies. Knowing "a bit about science" is a familiar and increasingly popular exemplar of this which C. P. Snow treats in his *Two Cultures*.[2] But if culture is anything it is a way of life, the way real people live and grow, the way ideals and moral imperatives are transmitted and infused. Culture is more *value* than knowledge ("a bit of science"). Dr. Bronowski, who shares with Snow the view that "humanists" tend to be ignorant of and removed from science (they cannot discuss the Second Law of Thermodynamics) understands more than Snow seems to that a fundamental unification of cultural outlook is what is required.[3] The connective tissue required, then, is cultural, social, institutional—not grafted on evening courses on Science.

In this connection, and closer to some of the general aims of this paper, Nevitt Sanford has said:

> The ethical systems of other professions, such as business or the military, have become models for whole societies. Why should not the practice of science become such a model? After we have shown, as we can, that joy and beauty have their places in this system? At any rate, anyone who takes it upon himself to be a scientist, and succeeds in living up to its requirements, may be willing for his behavior to become a universal norm.[4]

This foreshadows the general theme of this essay: the recognition that the *institution* of science can and should provide a viable model for other institutions not solely concerned with developing knowledge. To demonstrate this proposition, this paper first discusses the criterion problem in relation to organizations.[5] An attempt is made to show that the usual criteria for evaluating organizational effectiveness, "enhancement of satisfaction on the part of industry's participants and improvement of effectiveness of performance,"[6] are inadequate, incorrect, or both as valid indicators of organizational "health." (For the moment let us use the term "health" in the same vague way as "effectiveness." Organizational health is defined later in this paper.) Next it is suggested that an alternative set of criteria, extracted from the normative and value processes of science, provides a more realistic basis for evaluating organizational perfomance. These criteria are related to those of positive mental health, for it will be argued that there is a profound kinship between the mores of science and the criteria of health for an individual. From this confluence is fashioned a set of psychologically based criteria for examining organizational health. Finally a discussion is presented of some of the consequences of these effectiveness criteria for organizational theory and practice.

The Search for
Effectiveness Criteria

There is hardly a term in current psychological thought as vague, elusive, and ambiguous as the term "mental health." That it means many things to many people is bad enough. That many people use it without even attempting to specify the idiosyncratic meaning the term has for them makes the situation worse . . . for those who wish to introduce concern with mental health into systematic psychological theory and research.[7]

. . . No one can say with any degree of certainty by what standards an executive ought to appraise the performance of his organization. And it is questionable whether the time will ever arrive when there will be any pattern answers to such a question —so much does the setting of an organization and its own goal orientation affect the whole process of appraisal.[8]

Raising the problem of criteria, the standards for judging the "goodness" of an organization seldom fails to generate controversy and despair. Establishing criteria for an organization (or, for that matter, education, marriage, psychotherapy, etc.) accentuates questions of value, choice, and normality and all the hidden assumptions that are used to form judgments of operation. Often, as Jahoda has said in relation to mental health criteria, the problem "seems so difficult that one is almost tempted to claim the privilege of ignorance."[9]

However, as tempting as ignorance can be, research on organizations —particularly industrial organizations—has heroically struggled to identify and measure a number of dimensions associated with organizational effectiveness.[10] Generally, these dimensions have been of two kinds: those dealing with some index of organizational performance, such as profit, cost, rates of productivity, individual output, etc., and those associated with the human resources, such as morals, motivation, mental health, job commitment, cohesiveness, attitudes toward employer or company, etc. In short, as Katzell pointed out in his 1957 review of industrial psychology, investigations in this area typically employ measures of *satisfaction* and *performance*.[11] In fact, it is possible to construct a simple twofold table that adequately accounts for most of the research on organizations that has been undertaken to date, as shown in Table 1. On one axis is located the criteria variables: organizational efficiency (the ethic of work performance) and member satisfaction (the ethic of "health"). On the other axis is located the two main independent variables employed, human and rationalized procedures. In other words, it is possible to summarize

TABLE 1

Major variables employed in the study of organizational behavior.

Independent variables	Criteria variables	
	Organizational efficiency	Satisfaction or health
Technology (rationalized procedures)	Management Science: Systems Research, Operations Research, Decision Processes etc.	Human Engineering
Human factors	Personal Psychology, Training, and other personnel functions	Industrial Social Psychology and Sociology

most of the research literature in the organizational area by locating the major independent variables (technological or human) on one axis and the dependent variables (efficiency or health) on the other.

This classification is necessarily crude and perhaps a little puzzling, principally for the reason that research on organizations lacks sufficient information concerning the empirical correlation between the two dependent variables, organizational efficiency and health factors. For a time it seemed (or was hoped) that personnel satisfaction and efficiency were positively related, that as satisfaction increased so did performance. This alleged correlation allowed the "human relations" school and the industrial engineers (Taylorism being one example[12]) to proceed coterminously without necessarily recognizing the tension between "happy workers" and "high performance." As Likert put it:

> It is not sufficient merely to measure morale and the attitude of employees toward the organization, their supervision, and their work. Favorable attitudes and excellent morale do not necessarily assure high motivation, high performance, and an effective human organization. A good deal of research indicates that this relationship is much too simple.[13]

Indeed today we are not clear about the relation of performance to satisfaction, or even whether there is any interdependence between them. Likert and his associates have found organizations with all the logical possibilities—high morale with low productivity, low productivity with low morale, etc. Argyris' work,[14] with a popular assist from William H.

Whyte, Jr.,[15] clouds the picture even further by postulating the inevitability of conflict between human need-satisfaction and organizational performance (as formal organizations are presently conceived). This creates, as Mason Haire has recognized,[16] a calculus of values: how much satisfaction or health is to be yielded for many units of performance?

Generally speaking, then, this is the state of affairs: two criteria, crudely measured, ambiguous in meaning, questionable in utility, and fraught with value connotations.[17] In view of these difficulties, a number of other, more promising, approaches have been suggested. The most notable of these are the criterion of multiple goals, the criterion of the situation, and the criterion of system characteristics.

The Criterion of Multiple Goals

This approach rests on the assumption that ". . . organizations have more than a single goal and that the interaction of goals will produce a different value framework in different organizations."[18] Likert, who is a proponent of the multiple criterion approach, claims that very few organizations, if any, obtain measurements that clearly reflect the quality and capacity of the organization's human resources. This situation is due primarily to the shadow of traditional theory, which tends to overlook the human and motivational variables and the relatively new developments in social science that only now permit measurements of this type. Likert goes on to enumerate twelve criteria, covering such dimensions as loyalty and identification with the institution and its objectives, degree of confidence and trust, adequacy and efficiency of communication, amount and quality of teamwork, etc.[19] By and large, Likert's criteria are psychologically based and substantially enrich the impoverished state of effectiveness criteria.[20]

The Criterion of the Situation

This approach is based on the reasoning that organizations differ with respect to goals and that they can be analytically distinguished in terms of goal orientation. As Parsons pointed out: "As a formal analytical point of reference, *primacy of orientation to the attainment of a specific goal is used as the defining characteristic of an organization* which distinguishes it from other types of social systems."[21]

In an earlier paper by Bennis[22] a framework was presented for characterizing four different types of organizations based on a specific criterion variable. These "pure" types are rarely observed empirically, but they serve to sharpen the difference among formally organized activities.

Table 2 represents an example of developing effectiveness variables on the basis of organizational parameters.

TABLE 2

Typology of organization.

Type of organization	Major function	Examples	Effectiveness criterion
Habit	Replicating standard and uniform products	Highly mechanized factories, etc.	No. of products
Problem-solving	Creating new ideas	Research organizations; design and engineering divisions; consulting organizations, etc.	No. of ideas
Indoctrination	Changing people's habits, attitudes, intellect, behavior (physical and mental)	Universities, prisons, hospitals, etc.	No. of "clients" leaving
Service	Distributing services either directly to consumer or to above types	Military, government, advertising, taxi companies, etc.	Extent of services, services performed

From W. G. Bennis, "Leadership Theory and Administrative Behavior: The Problem of Authority," Admin. Sci. Quart. 4, (Dec. 1959): 299.

The Criterion of System Characteristics

This approach, most cogently advanced by sociologists, is based on a "structural-functional" analysis. Selznick, one of its chief proponents, characterizes the approach in the following way:

> Structural-functional analysis relates contemporary and variable behavior to a presumptively stable system of needs and mechanisms. This means that a given empirical system is deemed to have basic needs, essentially related to self-maintenance; the system develops repetitive means of self-defense; and day-to-day activity is interpreted in terms of the function served by that activity for the maintenance and defense of the system.[23]

Derivable from this system model are basic needs or institutional imperatives that have to be met if the organism is to survive and "grow." Selznick, for example, lists five:

> (1) The security of the organization as a whole in relations to social forces in its environment. (2) The stability of the lines of authority and communication. (3) The stability of informal relations within the organization. (4) The continuity of policy and of the sources of its determination. (5) A homogeneity of outlook with respect to the meaning and role of the organization.[24]

Caplow, starting from the fundamental postulate that organizations tend to maintain themselves in continuous operation, identifies three criteria of organizational success: the performance of objective functions, the minimization of spontaneous conflict, and the maximization of satisfaction for indviduals.[25] Obviously, with the exception of the second criterion, these resemble the old favorites, performance and satisfaction.

The preceding summaries do not do full justice to the nuances in these three approaches or the enormous creative effort that went into their development. Nor do they include the ideas of many thoughtful practitioners.[26] Despite these limitations, the discussion of multiple criteria, situational parameters, and system characteristics represents the main attempt to solve the criterion problem.[27]

Inadequacy of Criterion Variables
for the Modern Organization

> One thing that is new is the prevalence of newness, the changing scale and scope of change itself, so that the world alters as we walk in it, so that the years of man's life measure not some small growth or rearrangement or moderation of what he learned in childhood, but a great upheaval. . . . To assail the changes that have unmoored us from the past is futile, and in a deep sense, I think it is wicked. We need to recognize the change and learn what resources we have.[28]
>
> The history of other animal species shows that the most successful in the struggle for survival have been those which were most adaptable to changes in their world.[29]

The present ways of thinking about and measuring organizational effectiveness are seriously inadequate and often misleading. These criteria are insensitive to the important needs of the organizations and out of joint with the emerging view of contemporary organization that is held by many organizational theorists and practitioners. The present techniques of evaluation provide static indicators of certain output characteristics (i.e. performance and satisfaction) without illuminating the processes by which the organization searches for, adapts to, and solves its changing goals.[30] However, it is these dynamic processes of problem-solving that provide the critical dimensions of organizational health, and without knowledge of them output measurements are woefully inadequate.[31]

This rather severe charge is based upon the belief that the main challenge confronting the modern organization (and society) is that of coping with external stress and change. This point hardly needs elaboration or defense. Ecclesiastes glumly pointed out that men persist in disordering their settled ways and beliefs by seeking out many inventions. The recent work in the field of organizational behavior reflects this need and interest; it is virtually a catalogue of the problems in organizational change.[32] In a 1961 monograph on managing major change in organizations, Mann and Neff stated the issue this way: "Among the most conspicuous values in American culture of the twentieth century are progress, efficiency, science and rationality, achievement and success. These values have helped to produce a highly dynamic society—a society in which the predominant characteristic is *change*."[33] Kahn, Mann, and Seashore, when discussing a criterion variable, "the ability of the organization to change appropriately in response to some objective requirement for change," remarked: "Although we are convinced of the theoretical importance of this criterion, which we have called organizational flexibility, we have thus far been unable to solve the operational problems involved in its use."[34]

The basic flaw in the present effectiveness criteria is their inattention to the problem of adapting to change. To illuminate some of the consequences of this omission, let us turn to one rather simple example. The example is drawn from an area of research that started at the Massachusetts Institute of Technology about 1949 on the effects of certain organizational patterns (communication networks) on problem-solving by groups.[35] Two of these networks, the Wheel and the Circle, are shown in the illustration below.

The results of these experiments showed that an organization with a structure like the Wheel can solve simple tasks (e.g. identification of the color of a marble that is common to all five group members) more rapidly, more clearly, and more efficiently than an organization like the Circle. Thus the Wheel arrangement is plainly superior in terms of the usual criteria employed to evaluate effectiveness. However, if we consider two other criteria of organizational effectiveness that are relevant to the concern with change-flexibility and creativity, we discover two interesting phenomena. First, the rapid acceptance of a new idea is more likely in

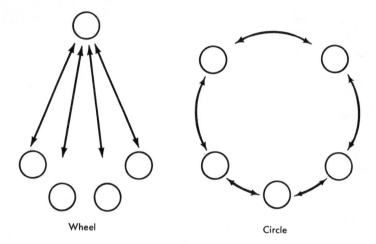

Wheel   Circle

Two Types of Communication Networks for Problem
Solving by a Group of Five Persons.

the Circle than in the Wheel. The man in the middle of the Wheel is apt
to discard an idea on the grounds that he is too busy or the idea is
impractical. Second, when the task is changed, for example by going
from "pure" color marbles to unusual color marbles (such as ginger-ale
color or blue-green), the Circle organization is better able to adapt to
this change by developing a new code.[36] As Leavitt pointed out:

> . . . by certain industrial engineering-type criteria (speech, clar-
> ity of organization and job descriptions, parsimonious use of paper,
> etc.), the highly structured, highly routinized, noninvolving cen-
> tralized net seems to work best. But if our criteria of effectiveness
> are more ephemeral, more general (like acceptance of creativity,
> flexibility in dealing with novel problems, generally high morale
> and loyalty), then the more egalitarian or decentralized type net
> seems to work better.[37]

If we view organizations as adaptive, problem-solving, organic structures, then inferences about effectivness have to be made, not from static
measures of output, though these may be helpful, but on the basis of
the processes through which the organization approaches problems. In
other words, no single measurement of organizational efficiency or satisfaction—no single time-slice of organizational perfomance—can provide
valid indicators of organizational health. An organization may be essentially
healthy despite measurements that reveal that its performance and satisfaction measurements are lower than last month's; it can be unhealthy
even if its performance and efficiency figures are higher than last month's.
Unhealthy and healthy, that is, in relation to the ability to cope with

change, with the future. Discussing the neurotic processes, Kubie makes the same point:

> There is not a single thing which a human being can do or feel, or think, whether it is eating or sleeping or drinking or fighting or killing or hating or loving or grieving or exulting or working or playing or painting or inventing, which cannot be either sick or well. . . . The measure of health is flexibility, the freedom to learn through experience, the freedom to change with changing internal and external circumstances, to be influenced by reasonable argument, admonitions, exhortations, and the appeal to emotions; the freedom to respond appropriately to the stimulus of reward and punishment, and especially the freedom to cease when sated. The essence of normality is flexibility in all of these vital ways.[38]

Any moment of behavior is unhealthy if the processes that set it in motion predetermine its automatic repetition, regardless of the environmental stimuli or consequences of the act. For example, it is plausible that lowering efficiency in order to adjust to some product change may be quite appropriate when market demands are considered. It is equally plausible that morale, or whatever measure is used to gauge the human factor, may similarly plummet during this period. In fact, maintaining the same level of efficiency and morale in new circumstances may be dysfunctional for the health of the organization.

Let us review the argument thus far. The main challenge confronting today's organization, whether it is a hospital or a business enterprise, is that of responding to changing conditions and adapting to external stress. The salience of change is forced on organizations because of the growing interdependence between their changing boundary conditions and society (a point that will be elaborated later) and the increasing reliance on scientific knowledge. The traditional ways that are employed to measure organizational effectiveness do not adequately reflect the true determinants of organizational health and success. Rather, these criteria yield static time-slices of performance and satisfaction, which may be irrelevant or misleading. These static, discrete measurements do not provide viable measures of health, for they tell us nothing about the processes by which the organization copes with its problems. Therefore, different effectiveness criteria have to be identified, criteria that reveal the processes of problem-solving. This point is corroborated by some recent works on organizational theory. Consider, for example, these remarks by Wilfred Brown, Chairman and Managing Director of the Glacier Metal Company:

> Effective organization is a function of the work to be done and the resources and techniques available to do it. Thus changes

in methods of production bring about changes in the number of work roles, in the distribution of work between roles and in their relationship to one another. Failure to make explicit acknowledgement of this relationship between work and organization gives rise to non-valid assumptions, e.g. that optimum organization is a function of the personalities involved, that it is a matter connected with the personal style and arbitrary decision of the chief executive, that there are choices between centralized and decentralized types of organization, etc. Our observations lead us to accept that optimum organization must be derived from an analysis of the work to be done and the techniques and resources available.[39]

The work of Emery and Trist, which has influenced the thinking of Brown, stressed the "socio-technical system," based on Bertalanffy's "open system" theorizing.[40] They conclude that:

> . . . the primary task of managing an enterprise as a whole is to relate the total system to its environment, and not internal regulation per se.[41]
> If management is to control internal growth and development it must in the first instance control the "boundary conditions"— the forms of exchange between the enterprise and the environment. . . . The strategic objective should be to place the enterprise in a position in its environment where it has some assured conditions for growth—unlike war the best position is not necessarily that of unchallenged monopoly. Achieving this position would be the primary task or overriding mission of the enterprise.[42]

In reference to management development, A. T. M. Wilson, Former Director of Tavistock Institute, pointed out:

> One general point of high relevance can be seen in these discussions of the firm as an institution. The tasks of the higher level managers center on problems in which there is a continuously high level of uncertainty; complex value decisions are inevitably involved; and this has a direct bearing on the requiremnts of personality for top level management . . .[43]

And H. J. Leavitt said on the same subject:

> Management development programs need, I submit, to be oriented much more toward the future, toward change, toward differences from current forms of practice and behavior. . . . We ought to allocate more of the effort of our programs to making our student a more competent analyst. We ought, in other words,

to try to teach them to think a little more like scientists, and indeed to know a good deal more about the culture and methods of scientists.[44]

What relevance have these quotations to the main theme of this essay? Note, first of all, that these theorists all view the organization (or institution) as an adaptive structure actively encountering many different environments, both internal and external, in their productive efforts. Note also the key terms: change, uncertainty, future, task, mission, work to be done, available resources, exchanges between the enterprise and environment. There is no dialogue here on the relation between "productivity" and "satisfaction," no fruitless arguments between the human relationists and scientific management advocates. Indeed, it seems that it is no longer adequate to perceive organization as an analogue to the machine as Max Weber indicated: ". . . (bureaucracy is like) a modern judge who is a vending machine into which the pleadings are inserted together with the fee and which then disgorges the judgment together with its reasons mechanically derived from the code."[45]

Nor is it reasonable to view the organization solely in terms of the sociopsychological characteristics of the persons involved at work, a viewpoint that has been so fashionable of late.[46] Rather, the approach that should be taken is that of these quoted writers: organizations are to be viewed as "open systems" defined by their primary task or mission and encountering boundary conditions that are rapidly changing their characteristics.[47] Given this rough definition, we must locate some effectiveness criteria and the institutional prerequisites that provide the conditions for the attainment of this criteria.

The Spirit of Inquiry as a Model for Organization

Findings are science's short-range benefits, but the method of inquiry is its long-range value. I have said that the invention of organization was Man's first most important achievement; I now add that the development of inquiry will be his second. Both of these inventions change the species and are necessary for its survival. But both must become a part of the nature of Man himself, not just given house room in certain groups. Organization is by now a part of every man, but inquiry is not. The significant product of science and education will be the incorporation within the human animal of the capability and habit of inquiry.[48]

Whether our work is art or science or the daily work of society, it is only the form in which we explore our experience which is different; the need to explore remains the same. This is why, at bottom, the society of scientists is more important than their discoveries. What science has to teach us here is not its techniques but its spirit: the irresistible need to explore.[49]

It has been asserted throughout this paper that organizations must be viewed as adaptive, problem-solving structures operating and embedded in complicated and rapidly changing environments. If this view is valid, then it is fair to postulate that the methodological rules by which the organization approaches its task and "exchanges with its environments" are the critical determinants of organizational effectiveness. These methodological rules or operating procedures bear a close resemblance to the rules of inquiry, or scientific investigation. Therefore, the rules and norms of science may provide a valuable, possibly necessary model for organizational behavior.

First, it should be stated what is meant and what is not meant by "science" in this context. It is not the findings of science, the vast array of data that scientists produce. Nor is it a barren operationalism—what some people refer to as "scientism"—or the gadgetry utilized for routine laboratory work. Rather it is what may be called the scientific "temper" or "spirit." It is this "spirit of inquiry," which stems from the value position of science, that such authors as Dewey, Bronowski, Geiger, and Sandford have emphasized must be considered if our world is to survive. This position says esentially that the roles of scientist and citizen cannot be sharply separated. As Waddington put it:

> The true influence of science is an attitude of mind, a general method of thinking about and investigating problems. It can, and I think it will, spread gradually throughout the social consciousness without any very sharp break with the attitudes of the past. But the problems for which it is wanted face us already; and the sooner the scientific method of handling them becomes more generally understood and adopted, the better it will be.[50]

Now it is necessary to look a bit more closely at what is meant by this "scientific attitude." Relevant here are two important aspects of the scientific attitude, one having to do with the methodology of science and one related to the social organization of science. The former is a complex of human behavior and adjustment that has been summed up as the "spirit of inquiry." This complex includes many elements, only two of which are considered here. The first may be called the hypothetical spirit, the feeling for tentativeness and caution, the respect for probable error. As Geiger says:". . . the hypothetical spirit is the unique contribution scientific method can offer to human culture; it certainly is the only prophylactic against the authoritarian mystique so symptomatic of modern nerve failure."[51]

The second ingredient is experimentalism, the willingness to expose ideas to empirical testing, to procedures, to action. The hypothetical stance without experimentalism would soon develop into a rather arid scholasticism. Experimentalism without the corrective of the hypothetical imagination would bring about a radical, "dustbowl" empiricism lacking significant insight and underlying structures capable of generalization. These two features, plus the corrective of criticism, is what is meant by the methodological rules of science; it is the spirit of inquiry, a love of truth relentlessly pursued, that ultimately creates the objectivity and intelligent action associated with science.

The second important aspect of the scientific attitude is that concerning the social organization of science, the institutional imperatives of the scientific enterprise. A number of social scientists, inspired by the work of Parsons[52] and Merton[53], have examined the society of scientific enterprise[54]. What they have said is important for the argument presented here. Only when the social conditions of science are realized can the scientific attitude exist. As Sanford pointed out:

> Science flourishes under that type of democracy that accents freedom of opinion and dissent, and respect for the individual. It is against all forms of totalitarianism, of mechanization and regimentation. . . . In the historical development of the ends that are treasured in Western societies there is reason to believe that science has had a determining role. Bronowski again: "Men have asked for freedom, justice and respect precisely as science has spread among them."[55]

or Parsons:

> Science is intimately integrated with the whole social structure and cultural tradition. They mutually support one another—only in certain types of society can science flourish and conversely without a continuous and healthy development and application of science such a society cannot function properly.[56]

What are the conditions that comprise the ethos of science? Barber identifies five that are appropriate to this discussion: Rationality, universalism, individualism, communality, and disinterestedness.[57] A brief word about each of these is in order. The goal of science is understanding, understanding in as abstract and general a fashion as possible. Universalism, as used here, means that all men have morally equal claims to discover and to understand. Individualism, according to Barber, expresses itself in science as anti-authoritarianism; no authority but the authority of science need be accepted or trusted. Communality is close to the utopian communist slogan: "From each according to his abilities, to each according to his needs." This simply means that all scientific peers have the right to share in existing knowledge; withholding knowledge and secrecy are cardinal sins. The last element, disinterestedness, is to be contrasted with the self-interest usually associated with organizational and economic life. Disinterestedness in science requires that role incumbents serve others and gain gratification from the pursuit of truth itself. These five conditions comprise the moral imperatives of the social organization of science. They are, of course, derived from an "ideal type" of system, an empirically imaginable possibility but a rare phenomenon. Nevertheless, insofar as they are imperatives, they do in fact determine significantly the behavior of scientific organization.

There are two points to be made in connection with this model of organization. The first was made earlier but may require reiteration: the spirit of inquiry can flourish only in an environment where there is a commitment toward the five institutional imperatives. The second point is that what is now called the "human relations school"[58] has been preoccupied primarily with the study of those factors that this paper has identified as the prerequisites of the science organization. In fact, only if we look at the human relations approach with this perspective do we obtain a valid view of their work. For example, a great deal of work in human relations has focused on "communication,"[59] "participation,"[60] and "decision-making." Over-generalizing a bit, we can say that most of the studies have been (from a moral point of view) predicated on and lean toward the social organization of science as has been outlined here. Note, for instance, that many studies have shown that increased participation, better communication (keeping worker "informed"), more "self-control," and decreased authoritarianism are desirable ends. Because of their emphasis on these factors, the researchers and theoreticians associated with human relations research have sometimes been perceived as "soft-headed," unrealistic, too academic, and even utopian. In some cases, the social scientists themselves have invited these criticisms by being mainly interested in demonstrating that these participative beliefs would lead to heightened morale and, on occasion, to increased efficiency. So they have been accused by many writers as advocates of "happiness" or a moo-cow psychology.[61]

These are invalid criticisms, mainly because the issue is being fought on the wrong grounds. The root of the trouble is that the social scientists have not been entirely aware or prescient enough to see the implications of their studies. Rather than debating the viability of socio-psychological variables in terms of the traditional effectiveness variables, which at this point is highly problematical, they should be saying that the only way in which organizations can develop a scientific attitude is by providing conditions where it can flourish. In short, the norms of science are both compatible and remarkably homogeneous with those of a liberal democracy. We argue, then, that the way in which organizations can master their dilemmas and solve their problems is by developing a spirit of inquiry. This can flourish only under the social conditions associated with the scientific enterprise, i.e. democratic ideals. Thus it is necessary to emphasize the "human side of enterprise," that is, institutional conditions of science, if organizations are expected to maintain mastery over their environment.[62]

Now, assuming that the social conditions of science have been met, let us return to the designated task of identifying those organizational criteria that are associated with the scientific attitude.

The Criteria of Science and Mental Health Applied to Organizations

Perhaps no other area of human functioning has more frequently been selected as a criterion for mental health than the individual's reality orientation and his efforts at mastering the environment.[63]

I now propose that we gather the various kinds of behavior just mentioned, all of which have to do with effective interaction with the environment, under the general heading of competence.[64]

. . . all aspects of the enterprise must be subordinated to . . . its *primary task*. It is not only industrial enterprises, however, which must remain loyal to their primary tasks. This is so of all human groups, for these are all compelled, in order to maintain themselves in existence, to undertake some form of appropriate action in relation to their environment. . . . An organism, whether individual or social, must do work in order to keep itself related to its external environment, that is, to meet reality.[65]

These quotations provide the framework for the following analysis. They express what has been the major concern throughout this paper: that, when organizations are considered as "open systems," adaptive structures coping with various environments, the most significant characteristic for understanding effectiveness is competence, mastery, or as the term has been used in this essay, problem-solving. It has been shown that competence can be gained only through certain adaptations of science: its attitude and social conditions. It is now possible to go a step further by underlining what the above quotations reveal, that the criteria of science bear a close kinship to the characteristics of what mental health specialists and psychiatrists call "health."

There is an interesting historical parallel between the development of criteria for the evaluation of mental health and the evolution of standards for evaluating organizational health. Mastery, competence, and adaptive, problem-solving abilities are words relatively new to both fields. In the area of organizational behavior these words are replacing the old terms "satisfaction" and "work competence." Similarly, an important change has taken place in the mental health field, which has had some of the same problems in determining adequate criteria. Rather than viewing health exclusively in terms of some highly inferential intrapsychic reconstitutions, these specialists are stressing "adaptive mechanisms" and "conflict-free," relatively antonomous ego-functioning, independent of id energies. The studies of White,[66] Rapaport,[67] Erikson,[68] Hartmann,[69] and other so-called ego-psychologists all point in this direction.

The main reason for the confluence of organizational behavior and mental health is at bottom quite simple. Both the norms of science and the methodology of psychotherapeutic work have the same goal and methodology: to perceive reality, both internal and external; to examine unflinchingly the positions of these realities in order to act intelligently. It is the belief here that what a patient takes away and can employ *after* treatment is the methodology of science, the ability to look facts in the face, to use the hypothetical and experimental methods—the spirit of inquiry—in understanding experience. Sanford has said in this connection:

> . . . most notably in Freud's psychoanalytic method of investigation and treatment. (This method is in my view, Freud's greatest, and it will be his most lasting contribution.) By the method I mean the whole contractual arrangement according to which both the therapist and patient become investigators, and both objects of careful observation and study; in which the therapist can ask the patient to face the truth because he, the therapist, is willing to try to face it in himself; in which investigation and treatment are inseparable aspects of the same humanistic enterprise.[70]

and in Freud's words:

> Finally, we must not forget that the relationship between analyst and patient is based on a love of truth, that is, on the

acknowledgement of reality, and that it precludes any kind of sham or deception.[71]

It is now possible to postulate the criteria for organizational health. These are based on a definition by Marie Jahoda, according to which a healthy personality ". . . actively masters his environment, shows a certain unit of personality, and is able to perceive the world and himself correctly."[72] Let us take each of these elements and extrapolate it into organizational criteria.

1. "Actively masters his environment": *Adaptability.* In the terms of this paper, this characteristic coincides with problem-solving ability, which in turn depends upon the organization's flexibility. Earlier it was pointed out that flexibility is the freedom to learn through experience, to change with changing internal and external circumstances. Another way of putting it, in terms of organizational functioning, is to say that it is "learning now to learn." This is equivalent to Bateson's notion of "deutero-learning," the progressive change in rate of simple learning.[73]

2. "Certain unit of personality": *The Problem of Identity.* In order for an organization to develop adaptability, it needs to know who it is and what it is to do; that is, it has to have some clearly defined identity.[74] The problem of identity, which is central to much of the contemporary literature in the mental health field, can in organizations be examined in at least two ways: (a) determining to what extent the organizational goals are understood and accepted by the personnel, and (b) ascertaining to what extent the organization is perceived veridically by the personnel.

As to the problem of goals, Selznick pointed out:

> The aims of large organizations are often very broad. A certain vagueness must be accepted because it is difficult to foresee whether more specific goals will be realistic or wise. This situation presents the leader with one of his most difficult but indispensable tasks. *He must specify and recast the general aims of his organization so as to adapt them, without serious corruption, to the requirements of institutional survival.* This is what we mean by the definition of institutional mission and role.[75]

The same point is made by Simon, Smithburg, and Thompson: "No knowledge of administrative techniques, then, can relieve the administrator from the task of moral choice—choice as to organizational goals and methods and choice as to his treatment of the other human beings in his organization."[76]

In addition to the clear definition of mission, which is the responsibility of the leader to communicate, there also has to be a working consensus on the organization of work. Wilfred Brown's work is extremely useful in this connection. He enumerates four concepts of organization: the *manifest* organization, the one that is seen on the "organization chart" and is formally displayed; the *assumed* organization, the one that individuals perceive as the organization (were they asked to draw their phenomenonological view of the way that things work); the *extant* organization, the situation as revealed through systematic investigation, say by a student of organizations; and the *requisite* organization, or the situation as it would have to be if it were "in accord with the real properties of the field in which it exists."

"The ideal situation," Brown goes on to say, "is that in which the manifest, the assumed, the extant, and the requisite are as closely as possible in line with each other."[77] Wherever these four organizational concepts are in contradiction, we find a case of what Erikson calls "identity diffusion."[78] Certainly this phenomenon is a familiar one to students and executives of organizations. Indeed, the great attention paid to the "informal group" and its discrepancy with the formal (difference between the manifest and the assumed organizations or between the manifest and the extant) testifies to this.

Another useful analogy to the mental health field shows up in this discussion. Many psychotherapeutic schools base their notions of health on the degree to which the individual brings into harmony the various "selves" that make up his personality. According to Fromm-Reichmann, ". . . the successfully treated mental patient, as he then knows himself, will be much the same person as he is known to others."[79] Virtually the same criterion is used here for organizational health, i.e. the degree to which the organization maintains harmony—and knowledge—about and among the manifest, assumed, extant, and requisite situations. This point should be clarified. It is not necessary to organizational health that all four concepts of organization be identical. Rather, all four types should be recognized and allowance made for all the tensions attendant upon their imbalance. It is doubtful that there will always be total congruence in organizations. The important factor is recognition; the executive function is to strive toward congruence insofar as it is possible.

3. "Is able to perceive the world and himself correctly": *Reality-Testing.* If the conditions for requisite organizations are to be met, the organization must develop adequate techniques for determining the "real properties" of the field in which it exists." The field contains two main boundaries, the internal organization and the boundaries relevant to the organization. March and Simon, in their cognitive view of organization, place great emphasis on adequate "search behavior." Ineffective search behavior—cycling and stereotypy—are regarded as "neurotic."[80]

However, it is preferable here to think about inadequate search behavior in terms of perception that is free from need distortion.[81] Abraham Maslow places this in perspective:

> Recently Money-Kyrle, an English psychoanalyst, has indicated that he believes it possible to call a neurotic person not only *relatively* inefficient simply because he does not perceive the real world as accurately or as efficiently as does the healthy person. The neurotic is not only emotionally sick—he is cognitively *wrong!*[82]

The requisite organization requires reality testing, within the limits of rationality, for successful mastery over the relevant environments.[83]

In summary, then, I am saying that the basic features of organization rely on adequate methods for solving problems. These methods stem from the elements of what has been called the scientific attitude. From these ingredients have been fashioned three criteria or organizational mechanisms, which fulfill the prerequisites of health. These criteria are in accord with what mental health specialists call health in the individual.

Undeniably, some qualifications have to be made. The mensuration problem has not been faced, nor have the concrete details for organizational practice been fully developed. Nonetheless, it has been asserted that the processes of problem-solving—of adaptability—stand out as the single most important determinant of organizational health and that this adaptability depends on a valid identity and valid reality-testing.[84]

Some Implications of the Science Model for Organizational Behavior

> There is one human characteristic which today can find a mode of expression in nationalism and war, and which, it may seem, would have to be completely denied in a scientific society. That is the tendency to find some dogma to which can be attached complete belief, forthright and unquestioning. That men do experience a need for certainty of such a kind can scarcely be doubted. . . . Is science, for all its logical consistency, in a position to satisfy this primary need of man?[85]

> We are not yet emotionally an adaptive society, though we try systematically to develop forces that tend to make us one. We encourage the search for new inventions; we keep the mind stimulated, bright, and free to seek out fresh means of transport, communication, and energy; yet we remain, in part, appalled by the con-

sequences of our ingenuity and, too frequently, try to find security through the shoring up of ancient and irrelevant conventions, the extension of purely physical safeguards, or the delivery of decisions we ourselves should make into the keeping of superior authority like the state. These solutions are not necessarily unnatural or wrong, but historically they have not been enough, and I suspect they will never be enough to give us the serenity and competence we seek . . . we may find at least part of our salvation in identifying ourselves with the adaptive process and thus share . . . some of the joy, exuberance, satisfaction and security . . . to meet the changing time.[86]

The use of the model of science as a form for the modern organization implies some profound reforms in current practice, reforms that may appear to some as too adventurous or utopian. This criticism is difficult to deny, particularly since not all the consequences can be clearly seen at this time. However, before necessity diminishes the desirability of using the science model, let us examine a few consequences that stand out rather sharply.

1. The problem of commitment and loyalty. Although the viewpoint does have its critics, such as William H. Whyte, Jr., most administrators desire to develop high commitment and loyalty to the organization. Can the scientific attitude, with its ascetic simplicity and acceptance of risk and uncertainty, substitute for loyalty to the organizations and its purpose? Can science, as Waddington wonders, provide the belief in an illusion that organizational loyalty is thought to provide? The answer to this is a tentative "yes and no." Substituting the scientific attitude for loyalty would be difficult for those people to whom the commitment to truth, to the pursuit of knowledge, is both far too abstract and far too threatening. For some, the "escape from freedom" is a necessity, and the uncertain nature of the scientific attitude would be difficult to accept. However, it is likely that even these individuals would be influenced by the adoption of the science model by the organization. Loyalty to the organization per se would be transformed into loyalty and commitment directed to the spirit of inquiry. Hence, a higher rate of mobility is envisaged for organizations based on movement towards those environments in which the social conditions of science exist. Gouldner, in another context, has discussed this difference between individuals in terms of the split of organizational roles into "locals and cosmopolitans."[87] The cosmopolitan derives his rewards from inward standards of excellence, internalized and reinforced through professional (usually scientific) identification. On the other hand, the local (what Marvick calls the "bureaucratic orientation"[88] derives his rewards from manipulating power within the hierarchy. The former are

considered to be better organization men than the latter. Loyalty within the scientific organizational conditions specified here, would be directed not to particular ends or products or to work groups but to identification with the adaptive process of the organization.

2. Recruitment and training for the spirit of inquiry. There are some indications that the problems of recruitment and training for the social organization of science are not as difficult as has been expected. For one thing, as Bruner has shown,[89] today's school children are getting more and better science teaching. It is to be hoped that they will learn as much about the attitude of science as they will about its glamour and techniques. In addition, more and more research-trained individuals are entering organizations.[90] As McGregor points out: "Creative intellectual effort by a wide range of professional specialists will be as essential to tomorrow's manager as instruments and an elaborate air traffic control system are to today's jet pilot."[91] Individuals trained in scientific methodology can easily adapt to, in fact will probably demand, more and more freedom for intellectual inquiry. If McGregor's and Leavitt and Whisler's[92] prognostications are correct, as they presently seem to be, then there is practically no choice but to prepare a social milieu in which the adaptive, problem-solving processes can flourish.

As to training, only a brief word needs to be said. The training program of the National Training Laboratories[93] and the work of Blake,[94] Blansfield,[95] and Shepard[96] are based rather specifically on developing better diagnosticians of human behavior. It is apparent from such training studies that the organization of tomorrow, heavily influenced by the growth of science and technology and manned by an increasing number of professionals, appears to have the necessary requirements for constructing organizations based on inquiry.

3. Intergroup Competition. Blake and Mouton, guided partly by the work of the Sherifs,[97] have disclosed for examination one of organization's most troublesome problems—intergroup conflict and collaboration. These perseverating conflicts, usually based on a corrupt practice of vested interests, probably dissipate more energy and money than any other single malady caused by humans. Intergroup conflict, with its "win-lose" orientation, its dysfunctional loyalty (to the group or product, not to the truth), its cognitive distortions of the outsider, and its inability to reach what has been called creative compromise, effectively disrupts the commitment to truth. By means of a laboratory approach Blake and Mouton have managed to break

> . . . the mental assumptions underlying win-lose conflict. Factually based mutual problem identification, fluidity in initial stages

of solution-proposing rather than fixed position taking, free and frequent interchange between representatives and their constituent groups and focusing on communalities as well as differences as the basis for achieving agreement and so on, are but a few of the ways which have been experimentally demonstrated to increase the likelihood of arriving at mutually acceptable solutions under conditions of collaboration between groups.[98]

What the authors do not explicitly say but only imply is that the structure of their experimental laboratory approach is based on the methods of inquiry that have been advocated in this paper. Theirs is an action-research model, in which the subjects are the inquirers who learn to collect, use and generalize from data in order to understand organizational conflict. Rational problem-solving is the only prophylaxis presently known to rid organizations of perseverating intergroup conflict.

Loyalty, recruitment and training, and intergroup hostility are by no means all the organizational consequences that this paper suggests. The distribution of power, the problems of group cohesiveness,[99] the required organizational fluidity for arranging task groups on a rational basis, and the change in organizational roles and status all have to be considered. More time and energy than are now available are needed before these problems can be met squarely. However, one thing is certain: whatever energy, competence, and time are required, it will be necessary to think generally along the directions outlined here. Truth is a cruel master, and the reforms that have been mentioned or implied may not be altogether pleasant to behold. The light of truth has a corrosive effect on vested interests, outmoded technologies, and rigid, stereotypic patterns of behavior. Moreover, if this scientific ethos is ever realized, the remnants of what is now known as morale and efficiency may be buried. For the spirit of inquiry implies a confrontation of truth that may not be "satisfying" and a deferral of gratification that may not, in the short run, be "efficient." However, this is the challenge that must be met if organizations are to cope better within their increasingly complicated environments.

---

1. "Muggeridge and Snow," *Encounter* 27 (1962): 90.

2. C. P. Snow, *Two Cultures and the Scientific Revolution* (New York: Mentor Books, 1962).

3. J. Bronowski, *Science and Human Values* (New York: Harper & Row, Publishers, 1959).

4. N. Sanford, "Social Science and Social Reform," presidential address for SPSSI, Annual Meeting of the American Psychological Association, Washington, D.C., Aug. 28, 1958.

5. For the purpose of this discussion, "organization" is defined as any institution from which one receives cash for services rendered. This paper deals with all such supra-individual entities, although reference is made mostly to industrial organizations.

6. R. A. Katzell, "Industrial Psychology," in *Annual Review of Psychology,* vol. 8, ed. P. R. Farnsworth (Palo Alto, Calif.: 1957), pp. 237–68.

7. M. Jahoda, *Current Concepts of Positive Mental Health* (New York: Basic Books, 1958), p. 3.

8. J. M. Pfiffner and F. P. Sherwood, *Administrative Organization* (Englewood Cliffs, N.J.: Prentice-Hall, 1960).

9. M. Jahoda, op. cit., p. 77.

10. P. Wasserman, *"Measurement and Evaluation of Organizational Performance,"* McKinsey Foundation Annotated Bibliography, Graduate School of Business Administration, Cornell University, Ithaca, N.Y., 1959.

11. R. A. Katzell, op. cit.

12. For a recent historical review, see H. G. J. Aitkin, *Taylorism at Watertown Arsenal: Scientific Management in Action 1908—1905* (Cambridge, Mass: Harvard University Press, 1960).

13. R. Likert, "Measuring Organizational Performance," *Harvard Bus. Rev.* 36 (1958): 41–48.

14. C. Agyris, "The Integration of the Individual and the Organization," paper presented at the University of Wisconsin, Madison, May 1961, and *Personality and Organization* (New York: Harper & Row, Publishers, 1957).

15. W. H. Whyte, Jr., *The Organization Man* (New York: Simon & Schuster, 1956).

16. M. Haire, "What Price Value?" *Contemp. Psychol.* 4 (1959): 180–82.

17. R. Kahn, F. C. Mann, and S. Seashore, "Human Relations Research in Large Organizations: II," *J. Soc. Issues* 12 (1956): 4.

18. Pfiffner and Sherwood, op. cit., p. 42.

19. Likert, op. cit.

20. See also Kahn, Mann, and Seashore, op. cit., "Introduction," for other suggestions for criteria.

21. T. Parsons, "Suggestions for a Sociological Approach to the Theory of Organizations, I," *Admin. Sci. Quart.* 1 (1956): 63–85, esp. p. 64.

22. W. G. Bennis, "Leadership Theory and Administrative Behavior: The Problem of Authority," *Admin. Sci. Quart.* 4 (1959): 259–301.

23. P. Selznick, "Foundations of the Theory of Organization," *Amer. Sociol. Rev.* 13 (1948): 28.

24. Ibid., pp. 29–30.

25. T. Caplow, "The Criteria of Organizational Success," in *Readings in Human Relations,* ed. K. Davis and W. G. Scott (New York: McGraw-Hill Book Co., 1959), p. 96.

26. See, for example, L. F. Urwick, "The Purpose of a Business," in *Readings in Human Relations,* ed. K. Davis and W. B. Scott (New York: McGraw-Hill Book Co., 1959), pp. 85–91.

27. Another approach, advocated by A. L. Comrey, is the deliberate (and often wise) avoidance of a definition of effectiveness of health by obtaining judgments of knowledgeable observers. "This method of defining 'effectiveness' seems to be the only

feasible course of action in view of the tremendous number of meanings involved in a conceptual definition of this term and the obvious impossibility of providing a criterion which would reflect all or most of these meanings." A. L. Comrey, "A Research Plan for the Study of Organizational Effectiveness," in *Some Theories of Organization,* ed. A. H. Rubinstein and C. J. Haberstroh (Homewood, Ill.: Dorsey Press, 1960).

28.   Robert Oppenheimer, "Prospects in the Arts and Sciences," *Perspectives USA* 11 (1955): pp. 5–14.

29.   J. Bronowski, *The Common Sense of Science* (New York: Modern Library, n.d.).

30.   B. Paul, "Social Science in Public Health," *Amer. J. Public Health* 46 (1956): pp. 1390–93.

31.   For other criticisms of the use of performance measures, see V. F. Ridgeway, "Dysfunctional Consequences of Performance Measurements," in *Some Theories of Organization,* ed. A. H. Rubinstein and C. J. Haberstroh (Homewood, Ill: Dorsey Press, 1960), pp. 371–77.

32.   See, for example, J. March and H. Simon, *Organizations* (New York: John Wiley & Sons, 1958), chap. 7; C. Argyris, "Organizational Development—An Inquiry into the Esso Approach," (Yale University, New Haven, Conn., July, 1960); H. Shepard, "Three Management Programs and the Theories Behind Them," in *An Action Research Program for Organizational Improvement* (Ann Arbor, Mich.: 1960); Foundation for Research on Human Behavior, J. R. Gibb and R. Lippitt, "Consulting with Groups and Organizations," *J. Soc. Issues* 15 (1959): 1–74; R. Lippitt, J. Watson, and B. Westley, *The Dynamics of Planned Change* (New York: Harcourt, Brace & World, 1958); W. G. Bennis, K. Benne, and R. Chin, *The Planning of Change* (New York: Henry Holt & Co., 1961); C. Walker, ed., *Modern Technology and Civilization* (New York: McGraw-Hill Book Co., 1961).

33.   F. C. Mann and F. W. Neff, *"Managing Major Change in Organizations"* (Ann Arbor, Mich.: Foundations for Research on Human Behavior, 1961).

34.   Kahn, Mann, and Seashore, op. cit., p. 4.

35.   H. J. Leavitt, "Effects of Certain Communication Patterns on Group Performance," *J. Abnormal Soc. Psych.* 46 (1951): 38–50.

36.   S. Smith, "Communication Pattern and the Adaptability of Task-Oriented Groups: An Experimental Study," unpublished paper (M.I.T., Cambridge, Mass., 1950).

37.   H. J. Leavitt, "Unhuman Organizations," address presented at the Centennial Symposium on Executive Development, School of Industrial Management M.I.T., Cambridge, Mass., April 27, 1961, p. 22.

38.   Ibid., p. 20.

39.   W. Brown, *Exploration in Management* (New York: John Wiley & Sons, 1960).

40.   R. R. Blake and J. S. Mouton, "Developing and Maintaining Corporate Health Through Organic Management Training," unpublished paper (University of Texas, Austin, 1961).

41.   F. E. Emory and E. L. Trist, "Socio-Technical Systems," paper presented at the 6th Annual International Meeting of the Institute of Management Sciences, Paris, France, September 1959, p. 10.

42.   Ibid., p. 12.

43.   A. T. M. Wilson, "The Manager and His World," paper presented at the Centennial Symposium on Executive Development, School of Industrial Management, M.I.T., Cambridge, Mass., April 27, 1961, p. 13.

44. H. J. Leavitt, "Unhuman Organizations," pp. 32–33. Although not quoted here, a book by Selznick is also directly relevant. See P. Selznick, *Leadership in Administration* (Evanston, Ill.: Row, Peterson, 1957).

45. R. Bendix, *Max Weber: An Intellectual Portrait* (Garden City, N.J.: Doubleday & Co., 1960).

46. For an elaboration of this point see Bennis, op. cit.

47. Wilson lists six "areas of social activity; each of which contains a number of significant social institutions and social groups. These areas may be rather summarily labelled as: (i) Government, (ii) Consumers, (iii) Shareholders, (iv) Competitors, (v) Raw material and power suppliers, and (vi) Groups within the firm" (Wilson, op. cit., p. 3). These represent some of the boundary conditions for the manager.

48. H. Thelan, *Education and the Human Quest* (New York: Harper & Row, Publishers, 1960), p. 217.

49. J. Bronowski, *Science and Human Values* (New York: Harper & Row, Publishers, 1959), p. 93.

50. C. H. Waddington, *The Scientific Attitude* (Baltimore: Penguin Books, 1941), p. xiii.

51. C. Geiger, "Values and Social Science," *J. Soc. Issues* 6 (1950): pp. 8–16.

52. T. Parsons, *The Social System* (New York: Free Press, 1951), chap. 8.

53. R. Merton, *Essays in Sociological Theory* (New York: Free Press, 1949), chap. 8; and *Social Theory and Social Structure* (New York: Free Press, 1949), chaps. 8 and 12.

54. B. Barber, *Science and the Social Order* (New York: Free Press, 1952); G. P. Bush and D. H. Hattery, *Teamwork in Research* (Washington, D.C.: American University Press, 1953); S. Marcson, "The Scientist in American Industry," (Princeton, N.J.: Industrial Relations Section, 1960); A. H. Rubinstein and H. A. Shepard, *Annotated Bibliography in Human Relations in Research Laboratories,* (Cambridge, Mass.: M.I.T. Press, 1956).

55. N. Sanford, op. cit., p. 9.

56. B. Barber, op. cit., p. 83.

57. L. Baritz, *The Servants of Power* (Middletown, Conn.: Wesleyan University Press, 1960).

58. W. G. Bennis, op. cit.

59. N. Berkowitz and W. G. Bennis, "Interaction in Formal Service-Oriented Organizations," *Admin. Sci. Quart.* 6 (1961): pp. 25–50.

60. D. McGregor, *The Human Side of Enterprise* (New York: McGraw-Hill Book Co., 1960).

61. L. Baritz, op. cit., bibliographies for chaps. 6, 9, and 10.

62. Shepard notes the irony that as research organizations expand their operations they become more like the classical, ideal-type bureaucracy. For another approach to the social conditions of science, see H. Shepard, "Superiors and Subordinates in Research." *J. Business* 29 (1956): 261–67.

63. M. Jahoda, op. cit., p. 53.

64. R. W. White, "Motivation Reconsidered: The Concept of Competence," *Psychol Rev.* 66 (1959): 297–333.

65. Eric Trist in Brown, op. cit., p. xvi.

66. R. W. White, op. cit.

67. D. Rapaport, "The Theory of Ego Autonomy: A Generalization," *Bull. Menninger Clinic* 22 (1958): pp. 13–35. See also "The Structure of Psychoanalytic Theory," *Psychol. Issues* 2 (1960): Monograph 6.

68. E. Erikson, "Identity and the Life Cycle," *Psychol. Issues* 1 (1959): Monograph 1.

69. H. Hartman, *Ego Psychology and the Problem of Adaption* (New York: International Universities Press, 1958).

70. N. Sanford, op. cit., p. 12.

71. S. Freud, "Analysis Terminable and Interminable," in *Collected Papers,* ed. E. Jones (New York: Basic Books, 1959).

72. M. Jahoda, op. cit., p. 51.

73. G. Bateson, "Social Planning and the Concept of Deutero-Learning," in *Reading in Social Psychology,* ed. T. M. Newcomb and E. L. Hartley (New York: Henry Holt & Co., 1947), pp. 121–28.

74. See Selznick, *Leadership in Administration,* chap. 3, for similar emphasis.

75. Ibid., p. 66.

76. H. A. Simon, D. W. Smithburg, and V. S. Thompson, *Public Administration* (New York: Alfred A. Knopf, 1950).

77. W. Brown, op. cit., p. 24.

78. E. Erikson, op. cit.

79. F. Fromm-Reichmann, *Principles of Intensive Psychotherapy* (Chicago: University of Chicago Press, 1950).

80. March and Simon, *Organizations,* op. cit., p. 50.

81. Katzell, "Industrial Psychology," op. cit.

82. M. Jahoda, op. cit., p. 50.

83. See March and Simon, op. cit., for a formal model of search behavior (p. 50) and an excellent discussion of organizational reality-testing (chap. 6).

84. Dr. M. B. Miles has suggested that an important omission in this approach is organization "memory" or storage of information. Organizations modeled along the lines suggested here require a "theory" based on an *accumulated* storage of information. This is implied, I believe, in the criterion of adaptability.

85. Waddington, *The Scientific Attitude,* op. cit., pp. 163–64.

86. E. Morison, "A Case Study of Innovation," *Eng. Sci. Monthly* 13 (1950): 5-11.

87. A. Gouldner, "Locals and Cosmopolitans: Towards an Analysis of Latent Social Roles, I," *Admin. Sci. Quart.* 2 (1957): 1–74.

88. D. Marvick, "Career Perspectives in a Bureaucratic Setting," *University of Michigan Governmental Study* 27 (Ann Arbor, Mich.: University of Michigan Press, 1954).

89. J. Bruner, *The Process of Education* (Cambridge, Mass.: Harvard University press, 1961).

90. On this point see F. H. Harbison, "Management and Scientific Manpower," paper presented at the Centennial Symposium on Executive Development, School of Industrial Management, M.I.T., Cambridge, Mass., April 27, 1961.

91. D. McGregor, "New Concepts of Management," *Technol. Rev.* 63 (1961): pp. 25–27.

92. H. J. Leavitt and T. L. Whisler, "Management in the 1980's," *Harvard Bus. Rev.* 36 (1958): pp. 41–48.

93. L. Bradford, ed., *Theories of T-Group Training* (New York: New York University Press, 1962).

94. Blake and Mouton, op. cit.

95. M. G. Blansfield and W. P. Robinson, "Variations in Training Laboratory Design: A Care Study in Sensitivity Training," *Personnel Admin.* 24 (1961): pp. 17–22.

96. H. Shepard, "Three Management Programs and the Theories Behind Them," op. cit.

97. M. Sherif and C. Sherif, *Groups in Harmony and Tension* (New York: Harper & Row, Publishers, 1953).

98. R. R. Blake and J. S. Mouton, "From Industrial Warfare to Collaboration: A Behavioral Science Approach," Korzybski Memorial Address, April 20, 1961.

99. It is suspected that group cohesiveness will decrease as the scientific attitude infuses organizational functioning. With the depersonalization of science, the rapid turnover, and some expected individualism, cohesiveness may not be functional or even possible.

A SYSTEM RESOURCE APPROACH TO ORGANIZATIONAL EFFECTIVENESS

Ephraim Yuchtman and Stanley E. Seashore

We are badly in need of an improved conceptual framework for the description and assessment of organizational effectiveness. Nearly all studies of formal organizations make some reference to effectiveness; the growing field of comparative organizational study depends in part upon having some conceptual scheme that allows comparability among organizations with respect to effectiveness and guides the empirical steps of operationalization and quantification.

Aside from these needs of social scientists, consideration should also be given to the esthetic and applied requirements of organization managers. They experience high emotional involvement, pleasurable or otherwise, in the assessment of the relative success of their organizations; they are, of course, intensively and professionally engaged, informally, in the formulation and testing of hypotheses concerning the nature of decisions

From *Administrative Science Quarterly* vol. 32, (Dec. 1967), pp. 377–95. Reprinted by permission of the authors and publisher.

and actions that alter organizational effectiveness. They need a workable conception of "effectiveness" to sustain their egos and their work.

The social scientist designing or interpreting an organizational study is presently in a quandary. Most of the research concerned with the problem has been devoted to the study of the *conditions* under which organizations are more or less effective. The classic paradigm consists of some measurement of effectiveness—productivity or profit, for example—as the dependent variable, and of various sociological and social-psychological measures as the independent variables. The independent variables are usually treated in a relatively sophisticated manner; little attention, however, has been given to the concept of effectiveness itself. The latter remains conceptually a vague construct; in consequence there is available a large amount of empirical data with little understanding of these data. As stated recently by Katz and Kahn:

> There is no lack of material on criteria of organizational success. The literature is studded with references to efficiency, productivity, absence, turnover, and profitability—all of these offered implicitly or explicitly, separately or in combination, as definitions of organizational effectiveness. Most of what has been written on the meaning of these criteria and on their interrelatedness, however, is judgmental and open to question. What is worse, it is filled with advice that seems sagacious but is tautological and contradictory.[1]

Similar conclusions, on the same or on different grounds, have been reached by other students of organizations.[2] While emphasizing different aspects of the problem, all agree that results from studies of organizational effectiveness show numerous inconsistencies and are difficult to evaluate and interpret, let alone compare. The inconsistencies arise, often, from discrepant conceptions of "organizational effectiveness." In the present paper an attempt is made, first, to show some of the limitations inherent in traditional approaches to organizational effectiveness and, second, to provide an improved conceptual framework for dealing with that problem.

Traditional Approaches to Organizational Effectiveness

In spite of the variety of terms, concepts, and operational definitions that have been employed with regard to organizational effectiveness, it is hardly difficult to arrive at the generalization that this concept has been traditionally defined in terms of goal attainment. More specifically, most investigators tend implicitly or explicity to make the following two assumptions: (1) that complex organizations have an ultimate goal ("mission," "function") toward which they are striving and (2) that the ultimate goal can be identified empirically and progress toward it measured. In fact, the orientation to a specific goal is taken by many as the defining characteristic of complex organizations. A few organizational theorists[3] avoid making these assumptions, but they represent the exception rather than the rule.

Beyond these two common assumptions, however, one may discern different treatments of the matter, especially with regard to the rationale and operations for identifying the goals of organizations. It is useful to distinguish between two major doctrines in this respect. The first may be called the "prescribed goal approach." It is characterized by a focus on the formal charter of the organization, or on some category of its personnel (usually its top management) as the most valid source of information concerning organizational goals. The second may be referred to as the "derived goal approach." In it the investigator derives the ultimate goal of the organization from his (functional) theory, thus arriving at goals which may be independent of the intentions and awareness of the members. The prescribed and derived doctrines will be referred to as the *goal approach* and the *functional approach,* respectively.

The Goal Approach to Organizational Effectiveness

The goal approach, which itself has taken many forms, is the most widely used by students of organizations. Some have adopted it only as part of a broader perspective on organizations.[4] Others have employed it as a major tool in their study of organizations.[5] The goal approach has been attacked recently on various grounds. Katz and Kahn, while noting that ". . . the primary mission of an organization as perceived by its leaders furnishes a highly informative set of clues," go on to point out that:

> Nevertheless, the stated purpose of an organization as given by its by-laws or in the reports of its leaders can be misleading. Such statements of objectives may idealize, rationalize, distort, omit, or even conceal some essential aspects of the functioning of the organization.[6]

The goal approach is often adopted by researchers because it seems to safeguard them against their own subjective biases. But Etzioni attacks precisely this assumption:

> The (goal) model is considered an objective and reliable analytical tool because it omits the values of the explorer and applies

the values of the subject under study as the criteria of judgment. We suggest, however, that this model has some methodological shortcomings, and it is not as objective as it seems to be.[7]

Furthermore, argues Etzioni, the assessment of organizational effectiveness in terms of goal attainment should be rejected on theoretical considerations as well:

> Goals, as norms, as sets of meanings depicting target states, are cultural entities. Organizations, as systems of coordinated activities of more than one actor, are social systems.[8]

We understand this statement as rejecting the application of the goal approach in the study of organizational effectiveness for two reasons: first, goals as ideal states do not offer the possibility of realistic assessment; second, goals as cultural entities arise outside of the organization as a social system and cannot arbitrarily be attributed as properties of the organization itself. A similar criticism is offered by Starbuck, who calls attention to a hazard in the inferring of organizational goals from the behavior of organizational members:

> To distinguish goal from effect is all but impossible. The relation between goals and results is polluted by environmental effects, and people learn to pursue realistic goals. If growth is difficult, the organization will tend to pursue goals which are not growth oriented; if growth is easy, the organization will learn to pursue goals which are growth oriented. What one observes are the learned goals. Do these goals produce growth, or does growth produce these goals?[9]

It should be noted that the authors cited above tend to treat the problem as a methodological one even though, as we will show, theoretical differences and uncertainties are present as well. In order to escape some of these methodological shortcomings, several investigators have attempted to rely upon inferential or impressionistic methods of goal identification. Haberstroh, for example, makes the distinction between the formal objectives and the "common purpose" of the organization, the latter serving as the "unifying factor in human organizations."[10] But how, one may wonder, can that factor be empirically identified? Haberstroh maintains that it can be discovered through a systematic inquiry into the communication processes of the organization and by knowledge of the interests of its leadership, especially those in key positions. An empirical investigation conducted in accordance with that advice resulted in a list of operational (task) goals that, according to the investigator's own acknowledgment, do not adequately represent his notion of the "common purpose" of the organization. The latter remains therefore a rather vague concept and, it may be added, not surprisingly so. If one assumes that Haberstroh's "common purpose" stands for those objectives that are shared by the organization's members, he is reminded by several students of organizations[11] that such objectives are generally highly ambiguous, if not controversial, and therefore difficult to identify and measure.

The same kind of criticism can be applied to those who rely on the organization's charter, whether formal or informal, as containing the main identifying features of the organization, including its goals. Such an approach is represented by Bakke; he refers to the organization's charter, in the broad sense of the term, as expressing ". . . the image of the organization's unique wholeness." Such an image is created by ". . . selecting, highlighting, and combining those elements which represent the *unique* whole character of the organization and to which uniqueness and wholeness all features of the organization and its operations tend to be oriented."[12] The reader is left puzzled about how to discover the goals of the organization even after knowing that they are contained somewhere in the "image of the organization's unique wholeness."

The difficulty of identifying the ultimate goals of an organization is illustrated by some of the research on mental hospitals and other "total" institutions, as discussed by Vinter and Janowitz and, particularly, by Perrow and Etzioni.[13] Many of these institutions have been judged to be ineffective since they fail to achieve their presumed therapeutic goals. Vinter and Janowitz demonstrate, however, that the goal of therapy is held only by a limited segment of the public, and that the institutions themselves are oriented mainly to custody, not therapy.

Etzioni elaborates upon this issue as follows:

> When the relative power of the various elements in the environment are carefully examined, it becomes clear that, in general, the sub-publics (e.g., professionals, universities, well-educated people, some health institutions) which support therapeutic goals are less powerful than those which support the custodial or segregating activities of these organizations. Under such conditions, most mental hospitals and prisons must be more or less custodial.[14]

This observation, like Starbuck's argument quoted above, amounts to saying that organizational goals are essentially nothing more than courses of action imposed on the organization by various forces in its environment, rather than preferred end-states toward which the organization is "striving." Such a perspective on the nature of organizational goals seems to undermine the rationale behind the use of goals as a yardstick for assessing organizational effectiveness. How, we may ask, can a given social unit be regarded as "effective" if it cannot even determine its goals for itself, i.e., if the reference is wholly to the needs of entities other than itself? It would seem that the capacity of an organization to attain its own goals is a consideration of higher priority than that of success in attainment of imposed goals. An adequate conceptualization of organizational effectiveness cannot therefore be formulated unless factors of organization-environment relationships are incorporated into its framework.

Finally, it is not only in its external environment that the organization is faced with a variety of forces exerting influence on its behavior. The organization itself is composed of a large variety of individuals and groups, each having its own conceptions about any claims on the organization. The managers of an organization do not wholly agree among themselves about the organizational goals; in addition it is not certain that these goals, even if agreed upon, would prevail. This complicated reality is highlighted by the analysis of Cyert and March. They warn against the confusion in understanding organizational behavior whenever any one individual or group, such as the top management, is selected to represent the organization as a whole:

> The confusion arises because ultimately it makes only slightly more sense to say that the goal of the business organization is to maximize profit than it does to say that its goal is to maximize the salary of Sam Smith, Assistant to the Janitor.[15]

These considerations, taken together, seem to cast a serious doubt on the fruitfulness of the goal approach to organizational effectiveness. This is not to suggest that the concept of organizational goals should be rejected *in toto*. For certain analytical purposes it is useful to abstract some goal as an organizational property. In the study of persons in organizational settings, the concept of goal is useful and perhaps essential.[16] In the study of organizational effectiveness, however, the goal approach has appeared as a hindrance rather than as a help.

The Functional Approach to Organizational Effectiveness

The functional approach to organizational effectiveness can be characterized as "normative" in the sense that the investor reports what the goals of an organization are, or should be, as dictated by the logical consistency of his theory about the relationship among parts of larger social systems. From this point of view, the functional, or derived goal, approach has an important advantage over the prescribed goal doctrine since it appears to solve the problem of identifying the ultimate goals of complex organizations: Given the postulates and premises of the functional model about the nature of organizations and their interconnectedness with the total social structure one can derive from it the specific goals of an organization, or of a class of organizations. This is evident mainly in the work of Parsons, one of the outspoken advocates of functional analysis, in his suggestions for a theory of organizations.[17] The Parsonian scheme also illustrates, however, a major weakness inherent in the functional approach. This weakness can be usefully discussed in terms of "frames of reference."

Organizations, or other social units, can be evaluated and compared from the perspective of different groups or individuals. We may judge the effectiveness of an organization in relation to its own welfare, or we may assess how successful the organization is in contributing to the well-being of some other entities. While the selection of a given frame of reference is a question of one's values and interests, the distinction among them must be clearly made and consistently adhered to. Vital as this requirement appears to be, one encounters various treatments of effectiveness that implicitly or explicity refer to different frames of reference interchangeably, as if effectiveness from the point of view of the organization itself is identical with, or corresponds to, effectiveness viewed from the vantage point of some other entity, such as a member, or owner, or the community, or the total society.

The point of departure for Parsons' analysis of complex organizations is the "cultural-institutional" level of analysis. Accordingly, "The main point of reference for analyzing the structure of any social system is its value pattern. This defines the basic orientation of the system (in the present case, the organization) to the situation in which it operates; hence, it guides the activities of participant individuals."[18] The impact of the value pattern, furthermore, is felt through institutional processes which ". . . spell out these values in the more concrete functional contexts of goal attainment itself, adaptation to the situation, and integration of the system."[19] These functional prerequisites, including the value pattern, are universally present in every social system. Their specific manifestations and their relative importance, however, vary according to the defining characteristic of the system and its place in the superordinate system. In the case of complex organizations, their defining characteristic is the primacy of orientation to the attainment of a specific goal. This goal, like all other organizational phenomena, must be legitimated by the value pattern of the organization. The nature of this legitimation is a crucial element in

Parsons' analysis; the following quotation shows its relevance for the present discussion as well:

> Since it has been assumed that an organization is defined by the primacy of a type of a goal, the focus of its value-system must be the legitimation of this goal in terms of the functional significance of its attainment for the superordinate system, and secondly, the legitimation of the primacy of this goal over other possible interests and values of the organization and its members.[20]

In terms of our analysis, this states explicitly that the focal frame of reference for the assessment of organizational effectiveness is not the organization itself but rather the superordinate system. Not only must the ultimate goal of the organization be functionally significant in general for that system but, in the case of a conflict of interests between it and the organization, the conflict is always resolved in favor of the superordinate system—since the value pattern of the organization legitimates only those goals that serve that system. In other words, the *raison d'être* of complex organizations according to this analysis, is mainly to benefit the society to which they belong, and that society is, therefore, the appropriate frame of reference for the evaluation of organizational effectiveness. In order to avoid misunderstanding in this respect the following illustration is provided by Parsons:

> For the business firm, money return is a primary measure and symbol of success and is thus part of the goal structure of the organization. But it cannot be the primary organizational goal because profit-making is not by itself a function on behalf of the society as a system.[21]

Now there is no argument that the organization, as a system, must produce some important output for the total system in order to receive in return some vital input. However, taking the organization itself as the frame of reference, its contribution to the larger system must be regarded as an unavoidable and costly requirement rather than as a sign of success. While for Parsons the crucial question is "How well is the organization doing for the superordinate system?", from the organizational point of view the question must be "How well is the organization doing for itself?"

It was suggested earlier that a major weakness of the goal approach has been its failure to treat the issue of organizational autonomy in relation to organizational effectiveness. This seems to be the Achilles heel of the functional approach as well. In Parsons' conception of organizations, and of social systems in general, there exists the tendency to overemphasize the interdependence among the parts of a system and thus, as argued by Gouldner, fail ". . . to explore systematically the significance of variations in the degree of interdependence," ignoring the possibility that ". . . some parts may vary in their dependence upon one another, and that their interdependence is not necessarily symmetrical."[22]

Gouldner's proposition of "functional autonomy" may be examined on several different levels. For example, one may regard the organization itself as the total system, looking for variations in the degree of autonomy among its own parts; this has been the focus of Gouldner's analysis. But the same line of analysis can be attempted at a different level, where society is taken as the total system. Here the investigator may be exploring variations in the degree of autonomy of various parts and sub-systems, an instance of which are complex organizations. Such an analysis underlies the typology offered by Thompson and McEwen, in which the relations between organizations and their environments are conceived in terms of the relative autonomy, or dominance, of the organization vis-à-vis its environment.[23]

The proposition of functional autonomy implies that organizations are capable of gearing their activities into relatively independent courses of action, rather than orienting themselves necessarily toward the needs of society as the superordinate system. Under such assumptions it is difficult to accept as a working model of organizations the proposition that the ultimate goal of organizations must always be of functional significance for the larger system.

Comparing the goal and the functional approaches, it can be concluded that both contain serious methodological and theoretical shortcomings. The goal approach, while theoretically adhering to an organizational frame of reference, has failed to provide a rationale for the empirical identification of goals as an organizational property. The functional approach, on the other hand, has no difficulty in identifying the ultimate goal of the organization, since the latter is implied by the internal logic of the model, but the functional model does not take the organization as the frame of reference. Furthermore, neither of the two approaches gives adequate consideration to the conceptual problem of the relations between the organization and its environment.

A System Resource Approach to Organizational Effectiveness

The present need, to which we address our attention, is for a conception of organizational effectiveness that: (1) takes the organization itself as the focal frame of reference, rather than some external entity or some particular set of people; (2) explicitly treats the relations between the organization and its environment as a central ingredient in the definition of effectiveness; (3) provides a theoretically general framework capable of encompassing different kinds of complex organizations; (4) provides some latitude for uniqueness, variability, and change, with respect to the specific operations for assessing effectiveness applicable to any one organization, while at the same time maintaining the unity of the underlying framework for comparative evaluation; (5) provides some guide to the identification of performance and action variables relevant to organizational effectiveness and to the choice for empirical use.

A promising theoretical solution to the foregoing problems can be derived from the open system model as it is applied to formal social organizations. This model emphasizes the distinctiveness of the organization as an identifiable social structure or entity, and it emphasizes the interdependency processes that relate the organization to its environment. The first theme supports the idea of treating formal organizations not as phenomena incidental to individual behavior or societal functioning but as entities appropriate for analysis at their own level. The second theme points to the nature of interrelatedness between the organization and its environment as the key source of information concerning organizational effectiveness. In fact, most existing definitions of organizational effectiveness have been formulated, implicitly or explicitly, in terms of a *relation* between the organization and its environment, since the attainment of a goal or the fulfillment of a social function imply always some change in the state of the organization vis-à-vis its environment. The crucial task, then, is the conceptualization of that relation. The system model, with its view of the nature of the interaction processes between the organization and its environment, provides a useful basis for such a conceptualization.

According to that model, especially as applied to the study of organization by Katz and Kahn,[24] the interdependence between the organization and its environment takes the form of input-output transactions of various kinds relating to various things; furthermore, much of the stuff that is the object of these transactions falls into the category of *scarce and valued resources*. We shall have more to say about "resources" below. For the moment it will suffice to indicate that the value of such resources is to be derived from their utility as (more or less) generalized means for organizational activity rather than from their attachment to some specific goal. This value may or may not correspond to the personal values of the members of the organization, including their conception of its goals. It should be noted also that scarce and valued resources are, for the most part, the focus of competition between organizations. This competition, which may occur under different social settings and which may take different forms, is a continuous process underlying the emergence of a universal hierarchical differentiation among social organizations. Such a hierarchy is an excellent yardstick against which to assess organizational effectiveness. It reflects what may be referred to as the "bargaining position" of the organization in relation to resources and in relation to competing social entities that share all or part of the organization's environment.[25]

We propose, accordingly, to define the effectiveness of an organization in terms of its bargaining position, as reflected in the ability of the organization, in either absolute or relative terms, to exploit its environment in the acquisition of scarce and valued resources.

The concept of "bargaining position" implies the exclusion of any specific goal (or function) as the ultimate criterion of organizational effectiveness. Instead it points to the more general capability of the organization as a resource-getting system. Specific "goals" however can be incorporated in this conceptualization in two ways: (1) as a specification of the means or strategies employed by members toward enhancing the bargaining position of the organization; and (2) as a specification of the personal goals of certain members or classes of member within the organizational system. The better the bargaining position of an organization, the more capable it is of attaining its varied and often transient goals, and the more capable it is of allowing the attainment of the personal goals of members. Processes of "goal formation" and "goal displacement" in organizations are thus seen not as defining ultimate criteria of effectiveness, but as strategies adopted by members for enhancing the bargaining position of their organizations.

The emphasis upon the resource-getting capability of the organization is not intended to obscure other vital aspects of organizational performance. The input of resources is only one of three major cyclic phases in the system model of organizational behavior, the other two being the throughput and the output. From this viewpoint the mobilization of resources is a necessary but not a sufficient condition for organizational effectiveness. Our definition, however, points not to the availability of scarce and valued resources as such, but rather to the bargaining position with regard to the acquisition of such resources as the criterion of organizational effectiveness. Such a position at a given point of time is, so far as the organization's own behavior is concerned, a function of all the three phases of organizational behavior—the importation of resources, their use (including allocation and processing), and their exportation in some output form that aids further input.

By focusing on the ability of the organization to exploit its environment in the acquisition of resources we are directed by the basic yet often neglected fact that it is only in the arena of competition over scarce and valued resources that the performance of both like and unlike organizations can be assessed and evaluated comparatively. To put it somewhat differently, any change in the relation between the organization and its environment is affected by and results in a better or worse bargaining position vis-à-vis that environment or parts therof.

It should be noticed that the proposed definition of effectiveness does not imply any specific goal toward which an organization is striving, nor does it impute some societal function as a property of the organization itself. Our definition focuses attention on *behavior,* conceived as continuous and never-ending processes of exchange and competition over scarce and valued resources.[26] We shall now discuss some of the concepts central to our definition of organizational effectiveness.

Competition and Exchange

Our emphasis upon the competitive aspects of interorganizational relations implies that an assessment of organizational effectiveness is possible only where some form of competition takes place. This raises the question of how general or limited is the scope of applicability of our definition, since interorganizational transactions take forms other than competion. An old and useful distinction in this respect has recently been formulated by Blau:

> A basic distinction can be made between two major types of processes that characterize the transactions of organized collectivities—as well as those of individuals, for that matter—competitive processes reflecting endeavors to maximize scarce resources and exchange processes reflecting some form of interdependence. Competition occurs only among like social units that have the same objectives and not among unlike units. . . . Competition promotes hierarchical differentiation between more or less successful organizations, and exchange promotes horizontal differentiation between specialized organizations of diverse sort.[27]

Blau's assessment that ". . . competition promotes hierarchical differentiation between more or less *successful* organizations" is, of course, in line with our definition of organizational effectiveness; furthermore, there is no question about the mainly competitive character of relations among "like" social units.

However, Blau's contention that competition occurs *only* among like organizations is an oversimplification. Indeed, it is difficult to point to any interrelated organizations that are not in competition with respect to some kinds of resources, and it is easy to point to organizations that are dominantly competitive, yet have some complementarity and interdependence in their relations. A university and a business firm, for example, may be involved in an exchange of knowhow and money, and still compete with respect to such resources as manpower and prestige. The type of pure complementarity of exchange is very limited indeed. We suggest, accordingly, that exchange and competition are the extremes of a continuum along which interorganizational transactions can be described. The proposed definition of effectiveness allows then for the comparative evaluation of any two or more organizations that have some elements of rivalry in their relations. Such a comparative evaluation becomes more meaningful—in the sense of encompassing the crucial dimensions of organizational behavior—as the variety and number of competitive elements in these relations increases. The clearest and most meaningful comparison obtains when the evaluated organizations compete directly for the same resources. This condition implies that the compared organizations are engaged in like activities and share to a large degree the same temporal and physical life space. In such cases the comparison is facilitated by the fact that the competition refers to the same kinds of resources and that the assessment variables—both of input and output—are measured in like units. Comparisons are also possible, however, in the case of organizations that do not compete directly, but that compete in environments that are judged to be similar in some relevant respects.

As the characteristic transactions between organizations come closer to the exchange pole of the continuum the problem of comparison becomes more complex: first, the elements of competition may be very few in number and peripheral in importance, thus making the comparison trivial; second, the more unlike the organizations, the more difficult it is to measure their performance units on common scales. In any case, the identification of the competitive dimensions in interorganizational transactions is the key problem in the assessment of organizational effectiveness. Some clarification and possible ways of solution for this problem can be achieved through an examination of the concept of "resources."

Resources

A key element in this definition is the term *resources*. Broadly defined, resources are (more or less) generalized means, or facilities, that are potentially controllable by social organizations and that are potentially usable—however indirectly—in relationships between the organization and its environment. This definition, it should be noted, does not attribute directionality as an inherent quality of a resource, nor does it limit the concept of resources to physical or economic objects or states even though a physical base must lie behind any named resource. A similar approach to "resources" is taken, for example, by Gamson. He argues that the "reputation" of individuals or groups as "influentials" in their community political affairs is itself a resource rather than simply ". . . the manifestation of the possession of large amounts of resources. . . ."[28]

One important kind of resource that is universally required by organizations, that is scarce and valued, and that is the focus for sharp competition, is energy in the form of human activity. The effectiveness of many organizations cannot be realistically assessed without some accounting for the organization's bargaining position with respect to the engagement of people in the service of the organization. One thinks, of course, of competition in the industrial or managerial labor market, but the idea is equally applicable to the competition, say, between the local church and the local political party, for the evening time of persons who are potentially active in both organizations.

Since human activity is such a crucial class of organizational resource, we elaborate on the meaning that is intended and one of the implications. We view members of an organization as an integral part of the organization with respect to their organizational role-defining and role-carrying activities, but as part of the environment of the organization with respect to their abilities, motives, other memberships, and other characteristics that are potentially useful but not utilized by the organization in role performance. An "effective" organization competes successfully for a relatively large share of the member's personality, engaging more of the personality in organizationally relevant ways, thus acquiring additional resources from its environment.

A number of other distinctions may usefully be made with respect to the resources that are involved in the effectiveness of organizations:

LIQUIDITY   Some resources are relatively "liquid" in the traditional economic sense of that term and are readily exchangeable by an organization for resources of other kinds. Money and credit are highly liquid, being exchangeable for many other (but not all) kinds of resources. By contrast, the resource represented by high morale (among members) is relatively low in liquidity; under some conditions it is not directly exchangeable at full value in transactions with other organizations but must be internally transformed, e.g., into products or services, before exchange. Some organizations are characterized by having a large proportion of their resources in relatively non-liquid forms.

STABILITY   Some resources are transient in the sense that they must be acquired and utilized continuously by an organization, while other resources have the property of being stored or accumulated without significant depreciation. An organization that acquires a rapidly depreciating resource and fails to utilize this resource within an acceptable period will suffer loss of part of the value. The current high turnover among technical staff in some industrial firms is an example of loss of effectiveness through failure to utilize transient resources. By contrast, money is a highly stable resource that can be stored indefinitely at small loss and can be accumulated against future exchange requirements. Political influence is a resource of notorious instability.

RELEVANCE   In principle, all resources are relevant to all organizations to the extent that they are capable of transformation and exchange. The degree of relevance, however, is of considerable interest, since identification of resources of high relevance offers a guide to a useful classification of organizations and serves to direct priority in comparative analyses to those kinds of resources that most clearly reflect the relative bargaining power of organizations. Degree of relevance also has a bearing upon the analysis of symbiotic relationships among organizations (high rates of exchange with relatively little bargaining and high mutual benefit) and upon the analysis of monopolistic forces (dominance of a given resource "market" and consequent enhancement of bargaining power). The degree of relevance of a given resource can be estimated on an *a priori* basis from a knowledge of the typical outputs of an organization and a knowledge of its characteristic throughput activities. Critical resources might be discerned from an analysis of changes in the pattern of internal organizational activity, for such changes can be interpreted to be a response to an enhanced requirement or a threatened deficit with respect to a given type of resource. Organizations are frequently observed to mobilize activities in a way that enhances their power to acquire certain resources. A judgment of future organizational effectiveness might accordingly be improved by information concerning the organization's ease of adaptation to shifts among classes of resources in their degree of relevance.

UNIVERSALITY   Some resources are of universal relevance in the sense that all organizations must be capable of acquiring such resources. The universally required classes include: (1) personnel; (2) physical facilities for the organization's activities; (3) a technology for these activities; and (4) some relatively liquid resource, such as money, that can be exchanged for other resources. The amount required of each class may in some cases be very modest, but all organizations must have, and must be able to replenish, resources of these kinds. The non-universal resources are, in general, those for which competition is limited, either because of irrelevance to many organizations or because the particular resource is ordinarily obtained amply through symbiotic exchange.

SUBSTITUTION   Organizations with similar typical outputs competing in a common environment do not necessarily share the same roster of relevant and critical resources. One reason for this is that the internal processes of organizational life may be adapted to exploit certain readily available resources rather than to acquire alternative scarce resources in hard competition. An example of this is seen in the case of a small, ill-equipped guerrilla army facing a force of superior size and equipment. While exploiting rather different resources, they may compete equally for the acquisition of territorial and political control.

A crucial problem in this context is the determination of the relevant and critical resources to be used as a basis for absolute or comparative assessment of organizational effectiveness. In stable, freely competitive environments with respect to relatively liquid resources, this determination may be rather easy to make, but under other conditions the determination may be problematic indeed. The difficulties arise primarily in cases in which the competing organizations have differential access to relatively rich or relatively poor environments, where symbiotic exchange relationships may develop, where the resources are not universal, and where the possibilities of substitution are great. In such situations, the analytic approach must employ not a static conception of the relationships between an organization and its environment but rather, a conception that emphasizes adaptation and change in the organizational patterns of resource-getting.

Optimization vs. Maximization

In their recent analysis of complex organizations, Katz and Kahn proposed defining organizational effectiveness as "the maximization of return to the organization by all means."[29] This definition shares with the one we propose an emphasis on resource procurement as the sign of organizational success; it differs, however, in invoking the notion of maximization, a concept we have avoided. The position taken here is that maximization of return, even if possible, is destructive from the viewpoint of the organization. To understand this statement it should be remembered that the bargaining position of the organization is equated here with the ability to exploit the organization's environment—not with the maximum use of this ability. An organization that fully actualizes its exploitative potential may risk its own survival, since the exploited environment may become so depleted as to be unable to produce further resources. Furthermore, an organization that ruthlessly exploits its environment is more likely to incite a strong organized opposition that may weaken or even destroy the organization's bargaining position. Thus, the short-run gains associated with overexploitation are likely to be outweighed by greater long-run losses. Also, the resource itself may lose value if over-exploited; for example, an effective voluntary community organization may enjoy extraordinary bargaining power in the engagement of prestigeful people, but this power may not safely be used to the maximum, because excessive recruitment risks the diminishing of the value of membership when membership ceases to be exclusive.

These considerations lead to the proposition that the highest level of organizational effectiveness is reached when the organization maximizes its bargaining position and optimizes its resource procurement. "Optimum" is the point beyond which the organization endangers itself, because of a depletion of its resource-producing environment or the devaluation of the resource, or because of the stimulation of countervailing forces within that environment. As stated by Thompson and McEwen:

> It is possible to conceive of a continuum of organizational power in environmental relations, ranging from the organization that dominates its environmental relations to one completely domnated by its environment. Few organizations approach either extreme. Certain gigantic enterprises, such as the Zaibatsu in Japan or the old Standard Oil Trust in America, have approached the dominance-over-environment position at one time; most complex organizations, falling somewhere between the extremes of the power continuum, must adopt strategies for coming to terms with their environment.[30]

We may add, however, that the need "for coming to terms with their environments" applies to organizations that approximate the dominance-over-environment extreme as well. A powerful enterprise like General Motors must exercise its potential power with much restraint in order to avoid the crystallization of an opposition which may weaken its bargaining power considerably, through legislation or some other means.

It is of course very difficult, if possible at all, to determine in absolute terms the organization's maximum bargaining position and the optimal point of resource procurement that is associated with that position. Since most organizations, however, fall short of maximizing their bargaining position, the optimization problem, though theoretically important, is only of limited empirical relevance. In practice, organizational effectiveness must be assessed in relative terms, by comparing organizations with one another. The above discussion on the nature of "resources" provides at best a general outline for carrying out such a task. A more detailed discussion and a preliminary effort to apply empirically the conceptual scheme presented here is reported elsewhere.[31] Briefly, the following steps seem necessary for a meaningful comparative assessment of organizational effectiveness: (1) to provide an inclusive taxonomy of resources; (2) to identify the different types of resources that are mutually relevant for the organizations under study; and (3) to determine the relative positions of the compared organizations on the basis of information concerning the amount and kinds of resources that are available for the organization and its efficiency in using these resources to get further resources.

Some Implications

We end this discussion with a few speculations about the impacts that might arise from a general acceptance and use of the conception of organizational effectiveness that we have proposed. These may affect theorists, empirical researchers and managers in various ways:

1. The rejection of the concept of an ultimate goal, and the replacement of this singular concept with one emphasizing an open-ended multidimensional set of criteria, will encourage a broadening of the scope of search for relevant criterion variables. Past studies have tended to focus too narrowly upon variables derived from traditional accounting practice or from functional social theory, or on narrowly partisan "goals" attributed to organizations. A conception of organizational effectiveness based upon organizational characteristics and upon resource-acquisition in the most general sense will encourage the treatment as criteria of many variables previously regarded as by-products or incidental phenomena in organizational functioning.

2. Past comparative studies of organizations have, in general, been of two kinds: (a) Comparison of organizations differing markedly in their characteristics, e.g. prisons and factories, so that issues of relative effectiveness were deemed irrelevant and uninteresting as well as impractical; and (b) comparisons among organizations of a similar type, so that they could be compared on like variables and measurement units. The conception we offer provides the possibility of making accessible for study the large middle range of comparisons involving organizations that have only limited similarities such that they compete with respect to some but not all of their relevant and crucial resources.

3. Case studies of single organizations will be aided by the provision of a conceptual basis for treating a more inclusive and more realistic range of variables that bear on the effectiveness of the organization.

4. The meaning of some familiar variables will need to be reassessed and in some cases changed. For example, distributed profit, a favorite variable for the comparative assessment of business organizations, will be more widely recognized as a cost of organizational activity and not as an unequivocal sign of success or goal achievement. Some managers have already adopted this view. Similarly, growth in size, usually interpreted as a sign of organizational achievement, can now be better seen as a variable whose meaning is tied closely to environmental factors and to the position of the organization with respect to certain other variables; the conception we have presented highlights the idea that growth in size is not in itself an unmitigated good, even though it may mean greater effectiveness under some conditions. In a similar fashion, it will be seen as necessary that the judgment of the meaning of each criterion variable rests not upon an absolute value judgment or a universal conceptual meaning, but rather upon the joint consideration of an extensive integrated set of organizational performance and activity variables.

---

1. Daniel Katz and Robert L. Kahn, *The Social Psychology of Organizations* (New York: John Wiley & Sons, 1966), p. 149.

2. Basil S. Georgopoulos and Arnold S. Tannenbaum, "A Study of Organizational Effectiveness," *Amer. Sociol. Rev.* 22 (Oct. 1957): 534–40; Mason Haire, "Biological Models and Empirical Histories of the Growth of Organizations," in *Modern Organization Theory,* ed. Mason Haire (New York: John Wiley & Sons, 1959), pp. 272–306; Amitai W. Etzioni, "Two Approaches to Organizational Analysis: A Critique and a Suggestion," *Admin. Sci. Quart.* 5 (Sept. 1960): 257–78; Robert M. Guion, "Criterion Measurement and Personnel Judgments," *Personnel Psychol.* (Summer 1961): 141–49; Charles Perrow, "Organizational Goals," in *International Encyclopedia of Social Sciences* (New York: Macmillan Co., 1968), pp. 854-66; Stanley E. Seashore, "Criteria of Organizational Effectiveness," *Michigan Bus. Rev.* 17 (July 1965): 26–30.

3. James G. March and Herbert A. Simon, *Organizations* (New York: John Wiley & Sons, 1958); Etzioni, op. cit.; Perrow, op.cit.; Katz and Kahn, op. cit.

4. Chester I. Barnard, *The Functions of the Executive* (Cambridge, Mass.: Harvard University Press, 1938); Peter F. Drucker, *The Practice of Management* (New York: Harper & Row, Publishers, 1954).

5. Robert Michels, *Political Parties* (New York: Free Press, 1949); William J. Baumol, *Business Behavior, Value and Growth* (New York: Macmillan Co., 1959); James K. Dent, "Organizational Correlates of the Goals of Business Management," *Person. Psychol.* 12 (Autumn 1959): 365–93; Carl M. White, "Multiple Goals in the Theory of the Firm," in *Linear Programming and the Theory of the Firm,* ed. Kenneth E. Boulding and W. Allen Spivey (New York: Macmillan Co., 1960) pp. 181–201; Bertram M. Gross, "What Are Your Organization's Objectives? A General-Systems Approach to Planning," *Human Relations* 18 (August 1965): 195–216.

6. Katz and Kahn, op. cit., p. 15.

7. Etzioni, op. cit., p. 258.

8. Etzioni, op. cit., p. 258.

9. William H. Starbuck, "Organizational Growth and Development," in *Handbook of Organizations,* ed. James G. March (Chicago: Rand McNally & Co., 1965), p. 465.

10. Chadwick J. Haberstroh, "Organization Design and Systems Analysis," in *Handbook of Organizations,* ed. James G. March (Chicago: Rand McNally & Co., 1965), pp. 1171–1211.

11. Abraham D. H. Kaplan, Joel B. Dirlam, and Robert F. Lanzillotti, *Pricing in Big Business* (Washington: Brookings Institution, 1958); Richard M. Cyert and James G. March, "A Behavioral Theory of Organizational Objectives," in *Modern Organization Theory,* ed. Mason Haire (New York: John Wiley & Sons, 1959), pp. 76–90.

12. E. Wight Bakke, "Concept of the Social Organization," in *Modern Organization Theory,* ed. Mason Haire (New York: John Wiley & Sons, 1959), pp. 16–75.

13. Robert Vinter and Morris Janowitz, "Effective Institutions for Juvenile Delinquents: A Research Statement," *Soc. Serv. Rev.* 33 (June 1959): pp. 118–30; Charles Perrow, "The Analysis of Goals in Complex Organizations," *Amer. Sociol. Rev.* 26 (Dec. 1961): 854–66.

14. Etzioni, op. cit., p. 264.

15. Cyert and March, op. cit., p. 80.

16. Alvin F. Zander and Herman M. Medow, "Individual and Group Levels of Aspiration," *Human Relations* 16 (Winter 1963): 89–105; Alvin F. Zander and Herman M. Medow, "Strength of Group and Desire for Attainable Group Aspirations," *J. Personality* 33 (Jan. 1965): 122–39.

17. Talcott Parsons, "Suggestions for a Sociological Approach to a Theory of Organizations—I," *Admin. Sci. Quart.* 1 (June 1956): 63–85; Talcott Parsons, *Structure and Processes in Modern Societies* (New York: Free Press, 1960), pp. 16–96.

18. Parsons, op. cit., 1956, p. 67.

19. Parsons, op. cit., 1956, p. 67.

20. Parsons, op. cit., 1956, p. 68.

21. Parsons, op. cit., 1956, p. 68.

22. Alvin W. Gouldner, "Organizational Dynamics," in *Sociology Today,* ed. Robert K. Merton et al. (New York: Basic Books, 1959), p. 419.

23. James D. Thompson and William J. McEwen, "Organizational Goals and Environment: Goal-Setting as an Interaction Process," *Amer. Sociol. Rev.,* 23 (Feb. 1958): 23–31.

24. Katz and Kahn, op. cit.

25. The differential amounts of success of organizations with regard to their bargaining positions implies the possibility of exploitation of one organization by another, a possibility which may endanger the stability of social order. This asymmetry in interorganizational transactions and its consequences for the problem of social order underlie the sociological interest in exchange processes and their normative regulation. As pointed out recently by Blau:
"Without social norms prohibiting force and fraud, the trust required for social exchange could not serve as a self-regulating mechanism within the limits of these norms. Moreover, superior power and resources, which often are the results of competitive advantages gained in exchange transactions, make it possible to exploit others." [*Exchange and Power in Social Life* (New York: John Wiley & Sons, 1964), p. 255.]
Blau's discussion is concerned mainly with the more limited case of exchange between individuals as social actors. Nevertheless, it points to the potential asymmetry

involved in exchange processes in general and the consequences of such asymmetry, namely, the emergence of a hierarchical differentiation among the interacting units with regard to their exploitative ability. For the purposes of the present discussion it is important to note that such an advantageous bargaining position, which may be dysfunctional for the system as a whole, is from the organization's point of view a sign of its success.

26. One reader of an early draft of this paper, Dr. Martin Patchen, inquired about the sources of directive energy in goal-less organizations. The answer is that persons who are members of the organization, and acting both within their role prescriptions and in idiosyncratic deviation from role prescriptions, impart personal values and goals which may modify the system in a directed way.

27. Peter Blau, *Exchange and Power in Social Life* (New York: John Wiley & Sons, 1964), p. 255.

28. William A. Gamson, "Reputation and Resources in Community Politics," *Amer. J. Sociol.* 72 (Sept. 1966): 121–31.

29. Katz and Kahn, op. cit., p. 170.

30. Thompson and McEwen, op. cit., p. 25.

31. Stanley E. Seashore and Ephraim Yuchtman, "The Elements of Organizational Performance," a paper prepared for a symposium on People, Groups and Organizations: An Effective Integration of Knowledge, Rutgers University, November 1966. (This paper appears in *Admin. Sci. Quart.,* 1967); Ephraim Yuchtman, "A Study of Organizational Effectiveness," Ph.D. diss., University of Michigan, 1966.

ADDITIONAL READINGS

A list of publications dealing with criteria of organizational effectiveness follows. The following discussion is intended to be a guide to some of the key works on this topic.

The earliest statements on criteria of organizational effectiveness were provided by Caplow, 1953; Likert, 1958; and Bass, 1952. Much has happened in the field since these statements were published. Concerted attention to the problem of criteria development has been given by scholars at the Universities of Michigan, Minnesota, and Ohio State. Some of the major publications from Michigan are: Bowers and Seashore, 1966; Georgopolous et al, 1960; Georgopolous and Tannenbaum, 1957; and Seashore, 1960, 1964, 1965, 1967, and 1968. Of these, the work by Georgopolous et al, 1960, is particularly worth noting. It provides a discussion and application of three models of organizational effectiveness around a common set of empirical data; numerous methodological and conceptual problems pertaining to operationalization and use of modern criteria of effectiveness are discussed. Some of the major publications from the University of Minnesota are: Dimick, Weitzel, and Mahoney,

1967; Mahoney, 1967;1967); and Weitzel (mimeographed, no date given). These publications deal largely with lists of criteria derived by factor analysis of responses to structured questionnaires given by executives participating in the executive development programs at the University of Minnesota. As these publications do not provide sufficient details about their methodologies, it is not possible to comment further about the usefulness or validity of the check-lists of criteria derived through factor analysis. The bibliography also contains two publications from Ohio: Peponsky et al, 1965, and Stogdill, 1965.

As is evident from prior discussions in this book, the notion of functional requirements pervades much of the writings pertaining to "systemic" criteria of effectiveness. Excellent discussions of this concept are found in Dobriner, 1969: 109–114, and Morse, 1961.

The publications by Barton, 1961, Price, 1968; and Wasserman, 1959, are particularly worth pursuing. The work by Barton is a pioneering attempt to systematically sort, operationalize, and measure major organizational inputs and outputs, and environmental, structural, and attitudinal variables per-tinent to measurement of organizational functioning and effectiveness. Price's work was referred to in Part I of this book. As regards criteria, Price has provided a challenging schema for conceptualizing organizational effective-ness in terms of five criteria of effectiveness: productivity, morale, con-formity, adaptiveness, and institutionalization. Holding organizational effec-tiveness to be the major dependent variable, these five criteria are classified as intervening variables and are in turn linked to various structural, political, environmental, and other variables pertinent to organizational functioning.

Wasserman provides a comprehensive annotated bibliography of pub-lications pertinent to the measurement and evaluation of organizational performance. It is divided into four parts: I—General and Theoretical Material, II—Measurement of Total Enterprise, III—Measurement of Functional Units of Organizations, and IV—Measurement of Individual Performance. Although excellent as a general source on this topic, the collection contains works published only prior to 1959.

Dealing with Criteria of Organizational Effectiveness

Anthony, R. N. 1960. "The trouble with profit maximization." *Harvard Bus. Rev.* 37: 126–34.

Barton, Allen H. 1961. "Organizational measurement and its bearing on the study of college environments." N.J.: College Entrance Examination Board.

Bowers, D. G., and Seashore, S. E. 1966. "Predicting organizational effective-ness with a four-factor theory of leadership." *Admin. Sci. Quart.* 11: 238–63.

Caplow, Theodore. 1953. "Criteria of organizational success." *Soc. Forces* 32: 1–9.

Charnes, A. and Stefry, A. C. 1965. "Quasi-rational models of behavior in organization research." *Manage. Sci. Res. Rep. no. 31.* Pittsburgh: Graduate School of Business Administration.

Comrey, A. L., Pfiffner, J. M., and High, W. S. 1952. "Factors influencing organizational effectiveness." *Personnel Psychol.* 5: 307–28.

———. 1954. "Factors influencing organizational effectiveness." *Fin. Tech. Rep.,* Office of Naval Research. Los Angeles: University of Southern California Press.

Cyert, R. M., and March, J. G. 1959. "A behavioral theory of organizational objectives." In *Modern organization theory,* ed. Mason Haire, pp. 76-90. New York: John Wiley & Sons.

Dent, James K. 1959. "Organizational correlates of the goals of business management." *Personnel Psychol.* 12: 365–93.

Dimick, David, Weitzel, William, and Mahoney, Thomas A. 1967. "Explicit and implicit managerial models." Mimeograph. Minneapolis: Industrial Relations Center, University of Minnesota.

Dobriner, William M. 1969. *Social structures and systems: A sociological overview.* Pacific Palisades, Calif.: Goodyear Publishing Co.

Dunnette, Marvin D. 1963. "A note on the criterion problem." *J. Appl. Psychol.* 47: 251–54.

Fiedler, F. 1960. *Tech. rep. no. 10.* Urbana, Ill.: Group Effectiveness Research Laboratory, Dept. of Psychology, University of Illinois.

Georgopoulos, Basil S., and Tannenbaum, Arnold S. 1957. "A study of organizational effectiveness." *Am. Sociol. Rev.* 22: 534–40.

Georgopoulos, B. S., Indik, B. P., and Seashore, S. E. 1960. "Some models of organizational effectiveness." Mimeograph. Ann Arbor, Mich.: Institute for Social Research, University of Michigan.

Ghorpade, J. V. 1970. "Study of organizational effectiveness: two prevailing viewpoints." *Pac. Sociol. Rev.* 13 (Sept.): 31–40.

Gross, Bertram M. 1965. "What are your organization's objectives? A general systems approach to planning," *Human Relations* 18: 195–216.

Guion, Robert M. 1961. "Criterion measurement and personnel judgments." *Personnel Psychol.* 14: 141–49.

Huston, C. L. 1962. "Company objectives: Blueprint or blue sky?" *Manage. Rev.* (Sept.).

Kaczka, Eugene, and Kirk, Roy V. 1967. "Managerial climate, work groups and organizational performance." *Admin. Sci. Quart.* 12: 253–72.

Katzell, R., Barrett, R. S., and Parker, T. C. 1961. "Job satisfaction, job performance, and situational characteristics." *J. Appl. Psychol.* 45: 65–72.

Klein, M. W. 1961. "Some considerations in the use of qualitative judgments as measures of organizational performance." *Sociol. Soc. Res.* 46: 26–35.

Kuethe, James L. 1964. "Conceptions of organizational worth." *Am. J. Sociol.* 70: 342–48.

Lewis, Joseph E. 1966. "Evaluation of the effectiveness of systems of command support." In *Operational research and the social sciences,* ed. J. R. Lawrence, pp. 263–74. London: Tavistock Publications.

Likert, Rensis. 1958. "Measuring organizational performance." *Harvard Bus. Rev.* 36: 41-50.

Mahoney, Thomas A. 1967a. "Managerial perceptions of organizational effectiveness." *Manage. Sci.* 14: B-76–B-91.

―――. 1967b. "Managerial criteria of organizational performance." Mimeograph. Minneapolis: Industrial Relations Center, University of Minnesota.

Martindell, Jackson. 1962. "The management audit." *Corporate Dir.* 9: 1–4.

McGregor, Douglas. 1964. "Can you measure executive performance?" *Int. Manage.* 20: 59–63.

Miner, John B. 1968. "Bridging the gulf in organizational performance." *Harvard Bus. Rev.* 46: 102–10.

Morse, Chandler. 1961. "The functional imperatives." In *The social theories of Talcott Parsons,* ed. Max Black, pp. 100–52. Englewood Cliffs, N.J.: Prentice-Hall.

Peponsky, H. B., Weick, K. E., and Riner, J. W. 1965. *Primer for productivity.* Columbus, Ohio: Ohio State University Research Foundations.

Perrow, Charles. 1961. "The analysis of goals in complex organizations." *Am. Sociol. Rev.* 26: 854–66.

―――. 1968. "Organizational goals." In *International encyclopedia of social sciences,* pp. 305–11. New York: Macmillan Co.

Phillips, Charles F. 1963. "What is wrong with profit maximization?" *Bus. Horizons* (Winter).

Price, James L. 1968. *Organizational effectiveness: An inventory of propositions.* Homewood, Ill.: Richard O. Irwin, Inc.

Proceedings of the Executive Study Conference. 1968. *Managing organizational effectiveness.* Princeton, N.J.: Educational Testing Service.

Seashore, Stanley E. 1964. *Assessing organizational performance with behavioral measurements.* Ann Arbor, Mich.: Foundation for Research on Human Behavior.

―――. 1965. "Criteria of organizational effectiveness." *Mich. Bus. Rev.* 17: 26–30.

Seashore, S. E., Indik, B. P., and Georgopolous, B. S. 1960. "Relationship among criteria of job performance." *J. Appl. Psychol.* 44: 195–202.

Seashore, S. E., and Yuchtman, E. 1967. "Factorial analysis of organizational performance." *Admin. Sci. Quart.* 12: 377–95.

―――. 1968. "The elements of organizational performance." In *People, groups and organizations,* ed. Bernard P. Indik and F. Kenneth Berrien, pp. 172–90. New York: Teachers College Press.

Stogdill, R. M. 1965. *Managers, employees organizations.* Columbus, Ohio: Bureau of Business Research, Ohio State University.

Tilles, Seymour. 1963. "How to evaluate corporate strategy." *Harvard Bus. Rev.* 41: 111–21.

Thompson, James D. 1967. *Organizations in action,* Chap. 6. New York: McGraw-Hill Book Co.

Thompson, James D. and McEwen, William J. 1958. "Organizational goals and environment: Goal setting as an interaction process." *Am. Sociol. Rev.* 23: 21–33.

Wasserman, P. 1959. *Measurement and evaluation of organizational performance.* McKinsey Foundation Annotated Bibliography. Ithaca, N.Y.: Graduate School of Business and Public Administration, Cornell University.

Weitz, Joseph. 1961. "Criteria for criteria." *Am. Psychol.* 16: 228–31.

Weitzel, William, and Mahoney, Thomas A. "Managerial models of organizational effectiveness." Mimeograph. Minneapolis: Industrial Relations Center, University of Minnesota.

White, Carl M. 1960. "Multiple goals in the theory of the firm." In *Linear programming and the theory of the firm,* ed. Kenneth E. Boulding and W. Allen Spivey, pp. 181–201. New York: Macmillan Co.

Zander, Alvin F., and Medow, Herman H. 1963. "Individual and group levels of aspirations." *Human Relations* 16: 89–105.

_____. 1965. "Strength of group and desire for attainable group aspirations." *J. Personality* 33: 122–39.

REVIEW OF RECENT
STUDIES ON
ORGANIZATIONAL EFFECTIVENESS

As SUBJECTS OF RESEARCH, formal organizations have attracted the attention of scholars from a variety of social science and other disciplines. Empirical research on organizations has varied considerably in terms of underlying concerns, levels of analysis, and research orientations. A predominant number of studies involving organizations have been "segmental" in the sense that they have focused upon studying the role of behavioral, structural, and other variables in the functioning of particular organizations. In such researches, the organization itself is not the focus of the study; rather, the aim of research is to isolate the role of particular behavior patterns, organizational subsystems, structural components, and other factors in the workings of the organization under consideration. For example, studies by Chris Argyris, 1962, 1964; Georgopoulos, 1965; Kaczka, 1967; Morse and Reimer, 1956; and Roberts, Miles, and Blankenship, 1968, have analyzed the role of various behavioral variables in organizational functioning. The role of structural factors in organizational functioning has been the concern of Etzioni, 1959; Jones, 1969; Rushing, 1968; and Tittle, 1964. The impact of technological and selected environmental variables on organizational functioning has been investigated by Baum, 1969; Christman, 1968; Grusky, 1963; Price, 1963; and Zald, 1967.

The segmental or partial studies of the type discussed above are a valuable source of data on the functioning of formal organizations. They can be potentially useful for the codification of knowledge about the role of various behavioral, structural, and other factors in organizational functioning. (Price's inventory of propositions on organizational effectiveness is based upon studies of this type [Price, 1968: 1–14].) However, the usefulness of the empirical findings of many of these studies is marred due to a major methodological flaw —they fail to work out systematically the manner in which the factor investigated is related to overall organizational functioning and effectiveness. If organizational goals, purposes or needs are discussed at all, they are treated in a cursory and simplistic fashion. The most commonly used criterion of organizational success is productivity, which is frequently taken to be the dependent variable; the particular factor investigated (behavioral, structural, or other) is taken to be the independent or intervening variable. Many of these studies fail to systematically clarify and explain the links between the variables investigated. Consequently, their research findings are of dubious value in understanding the complex interplay of forces underlying organizational functioning and effectiveness.

In contrast to the segmental or partial studies of the type discussed above, another group of studies has emerged over the years which has focused upon the organization itself as the subject of research. This approach is evident in the works of Abegglen, 1958; Blau, 1955; Cressey, 1961; Jaques, 1952; Lipset, Trow, and Coleman, 1956; Michels, 1962; Rice, 1958; and Selznick, 1948b. A distinguishing feature of these studies is the attempt to explore and understand the functioning of their respective organizations as total systems. Behavioral, structural, or other variables are investigated only if they have a bearing on the functioning of the organization under consideration. The variations within these studies reflect differing interests and purposes of the researchers. Thus, the studies by Selznick and Rice cited above deal with the examination of the relationship between the organizations investigated and their institutional and cultural environments. Abegglen's study deals with the unique features of the Japanese factory system. In spite of such variation, however, a common feature of such studies is the focus upon the organization itself as the subject of research.

Studies of total organizations of the type noted above have made landmark contributions towards the development of modern organization theory. Their scope and coverage have provided a broad base for the formulation of further propositions and theorizing about the functioning of organizations. (Review of the contributions of the studies noted above and other "generalist" studies toward the development of modern organization theory are found in Etzioni, 1960; Berelson and Steiner, 1964; Schein, 1965; and Leavitt, 1963.) The major limitation of such studies is the primarily exploratory nature of the data that they have supplied. This stems from the relatively "loose" research designs used in the conduct of many of these investigations. By and large, studies of total organizations of the type cited above have relied upon intensive case studies of one or a small number of organizations. The dimensions investigated have been loosely stated; they have sometimes emerged in the course of investigation. Heavy reliance has been placed in many cases on qualitative data acquired through observational accounts by individual scholars, documents, and other secondary sources. Such evidence may be considered "tentative," or even suspect, by those who place high reliance on large samples, quantitative analysis, and systematic experimentation.

In terms of the overall interest and concern of this book, perhaps the most pertinent are a small group of recent studies aimed specifically at the assessment of the effectiveness of particular organizations. These studies have used relatively "tight" research designs, spelling out in advance their criteria of effectiveness and methodology of analysis. The selections by Georgopoulos and Tannenbaum, and Friedlander and Pickle, included in this part, are examples of this type of research. The study by Georgopoulos and Tannenbaum analyzes the effectiveness of a delivery service organization in terms of three criteria of effectiveness: productivity, flexibility, and intra-organizational strain. The study by Friedlander and Pickle deals with a sample of ninety-seven small business organizations composed of retail, service, manufacturing, and mineral extraction establishments. The analysis of effectiveness is approached in terms of multiple criteria of effectiveness reflecting a variety of frames of reference: societal, owners', and employees'.

The studies by Georgopoulos and Tannenbaum and Friedlander and Pickle included in this part are illustrative of a small group of recent studies on organizational effectiveness. Other studies of this type are exemplified in the works of Yuchtman, 1966, and Ghorpade, 1968.

Viewed against the broader spectrum of organizational studies, these organizational effectiveness studies fall somewhere between the narrow segmental or partial studies and the total organizational studies reviewed earlier. Their focus is upon organizations as total entities. However, they use relatively "tight" research designs, spelling out in advance their criteria of effectiveness and methodology of analysis. The sample of organizations studied is relatively large.

Organizational effectiveness studies of the type reproduced in this part have potential for advancing the field of organization theory. To begin with, they represent an attempt to break away from the "goal model" which has dominated and constricted organizational analysis over the years (Etzioni, 1960). These studies demonstrate that the concept of organizational effectiveness can be broadened to include "systemic" criteria of effectiveness, yielding data on the overall "health" and long-term survival potential of the organizations studied. Also, insight is provided into how "soft" behavioral criteria can be made operational in a research situation. Factors such as organizational flexibility and intra-organizational strain have been successfully incorporated and used as criteria of organizational effectiveness. Furthermore, organizational effectiveness studies are capable of furthering theoretical integration of the field of organization theory. By their very nature, such studies raise questions about ends and means, purposes and needs, and interrelationships between the organization, its environment, and subsystems. The empirical data supplied by such studies can be potentially beneficial for attempts at theoretical integration initiated by scholars such as Price, 1968; Thompson, 1967; and others.

Even though organizational effectiveness studies have much potential for advancing knowledge about organizations, the usefulness of the empirical findings of the two studies reproduced here is marred by certain methodological orientations of the researchers. The reference here is to the almost complete faith placed upon data acquired through questionnaires dealing with the topics investigated. It is significant to note that most of the data on "hard" as well as "soft" variables is in the form of judgments, opinions, and estimates provided by "experts" and other personnel related to the organizations studied.

While such practices may be justified for initial exploratory purposes, they need not be accepted as a permanent ingredient of a methodology for the study of organizational effectiveness. Responses to structured, scaled questionnaires are not the only source of data on organizational functioning. Understanding of the dynamics underlying the functioning of particular organizations can be gained from a host of alternate sources such as organizational records, operating policies and practices, study of relevant incidents and events, observation, and records maintained by outside organizations. For an elaboration of this point, see Webb et al., 1966.

A STUDY OF
ORGANIZATIONAL EFFECTIVENESS

Basil S. Georgopoulos and Arnold S. Tannenbaum

Organizational effectiveness is one of the most complex and least-tackled problems in the study of social organizations. Many difficulties arise with attempts to define the concept of effectiveness adequately. Some stem from the closeness with which the concept becomes associated with the question of values (e.g., "management" versus "labor" orientations). Other problems arise when researchers choose *a priori* criteria of effectiveness that seem intuitively right, without trying systematically to place them within a consistent and broader framework. In effect, specific criteria that might be proper in one case may be entirely inappropriate to other organizations. The question arises whether it is possible to develop a definition of effectiveness and to derive criteria that are applicable across organizations and can be meaningfully placed within a general conceptual framework.

Reprinted from the *American Sociological Review,* vol. 22 (Oct. 1957), pp. 534–40 by permission of the authors and the American Sociological Association.

This article has three objectives: (1) to examine the concept of effectiveness and to provide a definition deriving from the nature of organizations; (2) to develop operational criteria and to measure the concept in a specific industrial setting; and (3) to evaluate these criteria and operations in terms of their organizational character, i.e., the extent to which they represent an organizational-level phenomenon, their reliability, and their agreement with independent expert judgment.

The Concept

The concept of organizational effectiveness (sometimes called organizational "success" or organizational "worth") is ordinarily used to refer to goal attainment. In this sense, it is a functional rather than a structural concept. Furthermore, it is probably most useful in comparative organizational research, i.e., in relational rather than absolute terms, but the concept could also be used developmentally to study the effectiveness of the same organization over time.

Traditionally, in the study of industrial organizations, effectiveness has been viewed and operationalized mainly in terms of productivity. In this connection, Thorndike has noted a general tendency on the part of personnel and industrial psychologists to accept as "ultimate criteria" of organizational success the following: organizational productivity, net profit, the extent to which the organization accomplishes its various missions, and the success of the organization in maintaining or expanding itself.[1] Other variables that have been used in various contexts as criteria of effectiveness include "morale," commitment to the organization, personnel turnover and absenteeism, and member satisfactions.[2]

With the exception of organizational productivity, however, practically all variables used as criteria of organizational effectiveness have been found inadequate and unsatisfactory. For example, previous findings regarding "morale" and member satisfaction in relation to effectiveness (effectiveness measured on the basis of productivity) have frequently been inconsistent, nonsignificant, or difficult to evaluate and interpret. The case of turnover and absenteeism is similar. A major problem in using these two variables as criteria of effectiveness is their differential sensitivity to such "third" considerations as the nature and volume of work to be processed, organizational level affected, and season of occurrence apart from the degree of such occurrence. Net profit is likewise a poor criterion in view of many unanticipated fluctuations external to the system, e.g., fluctuations in the general economy, markets, sales, and prices.

In view of these and related inadequacies, the role of other potential criteria of organizational effectiveness should be studied. On this point, and in addition to productivity, Kahn and Morse have suggested the variables of organizational flexibility and maximization of member potential,[3] but no work has been done in this direction. Elsewhere, Bass has proposed as criteria the extent to which an organization is of value to its members, and the extent to which the organization and its members are of value to society.[4] For theoretical reasons, however, it is preferable to look at the concept of organizational effectiveness from the point of view of the system itself—of the total organization in question rather than from the standpoint of some of its parts or of the larger society. Furthermore, proposed criteria should be system-relevant as well as applicable across organizations. It is most satisfactory, moreover, if such criteria are derived from a common framework to which the concept of organizational effectiveness can be meaningfully related.

General Criteria of Effectiveness

A distinguishing characteristic of nearly all variables which have been used as criteria of effectiveness is that, whether directly or indirectly, they tie in with organizational objectives. This relationship, however, is only a necessary condition. Not all criteria that fulfill this requirement are appropriate. Many cannot be applied across organizations (e.g., some organizations have no problems of turnover and absenteeism or may even be overstaffed), and many do not logically conform to a generally accepted conception of organizations.

It is our assumption that all organizations attempt to achieve certain objectives and to develop group products through the manipulation of given animate and inanimate facilities. Accordingly, definitions of organizational effectiveness must take into consideration these two aspects: the objectives of organizations and the means through which they sustain themselves and attain their objectives, particularly those means that usually become functionally autonomous (i.e., that come to assume the character of and function as organizational goals). In short, the study of organizational effectiveness must contend with the question of organizational means and ends.

Assuming that the organizational system maintains itself, the most general and most important common objectives of organizations are: (1) high output in the sense of achieving the end results for which the organization is designed, whether quantitatively or qualitatively; (2) ability to absorb and assimilate relevant endogenous and exogenous changes, or the ability of the organization to keep up with the times without jeopardizing its integrity; and (3) the preservation of organizational resources, of human and material facilities.[5] It should be both feasible and fruitful to study organizational effectiveness by gearing our criterion variables to these general aspects of organization.

We define organizational effectiveness as the extent to which an organization as a social system, given certain resources and means, fulfills its objectives without incapacitating its means and resources and without placing undue strain upon its members. This conception of effectiveness subsumes the following general criteria: (1) organizational productivity; (2) organizational flexibility in the form of successful adjustment to internal organizational changes and successful adaptation to externally induced change; and (3) absence of intraorganizational strain, or tension, and of conflict between organizational subgroups. These three criteria both relate to the means-ends dimension of organizations and, potentially, apply to nearly all organizations. The first relates to the movement of the organization toward its goals (locomotion); the others relate to the requirements of organizational survival in the face of external and internal variability, and to the dimension of preservation (or incapacitation) of organizational means. In an attempt to evaluate the present approach, we have used these criteria in the study of a large-scale organization, which we feel is particularly suitable to our investigation because of the simplicity of its structure.

Method, Operations, and Measures

The organization studied is an industrial service specializing in the delivery of retail merchandise. It is unionized and operates in several metropolitan areas, on a contract basis with department stores. In each area there is a company plant, under a plant manager, which is divided into a number of divisions, each division encompassing a number of smaller organizational units called stations. These constitute the basic operating units of the company.

The plant structure is replicated in every case, i.e. the stations are structurally homogeneous and organizationally parallel. They all perform the same kind of activity, employ uniform-standard equipment, draw upon the same type of resources, and function on the basis of uniformly established work standards. A typical station has a station manager, a day supervisor, a night supervisor, and about thirty-five workers. Approximately three-fourths of the workers are truck drivers who transport and deliver packages to private residences; the remaining workers sort and load the merchandise prior to delivery. Thirty-two such stations, representing five company plants, are included in the study.

In each case data were collected from all station members, supervisory as well as nonsupervisory.[6] The average questionnaire return rate for supervisory personnel was 97 per cent and for nonsupervisory 87 per cent (the questionnaires were administered on location). No station having a return rate lower than 75 per cent of its nonsupervisory members is represented in the sample. The operations and measures for the concept of organizational effectiveness and for the three criteria are based on this sample.

Independent judgments were obtained from a group of experts concerning the relative overall effectiveness of the various stations in the five plants. It was on this basis that the thirty-two stations were selected for study. The expert raters had first-hand knowledge of the stations they rated but were not directly involved in station operations. Included among the raters were the plant manager, the assistant plant manager, some division managers, and other key plant personnel, comprising a total of six to nine experts in each of the five company plants.

Special forms and instructions, developed in consultation with the top management of the company, were sent to the various raters separately. These requested the rater to list all stations in the plant, to cross out those stations he was not able to evaluate, and to judge the remaining stations by placing them into five categories of overall effectiveness, ranging from "best" to "poorest." The raters were asked to use as a time basis the six month period preceding the evaluation. The following excerpts from the instructions indicate the frame of reference for the concept of effectiveness as presented to the raters:

> You are to rank *the performance of the station as a whole* as distinct from the performance of any of the people in it. . . . You may want to take into consideration such things as: how satisfied you are personally with the *total* situation in the station; how well it is measuring up to the expectations and goals of (the company) considering the particular difficulties it faces; also recent progress and development; the way problems are handled; communications, costs, efficiency, morale, performance in relation to standards, etc. The important thing is that all these things taken together and considered as a whole will be the basis for the ranking. . . . Fill the form without checking your opinions with anyone and then send it directly to (the research staff). Your individual rankings will be treated as confidential and only the summary findings will be used for the purposes of the study.

Additional instructions were given about the mechanics of placing the stations in five effectiveness categories.

All raters submitted their independent evaluations of the stations under their jurisdiction, and their judgments were analyzed. All stations about which there was consistent agreement among raters (i.e., cases clearly falling at either of the two extremes or the middle of the five effectiveness categories), as judged by three members of the research staff, were retained as candidates for inclusion in the sample. A list of these stations was then submitted to each of the two regional managers of the organization. Each manager and one more expert classified the performance of the listed stations as "above average," "average," or "below average," using a procedure similar to that of the first group of raters. After eliminating a few units of ambiguous effectiveness standing, a representative sample of thirty-two stations resulted.

The effectiveness score for each station was computed by combining and averaging the judgments of all raters.[7] The range on effectiveness was from 1.0, signifying units of highest possible effectiveness, to 4.8, with 5.0 being the lowest possible score. It should be noted that the distribution of the sample on effectiveness was later found to be positively related with the mean responses of nonsupervisory station personnel to the question: "How do you feel your station compares with other similar stations in getting the job done?" Apparently those directly involved with the operations of the organization can make judgments about the performance of their respective units and they seem to use similar frames of reference. A similar finding has been reported by Comrey, Pfiffner, and Beem.[8]

Station productivity, the first of the three criterion variables of organizational effectiveness, was measured on the basis of standard, company-wide records of performance vis-à-vis established work-standards. This measure is expressed in units of time consumed by the worker below or above what is "allowed" according to the standard. The average productivity of all drivers[9] during the month preceding the field study[10] was taken to represent the organizational productivity of that station. (Incidentally, it should be noted that no problems of quality of output are involved.) On the basis of a standard of 2.00, the range of the obtained distribution of the sample on productivity was from 0.81, signifying the highest producing station, to 2.93 signifying the lowest producing station. An interval of .30 in the present scale is equivalent to 18 minutes of deviation from the established work standard.

Intraorganizational strain was conceptualized as the incidence of tension or conflict existing between organizational subgroups. This criterion was operationalized and measured in terms of responses by nonsupervisory station personnel to the following question: "On the whole, would you say that in your station there is any tension or conflict between employees and supervisors?" The respondent could choose, on a five-point scale, one of five alternatives ranging from there is "a great deal of tension" to "no tension at all." The average nonresponse rate to this question was 6.6 per cent. The mean of the responses in each station represents the score of intraorganizational strain characterizing that station. The range of these scores for the sample was from 2.46, signifying the highest strain station, to 4.50 signifying the lowest strain station. It is interesting to note that station supervisors generally agree with the consensus of their subordinates about the degree of strain characteristic of their station.

Organizational flexibility, the third and last criterion, was conceptualized as the extent to which the organization is able to adjust to internally induced change and to adapt to externally induced change. Two measures were used, one for each of these two aspects of flexibility, and the results were then combined into a single measure.[11] The first was based on the following question: "From time to time changes in methods, equipment, procedures, practices, and layout are introduced by the management. In general, do you think these changes lead to better ways of doing things?" The response alternatives, forming a five-point scale, ranged from "they are always an improvement" to "they never improve things" with an additional "I can't judge" category. The average nonresponse rate, including "I can't judge" responses, was 7.3 per cent. The second measure was based on the question: "In general, how well do you think your station handles sharp changes in volume during peak periods?" The response alternatives here ranged from "excellent" to "very poor," also forming a five-point scale. The nonresponse rate to this question was 3 per cent.

The flexibility score assigned to a given station was obtained by computing the mean of the responses of nonsupervisory station personnel for each of the two questions, and by adding the two means and dividing the result by two. The obtained sample distribution on flexibility ranges from a score of 1.78, signifying high flexibility, to a score of 2.99, signifying the least flexible station on a five-point scale. Again, as in the case of strain, station supervisors generally agree with their respective subordinates about the flexibility of their station.

Empirical Evaluation

The operations and measures used are evaluated in terms of three major considerations. Since effectiveness is viewed in terms of three criteria, the question arises (1) whether in fact each criterion is significantly related to the appraisal of effectiveness by experts, i.e. whether our operations correspond to such an independent standard; (2) whether the criteria are significantly interrelated and if so, what their joint reliability is. Since the concept of organizational effectiveness is by definition as well as logically and theoretically a group concept, the question arises (3) whether our criterion measures represent group phenomena.

The results of our study are presented in Table 1. Based on an N of thirty-two stations, these rank-order correlations are significant at the .05 level or better. In short, as was expected, each of the three criteria is found to be related to an independent assessment of organizational effectiveness by experts. These results lend support to the validity of the three criteria.

TABLE 1

Rank-Order correlations among criterion variables and organizational effectiveness

	Criterion variables		
	Station productivity	Station intergroup strain	Station flexibility
Station effectiveness	.73*	−.49	.39
Station productivity	. . .	−.48	.35
Station intergroup strain	. . .	. . .	−.70

*All correlation coefficients are statistically significant at the .05 level or better, based on an N of thirty-two organizational units (stations).

Table 1 also shows that the three criteria are significantly interrelated. Based on the reported relationships, the overall reliability[12] of the three criteria is found to be .77. These findings provide support for the statistical reliability of the criteria, theoretically considered in combination. The prediction of the independently obtained measure of organizational effectiveness was attempted by combining the three criterion measures into a single index.

To construct this index, the station productivity scores were transformed into five-point scale scores, with 1.00 signifying the highest and 5.00 the lowest theoretically possible productivity.[13] With the inversion of the intraorganizational strain scale, this operation resulted in station productivity scores on a scale equivalent to the scales used for the measurement of strain and flexibility. Thus, for each of the thirty-two sample units, three different scale scores became available, each representing one effectiveness criterion. These scores were averaged resulting in a criterion index score for each station in the sample.

This index score indicates the extent to which a given organizational unit is effective, or the extent to which it is productive, flexible, and devoid of internal strain. The range of criterion index scores for the sample was found to be from 1.69, the most favorable score, to 3.11, least favorable, on a five-point scale. The sample distribution on this criterion index was then related to the distribution of the sample on station effectiveness, and a correlation coefficient of .68 was obtained between the two distributions. When corrected for attenuation (This can be done since we know the reliability of the criterion index.), this coefficient becomes .77. This suggests that, by means of the present criterion index, one could predict to organizational effectiveness, as judged by experts, explaining about 46 per cent (or, theoretically, when corrected for attenuation, about 59 per cent) of the existing variance.[14] In short, this is the part of variance on station effectiveness that could be accounted for in terms of the employed criterion index.

Finally, to answer the question of whether our three criteria of effectiveness represent organizational rather than individual phenomena, the productivity criterion was chosen for further study. This was done because productivity in the present study contributes more to the explained variance in effectiveness than either strain or flexibility, and because the station productivity measure was derived by averaging the productivity of individuals. Unlike the flexibility and strain measures, which were derived from responses to questions that explicitly referred to organizational aspects, the station productivity criterion had as its initial referent the individual worker. Therefore, the criterion of productivity is the most doubtful from the standpont of whether or not it represents an organizational phenomenon.

The productivity criterion was further studied by analysis of variance to determine whether the stations or the individuals in them constitute the primary source of productivity variance. Twenty-seven stations, distributed among four company plants and encompassing a total of 685 individual workers whose productivity had been ascertained, were used. Suitable productivity scores were not available in the case of the remaining five stations, which belong to the fifth company plant studied.

Table 2 presents the results of this analysis. These results indicate that the between-stations variance on productivity is far greater than the within-stations variance. The obtained F-ratio of 5.82 is statistically significant beyond the .001 level. This confirms our initial expectation that the productivity criterion measure represents an organizational (station) rather than individual level phenomenon. This evidence, however, is not adequate for it is conceivable that the results might vary from plant to plant. To test this possibility, similar analyses of variance were also performed

TABLE 2

Analysis of variance on productivity for twenty-seven ungrouped stations.*

Source of variance	Sum of squares	d.f.	Mean square (variance)	F-ratio
Between stations	10,142	26	390	F = 5.82
				p < .001
				$F_{.99(26,658)}$ = 1.90
Within Stations	40,438	658	67	
Total	50,580	684		

*These stations are similar organizational units distributed among four, larger company plants.

separately for each of the four company plants represented in the sample of twenty-seven stations.[15] In each case the between-stations variance on productivity was found to be significantly greater than the within-stations variance; i.e., grouping the stations into plants makes no difference in this respect. Therefore, we are reasonably assured that the productivity criterion measure represents an organizational rather than an individual phenomenon.

Summary

The concept of organizational effectiveness is an important and widely used notion in the study of social organization. A considerable gap, however, exists between theoretical and empirical approaches. Because there is little theory that adequately treats this concept, research efforts have generally proceeded unsystematically, without sufficient consideration of the conceptual aspects of the phenomenon, and in terms of ad hoc criteria not systematically related to theoretical frameworks consistent with our knowledge of organizations.

The objective of the present research was to examine and define the concept, and to investigate some of its operational aspects by developing and testing criteria in an industrial setting. These criteria of effectiveness stem from a commonly accepted view of organizational requirements and are generally applicable across organizations. Based on this view, the study of organizational effectiveness would require that emphasis be placed on the means-ends dimension of organizations, and that the criteria of organizational flexibility, productivity, and strain be taken into consideration.

In the present case, organizational effectiveness was conceptualized as the extent to which an organization, as a social system, fulfills its objectives without incapacitating its means and resources and without placing undue strain upon its members. The problem was approached in terms of the criteria of organizational productivity, intraorganizational strain, and organizational flexibility, which were derived from a common framework. In the present study, the relevant operations proved reliable and the criteria related significantly to an independent evaluation of effectiveness by experts. These criteria represent important aspects of organizational functioning and deserve further attention in the study of organizational effectiveness.

---

1. R. L. Thorndike, *Personnel Selection: Test and Measurement Techniques* (New York: John Wiley & Sons, 1949), pp. 121–124.

2. See, for example, R. L. Kahn, "The Prediction of Productivity," *J. Soc. Issues* 12 (1956): 41–49; R. L. Kahn and N. C. Morse, "The Relationship of Productivity to Morale," *J. Soc. Issues* 7 (1951): 8–17; Daniel Katz and R. L. Kahn, "Human Organization and Worker Motivation," in *Industrial Productivity,* ed. L. R. Tripp (Madison, Wis.: Industrial Relations Research Association, 1951). See also the following, published at the Institute for Social Research, University of Michigan, Ann Arbor: Daniel Katz, N. Maccoby, and N. C. Morse, *Productivity, Supervision, and Morale in an Office Situation* (1950); Daniel Katz, N. Maccoby, G. Gurin, and L. G. Floor, *Productivity, Supervision, and Morale Among Railroad Workers* (1951); N. C. Morse, *Satisfaction in the White-Collar Job* (1953); S. E. Seashore, *Group Cohesiveness in the Industrial Work Group* (1955).

3. R. L. Kahn and N. C. Morse, op. cit., p. 16.

4. B. M. Bass, "Ultimate Criteria of Organizational Worth," *Personnel Psychol.* 5 (Autumn 1952): 157–73.

5. Satisfaction of member needs beyond some minimum critical level, and the maintenance of sufficient member motivation and of an effort-reward balance constitute important problems for all organizations. And, it is under this concept of preservation (or incapacitation) of resources that such variables as turnover, absenteeism, morale, and satisfaction could be viewed as "criteria" or correlates of effectiveness.

6. The major background characteristics of the nonsupervisory station personnel, as of July, 1955, were as follows: all workers are male; nearly all workers are unionized (95 per cent); 81 per cent are between 26 and 49 years old; 82 per cent are married; 77 per cent have gone beyond grade school; 85 per cent have been on the same job for at least one year, 84 per cent have been working in the same station for at least one year, and 73 per cent have been with the company for three years or more. Three-fourths of the workers express "fair" or better than fair satisfaction with their wages, but 42 per cent are "very little" or not at all satisfied with their chances for advancement in the company (probably due to the fact that upward mobility is extremely limited because of the structure of this organization).

7. Stations judged as "above average" by the second group of raters were assigned a scale value of 1, "average" stations 3, and "below average" stations 5 to achieve equivalence of scales for the two rater groups.

8. A. L. Comrey, J. M. Pfiffner, and H. P. Beem, "Factors Influencing Organizational Effectiveness," *Personnel Psychol.* 5 (Winter 1952): 307–28.

9. Drivers constitute three-fourths of all members and operate under uniformly established work standards. The remaining workers operate either under no work standards or under a group standard that may vary from station to station. However,

their productivity is reflected in that of the drivers since these workers process exactly the same work volume that the drivers deliver.

10. This particular month was chosen because it was the most recent month for which data could be made available to the researchers, and because it was a "normal" month in terms of work volume. All months, except December, are considered "normal."

11. The rank-order correlation between these two flexibility measures was found to be .71 for the study sample of thirty-two stations, suggesting a strong association between the two aspects of organizational flexibility represented by the two measures.

12. This reliability was computed on the basis of the relationships appearing in Table 1. For the formula used to compute the reliability coefficient, see J. P. Guilford, *Fundamental Statistics in Psychology and Education* (New York: McGraw-Hill Book Co., 1942), p. 282.

13. The theoretical scale limits in this transformation were set so as to correspond to the productivity scores of the highest and lowest producing individual worker in the sample. It was assumed that no station can have a higher productivity than the highest producing individual worker in the sample, nor a lower productivity than the lowest producing worker.

14. A less satisfactory way to answer the same question empirically would have been to compute the multiple correlation coefficient between the three criteria and effectiveness on the basis of the obtained correlational findings, without constructing an index. This was computed and found to be .75, suggesting that, in the present study, about 56 per cent of the variance in effectiveness can be accounted for in terms of the joint contribution of the three criteria—productivity, strain, and flexibility. This finding is similar to that obtained by using the criterion index.

15. The specific results from this analysis are as follows: for Plant A, consisting of 12 stations and 373 individual workers, the F-ratio is 3.67 and $p < .01$; for Plant B, consisting of 5 stations and 136 individuals, F is 6.31 and $p < .01$; for Plant C, consisting of 6 stations and 99 individuals, F is 6.57 and $p < .01$; and for Plant D, consisting of 4 stations and 77 individuals, F is 3.50 and $p < .05$. Thus, in all cases, the between-stations variance on productivity is significantly greater than the within-stations variance, as expected.

COMPONENTS OF EFFECTIVENESS
IN SMALL ORGANIZATIONS

Frank Friedlander and Hal Pickle

A primary focus for those interested in understanding or changing organizations has been upon the internal dynamics of the organization. This focus has led to emphasis on methods of enhancing the worth of the employee (to himself or to the organization) through selection, training, group participation, job restructuring, etc.; and consequently to criteria of effectiveness that are limited to the internal dynamics of the organization. The criteria have typically been of two kinds: those dealing with individual human resources such as motivation, mental health, cohesiveness, satisfaction, etc.; and those concerned with individual performance, such as amount produced, quality of output, error rate, etc. The generally low relationship between these two sets of criteria has been disturbing for the researcher and has resulted in numerous dilemmas for the practitioner.[1] Since these two criteria have for the most part been

From *Administrative Science Quarterly*, (Sept., 1968), pp. 289–304. Reprinted by permission of the authors and publisher.

uncorrelated, it appears useless to attempt to maximize them both. On the other hand, favoring one over the other produces either inefficiency for the organization or dissatisfaction for the individual. This dilemma has spurred some researchers to expand the scope of their analyses to encompass situational determinants of the satisfaction performance relationship.[2] Others have, in one way or another, explicitly recognized the inescapable tension between the individual and the organizational goals[3] and have concentrated upon the reduction of these tensions.

For the most part, theories and research concerned with individual performance, employee satisfaction, and reduction of tension between individual and organizational goals are dealing only with internal aspects of the events, relationships, and structures that make up the total organizational system. If the organization is viewed as an open-energy system, however, it is apparent that it is dependent for survival and growth upon a variety of energy transfers not only within the organization, but also between the organization and its external environment.[4] It is obvious, then, that the internal and external dynamics of the organization are complementary and interdependent. Modifications in one of these structures have an impact upon the other. This perspective of the organization is similar to the model proposed by Parsons,[5] in which four fundamental processes are specified for every social system: adaptation, goal achievement, integration, and latency. These functions provide a structural framework within which internal and external relationships may be explored.

A perspective that includes the organization's societal relationships can account for the full cycle of energy, since it incorporates both the importation of energy from this societal environment and the output of energy into that environment. The relationship between organization and environment is recognized by several research workers. For example, Bennis[6] claims that bureaucracy is least likely to cope and survive if unable to adapt to a rapidly changing, turbulent environment. Emery and Trist[7] stress that the primary task of managing an enterprise as a whole is to relate the total organizational system to its environment, and not just internal regulation. If the organization is to survive and grow, it must control its boundary conditions—the forms of exchange between the enterprise and the environment. Strother[8] reverses the direction of this influence process by claiming that one must allow for control of the organization by an outside and changing environment. Pepinsky, Weick, and Riner[9] observe that the organization must adapt to regulatory control by the environment. Typical models of organization behavior, however, treat the organization as a closed system and concentrate upon principles of internal functioning as if these problems were independent of the external environments.[10]

System Effectiveness

Parallel to the need to understand the total organization system as interdependent with its environment is the establishment of criteria of organizational effectiveness that reflect these interdependencies. Such criteria include those with some element of the organization's contribution *to society* and those that describe effectiveness in terms of maximization of return *from society* to the organization. Bass,[11] for example, suggests that an organization be evaluated in terms of its worth to the individual worker and the value of the worker and the organization to society. Similar criteria suggested by Davis[12] include broad social values, economic values, and personal values. The emphasis is in a reversed direction for Katz and Kahn,[13] who describe organizational effectiveness as referring to the maximization of return to the organization by all means—technological, political, market control, personnel policies, federal subsidies, etc.

Most behavioral scientists have come to realize that organizational effectiveness is not a unitary concept. Guion, for example, points out that "the fallacy of the single criterion lies in its assumption that everything that is to be predicted is related to everything else to be predicted—that there is a general factor in all criteria accounting for virtually all of the important variance in behavior at work and its various consequences of value."[14] The assumption of unitary criteria of organizational effectiveness has its counterpart in the concept of utility maximization, in which utility is defined as the value to an individual of all things he can possibly enjoy or possess. All of the nonmonetary components are assumed to be translatable into a single utility scale, which allows trade-offs between the nonmonetary and monetary components. The behavioral theory of the firm, by contrast, is rooted in the "satisficing" concept of individuals searching until a satisfactory (not an optimal) solution is found.[15] Individuals are not likely to combine their various sources of satisfaction into a single function, and certainly are not likely to maximize such a function. They are likely to seek satisfactory solutions in the several areas of their activities, with few trade-offs.

These differences in assumptions parallel those of organizational behavior, not only in terms of the internal dynamics of the organization, but also in terms of the criteria of organizational effectiveness. In the behavioral theory of organizations, it is assumed that goals are formulated for organizational activity in several areas. The rational-man assumptions of economics for the individual become profit maximization for the organization. If organizational goals are extended beyond profit maximization, the organizational utility function must incorporate effectiveness in these other areas.[16] If satisficing in these several activities rather than profit maximization is an organization goal, relative independence in their attainment might be expected.

Although the degree-of-fulfillment terminology is used in this article, fulfillment is probably more accurately represented in terms of the degree to which the organizational or environmental component is satisficed. Furthermore, it is probable that the expectations which a component holds of the organization in general, and the specific organization with which it transacts, affect the degree to which that component it satisficed with the organization.

Clearly, effectiveness criteria must take into account the profitability of the organization, the degree to which it satisfices its members, and the degree to which it is of value to the larger society of which it is a part. These three perspectives include system maintenance and growth, subsystem fulfillment, and environmental fulfillment. Each is obviously composed of several related components, and each component is hypothetically related to the other. The degree to which these several components of organizational effectiveness are interrelated is a primary focus of this paper.

The purpose of this study, then, was to explore the concept of total organizational effectiveness by studying the relationships between internal and external system effectiveness. Internal system components were those within the formal boundaries of the organization. Societal components with which the organization transacts by exporting and importing energy were considered part of the larger environment in which the organization is located. Effectiveness was viewed as the degree to which the needs of components were fulfilled (or satisfied) in their transactions with the organization. The specific interest was in the degree of interdependence in the satisfaction of components.

The particular subsystem components chosen for study do not exhaust the variety of components, but were selected to include seven of primary importance for the maintenance and growth of the organization in its society: the owner, the employees, and five societal components—the customers, the suppliers, the creditors, the community, and the government.[17]

Data

Sample

Small organizations were preferred as sample units in the study, because it was felt that whatever relationships exist among components might be explored more adequately, since the links among these components are presumably shorter and less numerous. The sample included ninety-seven small businesses, each with only one level of management, and each employing from four to about forty employees.

A random stratified technique was used. The distribution of types of small businesses in the United States was determined from various census data and this distribution was approximated in a random selection of small businesses within the state of Texas. Since responses from two of the initial ninety-seven business organizations were suspect, two additional organizations were substituted for these. The final sample of ninety-seven small businesses was composed of fifty-four retail establishments, twenty-six service establishments, eight wholesale establishments, six manufacturers, and three mineral extraction firms.

Societal Components

The data for measuring the degree of fulfillment for each of the five societal components for each of the ninety-seven organizations were gathered by questionnaires and interviews. All data were collected in quantified form, either in a Likert-type, multiple-choice format, or in specific dollar amounts or frequency information.

Initially, satisfaction for each of the five societal components was measured by from five to thirty-seven items. Correlation coefficients were then computed among all items within each of the five components. Items within each of the five components which correlated highly with each other were then selected to represent that component, so as to maximize its internal consistency or cohesion. The items so selected were then given equal weight and averaged to form mean scores for each of the components. As a final check on this process and on the internal consistency of each component scale, reliability coefficients for internal consistency[18] were computed for each scale with the following results: customers, .96; suppliers, .77; owners, .92; communities, .65; and governments, .60. This method of scale construction, based upon maximizing the internal consistency of items within each scale, yielded improved results over some of our earlier procedures which did not utilize this method.

The data gathered and the methods used follow:

COMMUNITY   Community fulfillment was measured in the general areas of membership and leadership in local and nonlocal organizations, the number of committees and drives that managers participated in during the past two years, and their attendance at community affairs such as fund-raising dinners, bazaars, etc. These data were obtained through a questionnaire survey administered to the managers in directed interviews.

GOVERNMENT   Relations with the federal, state, and local government were measured through the administration of a questionnaire to managers. Items concerned questioning by officials of the Internal Revenue Service on income tax returns, penalties paid on local, state, or federal taxes, or reprimands or censures by tax officials. In general, these items reflected the degree to which the organization carried out its explicit and implicit responsibilities with governmental agencies.

CUSTOMERS   Customers were surveyed by the use of a questionnaire administered in an interview. The sample size for each organization was proportional to its total number of customers within a framework of a minimum of fifteen and a maximum of twenty-five customers per organization. Customers rated the respective business on a five-point scale on each of the following features: quality of goods or services; quantity of goods or services available; neatness, cleanliness, and uniformity of appearance of product; management's knowledge of product or service; speed of service; dependability of business; rank of this business in relation to others in its field; helpfulness, friendliness, and appearance of employees.

SUPPLIERS   Supplier fulfillment was measured in the following areas: promptness of payment of accounts, fairness in transactions, receptiveness to suggestions, and overall evaluation as a customer. Of 403 survey questionnaires mailed, 208 were completed and returned, representing a return of approximately 52 per cent.

CREDITORS   Levels of creditor fulfillment with each organization were obtained from statistical data gathered during interviews with banks, retail merchant associations, and Dun and Bradstreet.

Owner Components

The degree of satisfaction for the owner of each organization was primarily financial. The score was composed of equal weights of the average yearly profit for the owner for the last ten years and the average yearly profit as a function of the hours per week that the owner worked for the organization. Since the correlation between these two measures was .95, the component was essentially a measure of owner financial profit.

Employee Component

The SRA Employee Inventory, a measure of employee satisfaction, was administered to all employees of each organization having ten or fewer employees. For organizations having more than ten employees, ten were randomly selected to represent the organization. A total of 513 inventories was completed, representing an average of 5.29 employees per organization.

Five types of employee fulfillment were measured within each organization. These types of fulfillment had been previously derived from a factor analysis of the SRA Employee Inventory.[19] Types of fulfillment included the following:

SATISFACTION WITH WORKING CONDITIONS   Nine items related to adequacy of working conditions, effects of these conditions on work efficiency, adequacy of equipment, reasonable hours of work, and absence of physical and mental pressures.

SATISFACTION WITH FINANCIAL REWARD.   Seven items related to adequacy of pay, effectiveness of personnel policies with respect to pay, and benefit programs and pay in comparison with other companies.

CONFIDENCE IN MANAGEMENT   Nineteen items related to management's organizing ability, its handling of employee benefit policies, its adequacy in two-way communication, and its interest in employees.

OPINION ABOUT IMMEDIATE SUPERVISION   Twelve items related to how well the supervisor organized his work, knowledge of the job, ability to get things done on time, supplying adequate equipment, letting employees know what was expected, emphasizing proper training, making employees work together, treating employees fairly, keeping his promises, giving encouragement, and interest in employee welfare.

SATISFACTION WITH SELF-DEVELOPMENT   Five items related to employee's feeling of belongingness, of participation, of pride in the company, of doing something worthwhile, and of growth on the job.

Results

Correlation coefficients were computed in order to explore the relationships among the components.[20] The relationships between external and internal criteria of organizational effectiveness were considered first. External criteria were those related to fulfillment of the needs of the five components of the societal system; internal criteria were those related to the five needs of the employees.

In a moderate number of instances, organizations were able to satisfice both societal needs and employee needs simultaneously, as indicated in Table 1. In almost all cases where significant relationships do exist, however, these are of a relatively low magnitude. Thus, while some mutual satisficing of employees and societal components does occur, the degree of this concurrent satisficing is rather low. Of the five societal components, only community and customer satisfaction seem to vary consistently (and positively) with the several types of employee satisfaction. In the case of

TABLE 1

Relationships among societal fulfillment, owner fulfillment, organizational size, and employee fulfillment.

Components fulfilled	Employee fulfillment				
	Working conditions	Financial rewards	Confidence in management	Immediate supervisor	Self-development
SOCIETAL COMPONENTS					
Community	.33*	.06	.28*	.23†	.24†
Government	—.09	.00	—.06	—.03	—.12
Customer	.11	.20†	.21†	.23†	.32*
Supplier	.10	.12	.16	.05	.10
Creditor	.09	—.03	.09	.15	.16
OWNER					
Financial profit	.12	.07	.20†	.22†	.23†
Organizational size					
(size of work force)	—.03	—.21	—.10	—.03	.01

* p < .01.
† p < .05.
N = 97.

community fulfillment, this finding is understandable. Organizations that recognize community needs and fulfill them are likely to be effective in providing similarly for their employees. Furthermore, in smaller communities, the membership of community and employee groups may overlap to a considerable degree. The reasons for the employee-customer satisfaction relationship are perhaps similar to those of the finding on the employee-community satisfaction relationship. Furthermore, in retail and service organizations, close contact between customers and employees may serve as a mechanism of contagion of satisfaction. Customer satisfaction may fulfill employee service needs, thereby causing employee satisfaction which, in turn, is sensed by customers. Finally, both the community and customer components represent more personal and less organized entities within the society. A management which takes action to increase employee fulfillment may thus tend also to focus upon increased customer and community satisfaction.

In the association between employee satisfaction and owner fulfillment, several significant relationships were found. Financially successful organizations were also those in which employees had confidence in management, held higher opinions of the supervisor, and sensed opportunities for self-development. Although these correlations were not of a high magnitude, they do point to the tempting conclusion that satisfied employees contribute toward (or are a product of) an organization profitable for the owner. The relationship is highest between owner fulfillment and employee self-development, a finding that seems understandable since the self-development measure reflects the employee's feelings of belongingness, participation, and pride in the company—a sense of "psychological ownership" in the organization. Previous findings in this area are ambiguous, however. Bass, McGhee, and Vaughan[21] found that satisfaction with one's particular job in the company did not seem particularly related to financial performance of the company. Katzell, Barrett, and Parker,[22] however, reported about three-fourths of their attitude items correlated positively with organizational performance and no items correlated negatively with performance. They also reported consistently negative relationships between job satisfaction and size of work force, a finding validated to some extent in this study. Table 1 reveals consistent (but generally not significant) negative relationships between organizational size (as measured by size of work force) and employee fulfillment. The single significant relationship indicates that employees are less satisfied with pay policies in organizations composed of larger work forces.

Since the relationships between internal and external criteria of organizational effectiveness were relatively weak, the relationships among the several external criteria were of interest, as well as those between external criteria and owner fulfillment and organizational size.

The relationships among the external components of the organizational system show no definite pattern, as indicated in Table 2. Only five of the fifteen relationships are significant. Customer satisfaction is correlated positively with supplier and owner fulfillment, which is understandable, since both are societal units with which the organization exchanges services directly for financial remuneration. This is also the case for exchanges with the employee components of the organization.

There was a negative relation between government and customer fulfillment, which was unexpected. It appears that organizations that focus upon goal achievement through customer interactions are less concerned with the adaptive functions of fulfilling governmental obligations. However, the adaptive function of fulfilling community needs does appear to be related to the goal of achieving organizational profitability; organizations whose managers are actively involved in community affairs are also those that are most profitable for the owner.

Perhaps one of the most direct exchanges leading to goal attainment

TABLE 2

Relationships among societal fulfillment, owner fulfillment, and organizational size.

Components fulfilled	Fulfillment of needs of					
	Government	Customer	Supplier	Creditor	Owner	Orig. size
SOCIETAL COMPONENTS						
Community	.00	−.04	.03	.03	.32*	.29*
Government		−.25†	−.11	.20†	−.11	−.07
Customer			.20†	.10	.21†	.20†
Supplier				.09	.08	.13
Creditor					−.02	.10
OWNER						.28*

* p < .01.
† p < .05.
N = 97.

is that between the owner and the customer of the organization. Table 2 indicates that organizations in which owner needs are fulfilled are also those in which customer fulfillment is high. The tempting conclusion is that the successful organization (for the owner) is one which satisfices customer needs also.

As might be predicted, government and creditor fulfillment were moderately correlated. The needs of both of these components can be viewed more as financial obligations of the organization. These needs are fulfilled as they are continually reduced to a minimum.

Organization size is also related to the ability of the organization to fulfill the needs of the societal component. The larger the organization (in number of employees), the more likely it is to fulfill the needs of its community, its owner, and its customers. Organizations with larger human and financial resources can be expected to provide greater support for the community in which they exist; they are able to offer a wider variety of products and services to customers, and thus greater psychological and financial satisfaction for the owner. Two notes of caution should be mentioned in connection with these inferences. First, one cannot be sure as to the causal direction of these relationships. It is possible that because an organization provides fulfillment for its community, owner, and customers, it has grown larger. It is more probable that causality changes its direction over time: at one time the organization grows because it fulfills societal needs; subsequently, society's needs are fulfilled to a greater extent because the organization is larger and offers greater resources.

Second, organizational size in this study was limited to organizations of forty employees. In organizations with many more than forty employees, it is probable that the size-fulfillment relationship becomes asymptotic; similar increments in size may produce decreasing gains in societal fulfillment.

Discussion

In this study we have attempted to avoid the dichotomy of satisfaction versus productivity, by which organizational effectiveness is traditionally gauged. This dichotomy has left both organizational researchers and practitioners with discomforting dilemmas, and resulted in a focus on internal criteria to the exclusion of the demands of the organization's environment. Instead, the organization has been conceived as interdependent components or subsystems through which energy is transferred; and energy exchange occurs both within the organization and also between it and its environment. In this light, organizational effectiveness is the extent to which all forms of energic return to the organization are maximized.

The five societal components upon which the organization is dependent for its survival and growth include the community, government, customers, suppliers, and creditors. The organization is also dependent upon maximizing energy transformation within the firm, a process in which its employees play a major role. A third component important in the survival and growth of the organization is its owner. The focus of the study was on the degree to which fulfillment of the needs of the organization's environmental components was related to fulfillment of the needs of the organization's internal subsystem components and whether organizational size was related to these.

Findings of this study indicate that there are only a moderate number of relationships between the degree to which the organization concurrently fulfills the needs of its internal subsystem components (its employees), its owner, and the components of its larger society. Concurrent fulfillment of the needs of the five societal components is also of a rather low magnitude.

Evidently, organizations find it difficult to fulfill simultaneously the variety of demands made upon them. Whether the organization *can* concurrently fulfill all or even a major share of the divergent demands made upon it is a provocative and hypothetical question. It is probable that organizations do not strive to maximize fulfillment of any one system component, but operate in accordance with a policy of satisficing several system components. A no-layoff policy, for example, may partially fulfill employee needs, but might do so at the cost of diminishing fulfillment of other societal components. Fulfillment of needs of the various organizational components must, therefore, be treated as separate and, apparently, independent. Components in the organization's system are linked together more by the flow of energic activities than by common goal attainment.

From a broader vantage, then, the manager's task is not only to coordinate functions within the organization, but to relate these internal functions to the organization's societal environment. Lack of concurrent maximization of the organization's components calls for greater focus upon the role of the manager as a systems balancer as well as a mediator of the boundaries of the organization.[23]

The inability of the organization to fulfill concurrently the needs of its societal components, its owners, and its employees, presents dilemmas for theorists in organizational behavior as well as for practitioners in industrial organizations. If prophesies and predictions[24] are correct, the tasks and goals of organizations will become far more complex in the future and will require greater adaptive and innovative capabilities. These increasing organizational complexities will demand the articulation and development of meta-goals that shape and provide the foundation for the goal structure. For example, one meta-goal might be the creation of a system for detecting new and changing goals of the organization or methods for deciding priorities among goals.

Finally, as Bennis[25] predicts, there will be an increase in goal conflict, more and more divergency and contradictoriness between and among effectiveness criteria. While at this date, the different effectiveness criteria among the variety of organizational functions appear unrelated and divergent, lethargy by management may allow these relationships to become negatively related to each other. Management's awareness of these relationships and of how they may change with differing goal structures seems a first step toward maximizing future organizational effectiveness.

1.   S. Seashore, *Assessing Organization Performance with Behavioral Measurements* (Ann Arbor, Mich.: Foundation for Research on Human Behavior, 1964).

2.   R. Katzell, R. S. Barrett, and T. C. Parker, "Job Satisfaction, Job Performance, and Situational Characteristics," *J. Appl. Psychol.* 45 (1961): 65–72.

3.   H. Levinson, "Role, Personality, and Social Structure in the Organizational Setting," *J. Abnormal Soc. Psychol.,* 58 (1959): 170–80; C. Argyris, *Interpersonal Competence and Organizational Effectiveness* (Homewood, Ill.: Dorsey Press, 1962); H. A. Shepard, "Changing Interpersonal and Intergroup Relationships in Organizations," in *Handbook of Organizations,* ed. James G. March (New York: Rand McNally & Co., 1964), pp. 1115–43.

4.   Daniel Katz and Robert L. Kahn, *The Social Psychology of Organizations* (New York: John Wiley & Sons, 1966).

5. Talcott Parsons, Edward Shils, Kaspar Naegle, and Jesse Pitts, *Theories of Society* (New York: Free Press, 1961), pp. 38–41.

6. Warren G. Bennis, "Organizational Developments and the Fate of Bureaucracy," address presented at the meetings of the American Psychological Association, Los Angeles, Calif., September, 1964.

7. F. E. Emery and Eric L. Trist, "Socio-Technical Systems," paper presented at Sixth Annual International Meeting of the Institute of Management Sciences, Paris, France, September, 1959.

8. G. B. Strother, "Problems in the Development of Social Science of Organization," in *The Social Science of Organizations,* ed. H. J. Leavitt (Englewood Cliffs, N.J.: Prentice-Hall, 1963), pp. 3–37.

9. H. B. Pepinsky, K. E. Weick, and J. W. Riner, *Primer for Productivity* (Columbus, Ohio: Ohio State University Research Foundation, 1965).

10. Katz and Kahn, op. cit.

11. Bernard M. Bass, "Ultimate Criteria of Organizational Worth," *Personnel Psychol.* 5 (1952): 157–73.

12. R. C. Davis, *Industrial Organization and Management* (New York: Harper & Row, Publishers, 1940).

13. Katz and Kahn, op. cit.

14. Robert M. Guion, "Criterion Measurement and Personnel Judgments," *Personnel Psychol.* 14 (1961): 141–49, esp. p. 145.

15. Herbert A. Simon, *Models of Man* (New York: John Wiley & Sons, 1957).

16. A. Charnes and A. C. Stedry, "Quasi-Rational Models of Behavior in Organization Research." *Management Sciences Research Report no. 31* (Pittsburgh: Graduate School of Industrial Administration, 1965).

17. While customers, suppliers, creditors, communities, and governments were grouped in the general category of the organization's societal environment, other models are obvious. In accord with Parsons' AGIL model (adaptation, goal attainment, integration, latency), for example, owners and customers are crucial to goal attainment of product exchange; creditors, communities, governments, and suppliers provide necessary resources and support for the organization and are thus instrumental in the organization's adaptation to its environment; and employees perform integrative functions within the organizational system. Talcott Parsons, Edward Shils, Kaspar Naegle, and Jesse Pitts, *Theories of Society* (New York: Free Press, 1961), pp. 38–41.

18. The internal consistency of each total societal component scale was computed using Kuder-Richardson's formula 20:

$$r_{tt} = \left[\frac{n}{n-1}\right]\left[\frac{\sigma T^2 - \Sigma pq}{\sigma_T{}^3}\right]$$

Essentially, this formula measures the proportion of the total scale variance $[\sigma_T{}^2]$, which is composed of the sum of the inter-item covariances $[T_{19}\ \sigma,\ \sigma^2]$. This formula was not applied to the creditor scale, since data were gathered from different types of statistical and financial records and were, therefore, not comparable.

19. Zile S. Dabas, "The Dimensions of Morale: An Item Factorization of the SRA Employee Inventory," *Personnel Psychol.* 11 (1958): 217-34.

20. To check for curvilinear relationships between variables, scatter plot outputs from computer runs were examined visually. In those cases where some curvilinearity was suggested, tests of curvilinearity were made. In no case was the appropriate coefficient (η) significant.

21.   Bernard M. Bass, Walter P. McGhee, and James A. Vaughan, "Three Levels of Analysis of Cost-Effectiveness Associated with Personnel Attitudes and Attributes," prepared for the *Proceedings of the Logistics Research Conference*, Warrenton, Virginia, Department of Defense, May 1965.

22.   R. Katzell, R. S. Barrett, and T. C. Parker, op. cit.

23.   K. Davis and R. L. Blomstrom, *Business and Its Environment* (New York: McGraw-Hill Book Co., 1966), and B. M. Bass, *Organizational Psychology* (Boston: Allyn and Bacon, 1965).

24.   W. Bennis, op. cit.

25.   Ibid.

ADDITIONAL READINGS

Additional readings for this part are divided into four sections. The first section contains a list of works which provide reviews of organizational studies conducted over the years. The second section lists studies which were referred to earlier as "segmental" or partial studies on formal organizations. The third section presents a list of total organizational studies on formal organizations, and the fourth section lists studies on organizational effectiveness.

General Reference Sources on Organizational Studies

Berelson, Bernard, and Steiner, Gary A. 1964. *Human behavior: An inventory of scientific findings*. New York: Harcourt, Brace & World.

Blau, Peter. 1962. "Studies on formal organizations: An editorial forward." *Am. J. Sociol.* 68: 289–90.

Blau, Peter M., and Scott, W. Richard. 1962. *Formal organizations*. San Francisco: Chandler Publishing Co.

203

Bowers, Raymond V., ed. 1966. *Studies on behavior in organizations.* Athens, Ga.: University of Georgia Press.

Etzioni, Amitai. 1964. *Modern organizations.* Englewood Cliffs, N.J.: Prentice-Hall.

Hammond, Phillip E., ed. 1964. *Sociologists at work.* New York: Basic Books.

Mayntz, Renate. 1965. "The study of organizations: A trend report and bibliography. *Current Sociol.* 13: 95–156.

March, James G., ed. 1965. *Handbook of organizations.* Skokie, Ill.: Rand McNally & Co.

Price, James L. 1968. *Organizational effectiveness: An inventory of propositions.* Homewood, Ill.: Richard D. Irwin.

Waldo, Dwight. 1961. "Organization theory: An elephantine problem." *Public Admin. Rev.* 21: 210–25.

Segmental or Partial Studies of Organizations

Argyris, Chris. 1962. *Interpersonal competence and organizational effectiveness.* Homewood, Ill.: Dorsey Press.

_____. 1964. "T-groups for organizational effectiveness." *Harvard Bus. Rev.* (Mar.-Apr.): 60–74.

Baum, Bernard, and Burack, Elmer. 1969. "Information technology, manpower development, and organizational performance." *Acad. Manage. J.* 12: 279–92.

Christman, Luther. 1968. "The role of nursing in organizational effectiveness." *Hospital Admin.* 13: 40–47.

Etzioni, Amitai. 1960. "Authority structure and organizational effectiveness." *Admin. Sci. Quart.* 4: 43–67.

Evan, W. M. 1963. "Indices of the hierarchical structure of industrial organizations." *Manage. Sci.* 9: 468–77.

Georgopoulos, Basil S. 1965. "Normative structure variables and organizational behavior: A comparative study." *Human Relations* 18: 155–70.

Grusky, O. 1961. "Corporate size, bureaucratization, and managerial succession." *Am. J .Sociol.* 67: 261–69.

_____. 1963. "Managerial succession and organizational effectiveness." *Am. J. Sociol.* 69: 21–30.

Hage, Jerald, and Aiken, Michael. 1967. "Relationship of centralization to other structural properties." *Admin. Sci. Quart.* 12: 49–72.

Hall, R. H. 1962. "Intraorganizational structural variables." *Admin. Sci. Quart.* 7: 295–308.

_____. 1963. "The concept of bureaucracy: An empirical assessment." *Am. J. Sociol.* 69: 32–40.

Jones, Halsey R. 1969. "A study of organization performance for experimental structures of two, three and four levels." *Acad. Manage. J.* 12: 351–36.

Kaczka, Eugene, and Kirk, Roy V. 1967. "Managerial climate, work groups, and organizational performance." *Admin. Sci. Quart.* 12: 253–72.

Morse, Nancy C., and Reimer, Everett. 1956. "The experimental change of a major organizational variable." *J. Abnormal Soc. Psychol.* 52: 120–29.

Price, James L. 1963. "The impact of governing boards on organizational effectiveness and morale." *Admin. Sci. Quart.* 8: 361–78.

Pugh, D. S., Hickson, D. J., Hinings, C. R., and Turner, C. 1969. "The context of organization structures." *Admin. Sci. Quart.* 14: 91–114.

Roberts, K., Miles, R. E., and Blankenship, L. V. 1968. "Organizational leadership, satisfaction and productivity: A comparative analysis." *Acad. Manage. J.* 11: 401–14.

Rosengren, William R. 1967. "Structure, policy and style: Strategies of organizational control." *Admin. Sci. Quart.* 12: 140–64.

Rushing, William A. 1968. "The effects of industry size and division of labor on administration." *Admin. Sci. Quart.* 12: 273–95.

Seashore, Stanley E., and Bowers, D. G. 1963. "Changing the structure and functioning of an organization: Report of a field experiment." *Monograph No. 33.* Ann Arbor, Mich.: Survey Research Center, University of Michigan.

Tittle, Charles R., and Tittle, Drollene F. 1964. "Structural handicaps to organizational effectiveness: A case study." *Proc. Southwest Sociol. Ass.* 14: 118–27.

Whyte, William Foote. 1948. *Human relations in the restaurant industry.* New York: McGraw-Hill Book Co.

Zald, Mayer N. 1967. "Urban differentiation, characteristics of boards of directors, and organizational effectiveness." *Am. J. Sociol.* 73: 261–72.

Total Organization Studies

Abegglen, James C. 1958. *The japanese factory.* New York: Free Press.

Argyris, Chris. 1954. *Organization of a bank.* New Haven, Conn.: Labor and Management Center, Yale University.

Blau, Peter M. 1955. *Dynamics of bureaucracy.* Chicago: University of Chicago Press.

Cressey, Donald R., ed. 1961. *The prison: Studies in institutional and organizational change.* New York: Holt, Rinehart & Winston.

Dalton, Melville. 1959. *Men who manage.* New York: John Wiley & Sons.

Gouldner, Alvin W. 1954. *Patterns of industrial bureaucracy.* New York: Free Press.

Jaques, Elliott. 1952. *The changing culture of the factory.* New York: Dryden.

_____. 1964. "Social analysis and the glacier project." *Human Relations* 17: 361–75.

Lipset, Seymour Martin. 1952. "Democracy in private government." *Brit. J. Sociol.* 3: 47–63.

Lipset, S. M., Trow, M. A., and Coleman, J. S. 1956. *Union democracy.* New York: Free Press.

McCleery, Richard H. 1957. *Policy change in prison management.* Ann Arbor, Mich.: Governmental Research Bureau; Michigan State University.

Michels, Robert. 1962. *Political parties.* New York: Free Press.

Rice, A. K. 1958. *Productivity and social organization: The ahmedabad experiment.* London: Tavistock Publications.

_____. 1963. *The enterprise and its environment.* London: Tavistock Publications.

Roethlisberger, Fritz J., and Dickson, William J. 1939. *Management and the worker.* Cambridge, Mass.: Harvard University Press.

Seashore, Stanley E., and Bowers, David G. 1963. *Changing the structure and functioning of an organization: Report of a field experiment.* Ann Arbor, Mich.: Survey Research Center.

Selznick, Phillip. 1948. *TVA and the grass roots.* Berkeley, Calif.: University of California Press.

_____. 1952. *The organizational weapon: A study of bolshevik strategy and tactics.* New York: McGraw-Hill Book Co.

Trist, E. L., and Bamforth, E. K. 1951. "Some social and psychological consequences of the Longwall method of coal getting." *Human Relations* 4: 3–38.

Warner, W. Lloyd, and Low, J. O. 1947. *The social system of the modern factory.* New Haven, Conn.: Yale University Press.

Woodward, Joan. 1965. *Industrial organization: Theory and practice.* London: Oxford University Press.

Selected Studies on Organizational Effectiveness

Ghorpade, J. V. 1968. "Study of relative effectiveness of joint stock and cooperative sugar factories located in Maharashtra, India. Unpubl. Ph.D. diss., University of California, Los Angeles.

Price, James L. 1968. *Organizational effectiveness: An inventory of propositions.* Homewood, Ill.: Richard D. Irwin.

Yuchtman, Ephraim. 1966. "A study of organizational effectiveness." Unpubl. Ph.D. diss., University of Michigan, Ann Arbor.

IV

METHODOLOGY

THE GROWING FOCUS upon organizations as subjects of research has resulted in numerous attempts to tackle the methodological problems involved in studying organizations. General discussions and reviews of pertinent literature on this topic are provided in Adams and Preiss, 1960; Caro, 1969; McGrath, 1964; Mechanic, 1963; and Vroom, 1967.

The expanding literature on methodology for organizational research does not as yet include a statement on the methodological problems involved in studying organizational effectiveness. The energies of organization theorists conducting research on this topic has thus far been directed largely at resolving broad theoretical issues and development of criteria of effectiveness. Discussions of methodology have thus far been incidental to resolution of broader theoretical problems and formulation of criteria of effectiveness.

The reading included in this part is this writer's contribution toward the development of a methodology for the study of organizational effectiveness. In undertaking this task, the writer has relied upon his experiences during a field study on organizational effectiveness recently conducted by him in India (Ghorpade, 1968).

TOWARD A METHODOLOGY FOR THE STUDY OF ORGANIZATIONAL EFFECTIVENESS

Jaisingh Ghorpade

The purpose of this discussion is to contribute toward the development of a methodology for the study of organizational effectiveness. In undertaking this task, the author seeks to draw upon experience gained by him in the conduct of a field study on organizational effectiveness.[1] This study was concerned with analyzing the effectiveness, in relative terms, of two types of sugar factories operating side by side in Maharashtra State in India: privately owned joint-stock sugar factories and state-sponsored cooperative sugar factories. Field work for this study (hereinafter referred to as the sugar industry study) lasted from October, 1964, to February, 1965. The complex of sugar factories which formed the subject of this study was composed of twenty cooperative and fourteen joint-stock sugar factories. The names, years of start, capacity, and location of these factories are given in Table 1. The relative effectiveness of the two organizational groups was assessed in terms of three criteria: (1) reduction in

TABLE 1
Sugar factories in operation in Maharashtra, June 1964.

Name of factory	Season factory started	Daily crushing capacity*	Location district
COOPERATIVES			
Ashok	1957/58	1000	Ahmednagar
Bhogawati†	1958/59	1000	Kolhapur
Chhatrapati	1956/57	1250	Poona
Dudhaganga†	1962/63	1000	Kolhapur
Ganesh	1957/58	1250	Ahmednagar
Girna	1958/59	1000	Nasik
Kopargaon	1955/56	1000	Ahmednagar
Krishna	1960/61	1250	Satara
Kumbhi-Kasari†	1962/63	1000	Kolhapur
Malegaon	1957/58	1250	Poona
Niphad	1963/64	1000	Ahmednagar
Panchganga	1957/58	1000	Kolhapur
Pravara	1950/51	1200	Ahmednagar
Rahuri	1957/58	1200	Ahmednagar
Sanjiwani	1963/64	1000	Ahmednagar
Shetkari†	1958/59	1000	Kolhapur
Shriram	1957/58	1200	Satara
Someshwar	1962/63	1000	Poona
Warana†	1959/60	1000	Kolhapur
Yeshwant	1962/63	1000	Sholapur
JOINT STOCK COMPANIES			
Belapur	1923/24	1200	Ahmednagar
Belvendi	1933/34	350	Ahmednagar
Brihan-Maharashtra	1938/39	1300	Sholapur
Changdeo	1941/42	800	Ahmednagar
Gangapur	1955/56	1000	Ahmednagar
Godavari (Laxmiwadi)	1941/42	1000	Ahmednagar
Godavari (Sakarwadi)	1939/40	1000	Ahmednagar
Kolhapur†	1933/34	1750	Kolhapur
Maharashtra	1934/35	1700	Sholapur
Phalton	1933/34	1000	Satara
Ravalgaon	1933/34	1200	Nasik
Saswadmali	1934/35	1000	Sholapur
Ugar†	1938/39	1200	Belgaum
Walchandnagar	1933/34	1750	Poona

*Number of tons of sugar cane crushed per day.
†These factories were visited during the field study.

economic power concentration: the extent to which each organizational group facilitated the dispersal of ownership and control of the sugar industry within the state; (2) employee enhancement: the extent to which each organizational group contributed towards the material and professional well-being of its workers; and (3) efficiency: measured in terms of two quantitative indices of operating efficiency—sugar losses and work-hour losses during selected seasons.[2] Data for this study were gathered through interviews with sugar factory personnel and others associated with the sugar factory complex in Maharashtra State and from secondary sources such as sugar industry publications, individual factory records, government reports, and prior studies on the sugar industry.[3] Further details about methodology used in the sugar industry study are presented as the need arises in the following sections of this report.

As indicated above, experience gained by this author in conducting field research for the sugar industry study forms the basis for this discussion on development of a methodology for the study of organizational effectiveness. However, as the author encountered a host of methodological issues and problems in conducting the above study,[4] it is essential to narrow the discussion down to a few selected issues in order to make it manageable. Therefore, instead of undertaking an exhaustive recounting of all the problems encountered, this discussion focuses upon the following issues: role of pilot studies, choice and use of informants, uses of interview data, and analysis of qualitative data. The choice of these issues was guided by two main considerations: first, relevance of these issues in regard to methodological aspects of studying organizational effectiveness (more has been said about this in the introductions to the sections dedicated to each of these issues); second, desire to avoid repetition and duplication of many worthwhile discussions which already exist. Although the task of studying organizational effectiveness has certain unique features to it, many of the methodological problems encountered are common to all field studies on organizations. For example, all organizational field studies have to make choices in regard to research designs (experimental or nonexperimental), statistical techniques for data reduction and analysis, size of sample and so on. Because of the general nature of such issues, it is difficult to say anything specific about their role in relation to a particular topic such as organizational effectiveness. The manner in which they are handled in a particular study depends upon situational factors such as the orientation of the researchers, availability of resources, willingness of organizational members to cooperate, and feasibility of manipulation of variables studied. The reader will find excellent explorations of such general issues in organizational research in the works of McGrath, Mechanic, Churchman and Emery, W. R. Scott, Seashore, and Zelditch.[5]

Pilot Studies

With reference to field investigations, the term pilot study refers to an exploratory project conducted during the preliminary stage of the research. As exploratory devices, pilot studies serve many functions in social research. They can be used as final checks for fully formulated research designs in order to discover possible flaws before time and resources are committed. Pilot studies can also be used in formative stages of research designs in order to assemble information about the availability of required data, test the adequacy of research instruments, and obtain estimates of time and resources required for the study.[6]

Although the importance of pilot studies is recognized by organization theorists at the theoretical level, they have not been used sufficiently in organizational research. Students of organizational effectiveness have been particularly remiss in making use of this highly valuable exploratory device. The most common practice has been to approach organizations with fully formulated research designs and to use them as subjects for the testing of abstract theories. This has sometimes resulted in many undesirable consequences in terms of quality of research output. The literature on organizational research is replete with examples of studies which have gotten bogged down in midstream due to discovery of situational and other factors not accounted for in the original design.[7]

Experience acquired by this writer in conducting field research for the sugar industry study has led him to conclude that pilot studies are an important ingredient of a methodology for the study of organizational effectiveness. In this case, the pilot study lasted for about three to four weeks. The main activities undertaken during the pilot study consisted of exploratory interviews with sugar factory personnel, government officials, union leaders, and others associated with the sugar industry, and examination of pertinent sugar industry publications, records and documents of individual factories, and other secondary sources of data on the sugar factory complex studied.[8]

The pilot project for the sugar industry study revealed a wealth of information which proved to be crucial for the formulation of a final research design. Some of the factors which were uncovered were peculiar to the cultural-institutional environment in which the factories were located; as these have little general application, they can be neglected here.[9] The most general factors which were discovered as a result of the pilot study can be discussed under the following headings: isolation of sources of potential strain and conflict in field relations; location of sources of data on the factories studied; and testing of the efficacy of the data-gathering instruments.

Sources of Strains and Conflict
in Field Relations

Systematic study and analysis of the functioning of formal organizations frequently requires the establishment and maintenance of on-going personal relations between the researcher and members of the host organizations. If the researcher is to fully understand the intricacies of the workings of complex organizations, he needs to enlist the active support and assistance of organizational members who are familiar with the operations of the organization. He needs further to be able to communicate in meaningful terms with his subjects, be they top managers, white-collar workers, or ordinary employees.

Researchers undertaking field studies of formal organizations and other social systems frequently encounter problems and barriers in establishing rapport with organizational members. Categorizations and discussions of field relations problems commonly faced by researchers have been provided by various scholars over the years. For example, Bruyn, Dalton, Scott, and Whyte[10] have discussed in general terms the problems faced by participant observers during the course of field investigations. Delany[11] has focused upon problems faced in gaining access to formal organizations. Chris Argyris[12] has discussed the role of personality variables which underlie communication blocks leading to defensive behaviors on the part of researchers and organizational members.

Commentaries of the type mentioned above are extremely helpful to the researcher embarking upon a study of organizational effectiveness. They provide itemization and some guidelines for the handling of field-relations problems commonly faced by organizational researchers. However, such discussions do not provide the student of organizational effectiveness with a categorization of the field-relation problems peculiar to his type of study. There is a general void in the literature pertaining to the field-relations problems characteristic to studies on organizational effectiveness.

Based upon experience gathered during the field research for the sugar industry study it is suggested that a major source of potential strain in field relations in organizational effectiveness studies stems from divergence in notions of organizational success or worth held by the researcher and members of the subject organization. In this case the investigator entered the field with a list of criteria based upon studies conducted in the United States. This list of criteria was composed of "hard" productivity and efficiency measures, as well as "soft" behavioral factors such as "morale," organizational flexibility, intraorganizational strain, and styles of leadership.[13] The original proposition about effectiveness was that the factory group which performed higher in terms of these criteria was to be judged relatively more effective, that is, had greater potential for attaining survival, stability, and growth.

Even though the preliminary list of criteria had much merit in theoretical terms,[14] they proved to be unacceptable to many persons associated with the sugar industry in Maharashtra. To begin with, serious barriers were encountered in explaining the meaning of these criteria to respondents. Terms such as "morale" and organizational flexibility are controversial and difficult to explain even in English. The job of translating them in operational terms in an indigenous Indian language proved to be insurmountable.[15] Also, even in cases where the language barriers were overcome, the preliminary list of criteria did not arouse much enthusiasm among the respondents interviewed. Top ranking government officials, sugar industry executives, and others interviewed during the pilot project tended to favor more "goalistic" criteria which tapped the immediate contributions of the two organizational systems in the task of national development. This was particularly so in regard to the cooperative factories which are looked upon primarily as a means for regional development, enhancement of welfare of workers and farmers, and generation of vertical social mobility of the lower caste groups. Many respondents expressed the fear that the use of criteria which tapped productivity and long-term organizational survival potential would tend to bias the study in favor of the older and relatively more mature private companies and neglect the immediate and worthwhile contributions of the newer cooperatives in the realm of national development. In fact, most respondents (even those who favored the cooperative factories over private companies) readily conceded that the private companies were probably more effective in terms of general managerial efficiency and productivity.

The divergence in viewpoints on organizational success between the investigator and persons associated with the sugar industry produced many strains in field relations in the initial phases of the study. The most general problem faced was difficulty of gaining cooperation in the conduct of the study from top policy-makers and others associated with this industry. Many respondents hesitated to give their support to a project which they did not consider worthwhile in terms of its ultimate potential contributions towards understanding of the relative worth of the two organizational systems within the cultural and institutional environment in which they operated. Some extremely tense moments were experienced by the investigator during initial attempts to arrive at a reconciliation of differences on notions of organizational success, particularly with blue-collar workers. The author remembers vividly a few encounters with workers which ended with unpleasantness. In one instance, the investigator inadvertently antagonized a group of about ten workers by appearing to challenge some commonly held notions about cooperative organizations. These workers were shown some preliminary empirical evidence which tended to show that the cooperatives were not in fact more successful than their private counterparts in regard to regional development, promotion of welfare of workers and farmers, and other socially desirable objectives. The reaction of the workers to this was one of disbelief and hostility; they accused the investigator of being a "capitalist stooge" bent upon discrediting the "peoples' cooperative movement." In another instance, a union leader was antagonized because he felt that not enough attention was being paid in the study to the immediate problems of the rank and file workers. He tended to perceive organizational effectiveness or success largely in terms of employee enhancement and development and did not see much sense in analyzing organizational productivity and social mobility. The outcome of such encounters was frequently to lose the cooperation of persons who had potential for being valuable informants. Some even went to the extent of campaigning against the investigator with their peers and superiors.

This has sought to illustrate the nature of strains stemming from divergence in viewpoints about organizational success held by the researchers and organizational members. Although the particular manifestations of this problem in the case illustrated were no doubt influenced by the cultural, political, and other factors surrounding the factories studied, the problem is of a general nature common to investigations involving the assessment of organizational effectiveness. Notions of organizational success held by researchers are influenced by their particular set of experiences, bias and preconceptions acquired outside the organization. For example, academic researchers frequently enter the field with theoretical interests in mind. They look upon the organization as a "subject" to be used in testing their particular theories and conceptual schemes; they may or may not have an interest in the long-term success of the organization. The notions of organizational success held by organizational members, on the other hand, are determined by their particular set of experiences and relationships within the organization. Factors such as length of service, financial stake in the organization's success, nature of personal experiences and ambitions can be presumed to play a part in organizational members' notions of effectiveness.

The manner in which strains arising from divergence in viewpoints about organizational success are resolved has implications for the overall success of the study. In this respect, the researcher is posed with a dilemma. On the one hand, he has to accommodate the desires, values, and notions about effectiveness held by organizational members. Neglecting these can result in lack of cooperation and enthusiasm from the organizational members. At the same time, the investigator has to incorporate in his study criteria which are general enough to have cross applications to other organizations and situations. Otherwise, his study may have no relevance beyond the case investigated.

There is, of course, no pat solution to this problem. The point here simply is that pilot investigations provide valuable tools for uncovering sources of potential strains and conflict. The manner in which they are handled will depend upon factors such as the orientation of the researcher, his relationship with the host organization, and level of analysis.[16]

Location of Data Sources

In organizational effectiveness research the term data can be used to denote any factor which in some manner influences the functioning of the organization under consideration. This includes such diverse factors as production and inventory control figures, formal organizational rules, informal norms and values of the organizational members, and attitudes of workers towards top management. The relevant consideration is that the factor under consideration be somehow influential in the functioning (or malfunctioning) of the organization under consideration.[17]

In a study dealing with organizational effectiveness it is quite unlikely that the researcher will be concerned with analyzing all the factors which have a bearing on organizational functioning. The criteria of effectiveness used provide the main guide for discriminating among the various factors or variables encountered. The selected criteria become the dependent variables; the research task involves isolating, analyzing, and measuring the factors associated with the criteria of effectiveness.

The amount of success attained in formulating and executing a research design depends largely upon the availability of required data for conducting the analysis. In this respect, it is suggested that pilot studies are an invaluable tool for the location of data sources. Although this point is obvious, it is frequently ignored by organizational researchers. All too often researchers go into the field making blanket assumptions about the availability or nonavailability of data on organizational functioning. This was a mistake made by this writer in conducting the sugar industry study. Because of factors such as India being an "underdeveloped" country, the predominantly rural location of sugar factories, and diversity of languages, it was assumed that reliable data on the functioning of sugar factories would not be available. It was, therefore, assumed that data would have to be "generated" by relying upon judgment of experts and other commonly used data-generating devices. The pilot project was instrumental in destroying these preconceptions and plans. Interviews with top-level sugar industry executives and other informants helped locate fairly sophisticated and usable data pertinent to the dimensions investigated in the study. For example, yearbooks published by the Sugar Technologists Association at Kanpur provided extensive productivity and efficiency data for about 90 per cent of the sugar factories in the nation. Individual factory records and governmental commission reports contained a wealth of information on labor relations, social backgrounds of sugar factory executives and leaders, and other subjects pertinent to the study. Secondary data of this type were supplemented by "first-hand" data gathered from interviews and questionnaires constructed during the field study.[18]

Systematic and deliberate explorations for data sources can add greatly to the quality of research on organizational effectiveness. The greatest benefit that such activity can yield is the uncovering of "hard" data on productivity, efficiency, individual-organizational transactions, and other dimensions commonly investigated in organizational effectiveness studies. This can aid in reducing reliance on judgments of experts, opinions of employees, and other "subjective" measures which are commonly used as substitutes for actual data. Another related benefit which pilot explorations for data can potentially yield is the widening of the types of data used in assessing effectiveness. The reference here is to almost complete faith placed in data acquired through interviews on the basis of structured questionnaires in recent studies on organizational effectiveness. More is said about this in a later section of this paper.

Efficacy of Data-Gathering Instruments

The types of data-gathering strategy used in a research situation is determined largely by the nature of data sought by the investigator. Strategy for gathering historical and other types of secondary data involves deliberate and systematic examination of sources such as organizational records, community and governmental publications, and industry documents. Frequently, it becomes essential to gather "first-hand" data, that is, data that is not "ready-made" or existing in printed form. These data commonly pertain to organizational processes relating to employee-organizational relations, political structures, attitudes and sentiments of workers, and so on. Such data are commonly gathered through interviews, observation, and other relatively "subjective" methods.

Pilot studies can be a valuable tool for judging the potential usefulness of data-gathering instruments and strategies. In the sugar industry study, the initial strategy for gathering "first-hand" data was composed of interviews on the basis of a structured questionnaire. This questionnaire contained a set of structured and scaled questions organized to elicit information on factors such as efficiency, intraorganizational strain, and "morale" derived from the original list of criteria of effectiveness.[19]

Exploratory interviews conducted during the pilot study revealed that the above strategy was unsuitable. A major problem, as revealed earlier, was difficulty of communication due to linguistic barriers. Also, the content of the questionnaire lost its relevance due to changes made in the criteria of effectiveness used. Furthermore, it was discovered that direct questioning on the basis of structured qeustions tended to produce dubious answers. The sugar factories in India are deeply immersed in politics; sugar factory personnel therefore tended to "close up" or give "pleasing answers" when questioned directly about their relations with their factories, their bosses, fellow employees, and other touchy matters.

As a result of experience gathered from the pilot study, it was decided to discard the preliminary structured questionnaire. Instead, a semi-structured instrument was devised which permitted relatively "open-ended" discussions and interaction. This questionnaire is illustrated and discussed in the section on uses of interview data below.

In general, the pilot study was responsible for some major changes in the design of the sugar industry study. It did not, of course, "solve" all the problems encountered in field relations and methods. However, it did uncover some major shortcomings in the original design and paved the way for construction of a research design and strategy which suited the circumstances of the investigation.

Informants in Organizational Effectiveness Research

In a broad literal sense, an informant is anybody who gives information to the researcher about the culture, group, or organization studied. This term, however, has a more limited and specific meaning in social research. In social research the term informant refers to ". . . an articulate member of the studied culture who enters into a more or less personal relationship with the investigator for a relatively long period of time."[20]

Informants have played an important part in organizational research. They have been a prime source of data in field studies on organizations conducted by Blau, Dalton, Lipset et al, Whyte,[21] and other social scientists. The importance of informants in organizational research stems from the complex nature of formal organizations. Researchers need to establish personal relations with "insiders" in order to be able to dissect the complex network of behavioral, structural, and other variables which comprise the concrete structure of formal organizations. Information about latent activities and interactions, covert practices and "deals," and informal rules and norms which govern organizational life can only be acquired from informants on the basis of long-term personal relations.

Although the importance of informants in organizational and other types of sociological research has been commonly recognized, little has thus far been done to provide guidelines for selection and use of informants. Using experience gained from the sugar industry study, the following discussion focuses upon two topics of particular concern to organizational researchers: potential informants, and profiles or characteristics of valuable informants.

Potential Informants

In a study dealing with organizational effectiveness, an informant may be defined as any person who is capable of providing data on the functioning of the organization under study. Defined broadly in these terms, the list of potential informants includes organizational members of various ranks, clients, customers, competitors, officials, and ordinary workers of governmental agencies, unions, and other organizations which have dealings with the subject organization.

As to which of the above mentioned groups will be contacted in a particular study will depend upon factors such as the criteria of effectiveness utilized, interests and orientation of the researcher, and level of analysis. It is important to emphasize, however, that the population of potential informants in organizational effectiveness research is extremely large and diverse. Quite frequently, researchers get themselves involved and stay with a particular sub-group related to the organization and thus fail to avail themselves of valuable data which lies dormant in the hands of persons who are not commonly available or are not part of the "formal" organization chart. This mistake was made by this writer during the preliminary phases of the sugar industry study. A preponderant amount of time was spent initially with employees and executives of the sugar factories visited. The moment of enlightment for this writer came after reviewing the contents of chance interviews with a government excise agent and a leader of a leftist labor union. Neither of those gentlemen were found in any particular spot within any particular factory. Rather, they dealt with the sugar factory complex within the district as a whole and came into contact with persons of all ranks associated with the factories. Their jobs exposed them to all phases of the sugar industry, including its "seamy" side. Both of these informants proved to be highly rich sources of data on the political processes within sugar factories, government-industry relations, union-management relations, and other issues relating to the overall functioning of the two organizational groups studied. Furthermore, they opened vistas for further investigation by directing the investigator's attention to the value of outside informants as sources of information of the factories investigated.

Profiles of Informants

Commentaries found in the literature pertaining to characteristics of desirable informants have taken the form of descriptions of informants found useful by scholars who have had the occasion to use such persons in their field work. Whyte recommends the use of persons who have observed significant events and are perceptive and reflective about their experiences. Such persons usually occupy important formal and informal positions within organizations.[22]

Dalton prefers to look upon his informants as "intimates" and "confidants." His idea of ideal informants are persons who:

> . . . (1) trusted me; (2) freely gave me information about their problems and fears and frankly tried to explain their own motivations; (3) had shown repeatedly that they could be counted on not to jeopardize the study; (4) accepted what I was able to tell them and refrained from prying into the information I was getting from others; and (5) gave me knowledge and aid (warnings, guidance, "tips") of the kind that, if known, would have endangered their careeers.[23]

Sjoberg recommends the use of "marginal men" as informants. A marginal man is defined as ". . . one who does not conform to, or adheres only partially to, the institutional expectations of the reference group in question." There are two principal types of marginal men:

> . . . (1) the deviant and/or maladjusted person who is either an "outcast" or is partially ostracized by other members of the social order; and (2) the marginal but highly organized and stable individual who, because he does not fully accept the definitions of any one role, serves as a link between systems or between various subgroups within a system.[24]

Back uses the term "sources" to describe informants, thus equalizing them with other sources of information such as documents. On the basis of test results and background information on informants used by the

U.S. Air Force in Germany and Japan, Back has isolated qualities of desirable informants: "(1) knowledgeability, (2) physical exposure to topics of interest, (3) effective exposure of interest in relevant topics, (4) perceptual abilities, (5) availability of information, (6) and motivation."[25]

The above discussion has presented profiles of informants used by various scholars in their field work on organizations. To this list this writer would like to add another type of informant: the cosmopolitan or a professional who is "low" on loyalty to the employing organization, high on commitment to specialized role skills, and likely to use an outer reference group orientation.[26] It is contended here that the cosmopolitan, as defined above, makes an exceptionally valuable informant in research dealing with organizational functioning and effectiveness. This contention stems from certain experiences gained during the field work for the sugar industry study. In this study, 145 persons were interviewed over a five-month period; this group consisted of sugar industry personnel of various ranks and others associated with the sugar industry (Table 2). From this group, the investigator leaned most heavily upon about fifteen

TABLE 2
Informants interviewed during the field study.

Positions	Number interviewed
Directors	20
Administrative	9
Accountants*	11
Agricultural Officers*	8
Chemists*	18
Engineers*	11
Labor Officers*	3
Clerical	14
Manual	41
Others†	10
	145

*Although the jobs of these informants were primarily professional or "staff" in nature, they usually performed administrative or "line" functions within their own departments and participated in organizational policy-formulation and decision-making.

†This category included civil engineers, medical officers, factory school teachers, union leaders, and other persons who were not commonly included in the factory organization chart.

*Summarized from Ghorpade, 1968, p. 126.

individuals who roughly fitted the description of cosmopolitans given above. These men were "top-notch" experts occupying key professional positions such as factory manager, chief engineer, chief chemist, and administrative officer. They belonged to and regularly attended meetings of professional associations of sugar technologists and administrators. All had read papers at professional meetings and some had even published scholarly articles and monographs in professional journals. All had changed jobs at least three times during the course of their careers; most had the experience of working for both joint stock as well as cooperative factories. They exhibited little "loyalty" to their employing organizations in the sense that their first commitment was to their jobs and professions rather than to any one sugar factory. They perceived themselves as "sugar technologists" and administrators rather than employees of any one factory.

The small group of cosmopolitan informants was found to be an exceptionally valuable source of data on the sugar industry as well as individual factories. To begin with, these men were willing to "speak out" and to delve into issues which the ordinary informant was reluctant to discuss. Because of governmental involvement in the operations of the sugar industry and other factors, the sugar factories were deeply immersed in politics.[27] Due to the resultant tenseness, suspicion, and even fear among sugar factory personnel, it was difficult to engage them in discussions about political process, internal relations, and other pertinent issues. Open and frank discussions were thus possible generally with cosmopolitan informants. This was because these men were not dependent upon any one employer for their livelihood; their professional reputation gave them a mobility which was lacking on the part of ordinary informants. Also, the cosmopolitan informants were a rich source of data on the operations of the sugar industry and technology. The professional expertise and knowledge of these men enabled them to provide the investigator with expert analysis of the workings of sugar factories. Furthermore, cosmo-politan informants were prime sources of data on the workings of individual factories. Having worked for several sugar factories during their careers and lacking "loyalty" to any one particular organization, they were able to clinically dissect the workings of their employing factories in a detached and objective manner.

The above discussion has sought to make a case for the use of cosmopolitans as informants in organizational effectiveness research. The manner in which the essentially cosmopolitan traits of professional orienta-tion, low loyalty to the employing organization, and outer group reference make the cosmopolitan a worthwhile informant was demonstrated by reference to field experience gained in the sugar industry study.

Uses of Interview Data in Organizational Effectiveness Research

An interview has been aptly described as a "conversation with a purpose." A research interview may be defined as a "two person conversation that is initiated by the interviewer for the specific purpose of obtaining information that is relevant to research."[28]

Interviews have been widely used for data-gathering in organizational research. A vast number of the field studies on organizations have either explicitly or implicitly made use of data gathered from interviews with organizational spokesmen, rank and file employees, experts and others associated with the organizations studied.[29]

Interviews comprised a major source of data of the sugar industry study. As revealed earlier, the initial interviews were conducted in terms of a structured questionnaire: this instrument was abandoned after the pilot study in favor of the relatively less structured questionnaire illustrated on p. 227.

The interviews conducted during the field study provided the investigator with a wealth of substantive information about the factories studied. They also shed some light on the methodological aspects of interviewing in organizational effectiveness. The following discussion comments briefly upon two issues: question formulation, and validity of qualitative judgments expressed by respondents on the functioning of the two organizational groups.

Question Formulation: Global Versus Specific Questions

Many factors influence the quality and usefulness of data gathered from interviews. One of the most important factors underlying success at interviewing is the format of the questionnaire, that is, the manner in which the questions are formulated, organized, and worded. An important choice facing the interviewer pertains to the degree of specificity of the questions asked: Should the interviewer ask global questions which require the respondents to generalize about the issue investigated? Or should he ask specific questions focusing upon details about the issue investigated? Global questions tend to be relatively "open-ended" giving the respondents opportunity to interject their personal viewpoints, interpretations and opinions. Specific questions, on the other hand, tend to be relatively "closed," restricting the answers of the respondents to particular details. Many times, specific questions are designed to provide respondents with a fixed number of alternative answers.[30]

Global as well as specific questions have been used widely in a variety of organizational studies. At one time there was a tendency to view these two types of questions as absolute alternatives, i.e., use either specific or global questions. It is now being realized, however, that both types of questions have legitimate places in organizational research; they merely serve different functions by generating different types of data.[31] The interviewing experience acquired from the sugar industry study tends to confirm this newer viewpoint on the role of these two types of questions in organizational research. In general, it was discovered that the relative usefulness of global and specific questions was dependent upon two main considerations: stage of the study, and characteristics of the respondents.

After the abandonment of the structured questionnaire used in the pilot study, respondents were asked global questions which permitted them considerable amount of latitude in discussing the issues involved (see questionnaire, particularly questions 1 and 3). These questions elicited a wealth of general information on factors such as notions of factory success held by respondents, their orientation to the two organizational groups, and other matters. Such information was crucial in developing criteria of organizational effectiveness and in designing further research strategies. As the study progressed, however, global questions began to be less and less useful. Their most general limitation was that they did not yield much "factual" data on the functioning of the two organizational groups. Barring responses given by cosmopolitan informants and a few others, global questions tended to elicit largely subjective data on feelings, attitudes, and sentiments. In order to avoid ending up with a meaningless "head count," therefore, it became essential as the study progressed to focus upon specific questions. Although all three of the questions in the instrument used were consistently asked, emphasis was placed in the later phases of the study on question 2.

The relative usefulness of global and specific questions tended also to vary with the characteristics of the respondents, that is, their educational backgrounds, positions within the organizations, years and quality of professional experience, and so on. In general, global questions yielded richer data from persons who occupied top-level managerial positions, had a college education, and possessed about five or so years of experience in managerial and administrative positions. Such persons were frequently able to use global questions as a basis for entering into enlightening discussions about the overall functioning of the factories studied as well as provide concrete information on particular issues. Global questions, however, proved to be less fruitful when interviewing blue-collar workers and even clerical personnel. At this level, the standard reaction to the

Questionnaire

1. As a worker (or officer) of this factory, what are some of the rewards and frustrations of your job?

2. Please comment upon the dynamics of the following in this organization and other sugar factories that you have worked for in the past:
   a. recruitment
   b. selection
   c. placement
   d. training
   e. decision-making
   f. coordination
   g. compensation
   h. leadership
   i. efficiency
   j. other

3. As you know, the sugar industry is composed of two types of organizations — private companies and cooperatives. Which of these two organizational types do you prefer and why?

first question in the questionnaire was expressions of dissatisfaction with pay, working conditions, and lack of opportunity for advancement in both organizational groups. The common reaction to the third question was expression of the belief that the cooperatives were somehow "better" or more "worthwhile" than the private companies. Informants at this level had to be posed with highly specific questions in matters pertaining to organizational relations and functioning (question 2). Even then the answers received were frequently in the form of yes or no, better or worse, higher or lower. Attempts to engage lower level workers in open-ended discussions were frequently frustrating and unrewarding.

Qualitative Judgments as Measures of Organizational Performance

Organizational members have provided social scientists with a variety of data on their employing organizations. Perhaps the most common type of data supplied by organizational members to academic researchers pertains to the dynamics of relationships underlying employee-organizational relations. Beginning with the now famous Hawthorne Experiments, researchers have accumulated volumes of data on employee reactions to different supervisory styles, job designs, authority structures, incentive schemes and a host of other issues. Such data have been commonly used to judge worker "morale," job satisfaction, worthwhileness of the company as a proper "environment" for individual growth and development and related topics. Organizational members have also furnished information on less personal issues such as organization-society relations and union-management contracts.[32]

In recent years organizational members have been relied upon increasingly as "judges" in rating the performance of their organizations. Because of difficulties encountered ni formulating valid and reliable quantitative measures of organizational outputs, social scientists have used judgments of top officials and experts as substitutes for physical measures of output, This practice has recently been followed in a variety of studies dealing with hospitals, delivery service, small business operations and other formal organizations.[33]

In spite of the practical attractions of qualitative judgments in studying organizational effectiveness, such measures are looked upon with skepticism by many social scientists. The major criticism against the use of such measures is that there is no basis for checking their validity and reliability. It is argued that if physical or "hard" measures of organizational outputs are available, then the use of qualitative judgments is redundant. On the other hand, if physical measures are not available it is impossible to verify the dimensions actually being measured by qualitative judgments.[34]

The results of the interview data of the sugar industry study provide a strong case against the use of qualitative judgments as primary data or as substitutes for actual criteria of organizational effectiveness. In this case, an analysis of the qualitative judgments or opinions expressed by the respondents interviewed about the relative effectiveness of the two organizational groups in terms of the criteria utilized revealed the following. A vast majority, over 90 per cent of the respondents rated the private companies to be more "efficient" than the cooperative factories; approximately 70 per cent indicated that the cooperatives did more for their workers than the private companies; and about 80 per cent rated the cooperative system as being more effective than the private companies in dispersing economic power and generating the vertical mobility of the "common man." These ratings cut across organizational as well as occupational lines:　blue-collar and white-collar workers as well as managerial personnel in private companies and cooperatives tended to perceive the two competing systems in the above terms. It needs to be confessed that even the investigator held the same beliefs prior to data-gathering and analysis.

It is interesting to report that the empirical results of the study confounded the expectations and ratings of the respondents on nearly every count. As regards operating efficiency, the private companies' performance was slightly better than the cooperative factories in terms of the two indices of efficiency utilized: sugar losses and work-hour losses over a four-year period—1961 to 1964 (see Table 3). However, the differences were not statistically significant.[35] This finding does not necessarily enable us to conclude in definitive terms that private and cooperative sugar enterprises operate at the same level of efficiency; the size of the sample, age differences among the organizational groups and other intervening variables stand as barriers in arriving at hard conclusions.[36] The results do, however, cast some doubts on the viewpoint held by many respondents or "judges" that the private companies were more efficient than the cooperative factories.

As regards employee-organizational relationships, the empirical results of the study again contradicted the judgments of the respondents. It was

TABLE 3
Comparative analysis of sugar losses and work hour losses
(Mann-Whitney U Test).

	Sugar losses Sum of ranks*	Work hour losses Sum of ranks*
Joint Stock Companies (n = 12)	125.5	118.0
Cooperatives (n = 12)	174.5	182.0
U Values†	48	40

*Derived by summing ranks of factories within each group in composite rankings of all factories included in the comparison.

†Critical values of U for a two tailed test of significance (n_1 = 12; n_2 = 12):

U values	Significance level
U = 31	P = .02
37	.05
42	.10

Source: *Sidney Siegel, Non-parametric Statistics for the Behavioral Sciences* (New York: McGraw-Hill Book Co., 1956), pp. 274-77.

discovered that wages and other direct financial rewards paid by the two organizational groups were quite standard—both organizational groups were required to adhere to minimum wages established by the government. Neither group exceeded the minimum required by official government policy. At the time of the study, the private companies actually provided a larger package of "fringe benefits" or indirect compensation to their employees than the cooperative group (Table 4). This was passed-off by proponents of the cooperative system as arising due to the newness of the cooperatives, and used by persons within the private sector to defend the "free-enterprise system."

The results pertaining to dispersal of power or social mobility are the most fascinating of all. The notion that the cooperative system is best suited for dispersing economic power and concomitantly promoting the upward mobility of the "common man" is deeply entrenched in India. It forms the basis of official industrial policy and is used widely by the Indian government for giving preference to cooperative enterprises over private companies in matters pertaining to licensing, financial assistance, and sponsorship. The study of mobility in this case was approached by analyzing the caste and ancestral occupations of the proprietors of all

TABLE 4
Indirect compensation paid by Maharashtrian sugar factories, 1960.

	Joint stock companies	Cooperatives
RENT-FREE HOUSING		
Number Providing	13	13
Workers Covered (per cent of labor force)	26.4	10.3
MEDICAL BENEFITS		
Dispensaries (number providing)	13	13
Workers Treated (daily average)	2,000	800
Hospitals (number providing)	6	0
Workers Treated (daily average)	150	0
EDUCATIONAL BENEFITS		
Montessori Schools	1	1
Primary Schools	13	9
Middle Schools	9	2
High Schools	9	4
Beneficiaries (approximate annual)	11,802	1,895

the private companies within the state and boards of directors of six cooperative sugar factories. It was hypothesized that if the commonly held notions were true, then the control of the private companies would be found to rest in the hands of caste groups who have traditionally dominated modern industry in India, that is, the merchant or business caste,[37] and the control of the cooperatives would be found to rest in the hands of the "common people" or the caste groups which comprised the lower strata of traditional village society (Table 5, divisions IV, V, VI). The results of the empirical study are presented in summary form in Table 6. In general, these data lend support to the first half of the hypothesis stated above—the private companies were owned and controlled predominately by the business castes. However, the data raise questions about the second half of the hypothesis. Only about 21 per cent of the cooperative directors were found to be members of caste-cum-occupational groups which traditionally comprised the lower strata of Indian society. A vast majority of the cooperative directors (67.2 per cent) were from families and castes whose ancestral occupations were concerned with land ownership, village government, and other feudal positions. These findings were interpreted to mean that the cooperatives brought about a horizontal rather than downward dispersal of economic power. Rather than perpetuate and enhance the economic hold of the business castes (Table 5, division III) that dominate industrial enterprise at the national level,[38] the cooperate sugar factories facilitated the entry and participation in modern industry of caste groups that had traditionally been identified with ruling and land ownership (Table 5, division I). The "common man" (Table 5, divisions IV, V, VI) was found to have little influence or "say-so" in the operations of either organizational system.

Returning to the methodological implications, the findings of this study present a case against the use of qualitative judgments of experts or informants as substitutes for actual measures of organizational performance. In this case, exclusive reliance upon judgments of the informants interviewed would have produced entirely different (and perhaps misleading) results than those revealed by empirical investigation. The results of any one study, however, cannot be sufficient to recommend courses of action for researchers working in different situations and with alternative orientations. Many times, it is not possible to devise actual or "hard" measures of effectiveness, and use of qualitative judgments may be the only course of action open. Rather than reject completely this method, therefore, perhaps it may be worthwhile to use such measures in conjunction with other types of measures. Alternatively, it may be feasible to devise statistical techniques for isolating contaminating factors arising from the judges' personality traits, habitual response sets,

TABLE 5
Social structure of traditional Indian village society.

A	B	C	D	E			F
Caste* divisions	Names of† castes	Traditional† occupations	Population†† (% village population)	Rank criteria and rankings			Overall power and influence in village affairs
				Varna status	Property ownership	Occupational prestige	
I. Dominant Castes	Rajputs Patidars Jats Marathas	Ruling, Landlords Administration Gentlemen Farmers Village Headmen	10-15	High (Kshatriya)	Very High	Very High	Very High
II. Brahmin Castes	Deshastha Saraswat Rarhi Nagar	Priests, Teachers Doctors, Lawyers Astrologers Accountants	5-10	Very High (Brahmin)	Medium	Very High	High
III. Business Castes	Baniya Marwadi Jain Pharsee	Merchants, Traders Shop-Keepers Money-Lenders Brokers	5-10	Medium (Vaisha)	High	Medium	Medium-High

Division	Caste (column B)	Occupation (column C)	Population %				
IV. Farming Castes	Kunbhi, Mali, Khati	Soldiers, Gardeners, Cultivators	25-30	Medium (Pseudo-Kshatriya)	Low	Medium	Low-Medium
V. Service Castes	Shimpi, Sutar, Nhavi, Lohar, Kumbhar, Telli, Parit	Tailors, Carpenters, Barbers, Blacksmiths, Potters, Oil Pressers, Laundrymen	20-25	Low (Vaisha-Shudra)	Low	Low	Low
VI. Harijan Castes	Mahar, Bhangi	Tanners, Sweepers, Laborers	5-10	Very Low (Shudra)	Very Low	Very Low	Very Low

*All the castes included in these divisions (column B) were not necessarily present in any one region of the country. Column B lists some of the most prominent and/or commonly found castes in northern regions. The listing of castes presented is not exhaustive; for more elaborate inventory of castes, see Hutton, 1961.

†The correspondence between castes and occupations was most pronounced in division V, service castes; the occupations listed in column C (parallel to division V, column A) are literal English translations of caste names listed in division V, column B. In all other cases, the castes listed in column B practiced one or more of the corresponding occupations listed in column C. Castes normally did not cross the occupational boundaries of other castes, except in the case of agriculture, which was open to all castes.

††Population percentages were based upon rough estimates provided by informants consulted during the field study; they represent proportions of village population composed of local representatives of the castes listed in column B.

TABLE 6

Caste and ancestral occupational backgrounds: Proprietors of fourteen joint stock companies, directors of six cooperative sugar factories, Maharashtra State, India.

		Joint stock company proprietors (n = 10) (per cent)	Cooperative factory directors (n = 67) (per cent)
Caste:	Maratha	10.0	56.7
	Brahmin	20.0	3.0
	Business Castes	60.0	19.4
	Kunbhi, Mali	10.0	17.9
	Service Castes	0.0	3.0
	Harijan	0.0	0.0
		100.0	100.0
Ancestral Occupation*			
	Chieftains, Landlords	10.0	67.2
	Brahmanic Professions	20.0	0.0
	Business, Money-lending	60.0	11.9
	Cultivation and Allied	10.0	17.9
	Services	0.0	3.0
	Menial Occupations	0.0	0.0
		100.0	100.0

*The term "ancestral occupation" refers to occupations followed by the individual's family over several generations.

and situational variables. A useful beginning in this respect has been made by Klein, Berkowitz, and Malone.[39]

Analysis of Qualitative Data

The types of problems faced in analyzing data are frequently determined by the research design used in the study. Relatively "tight" research designs such as experiments and structured questionnaire surveys invariably yield quantitative data which lend themselves to analysis with the use of conventional statistical and other quantitative techniques. The problem of data analysis, however, becomes progressively more difficult with the "looseness" of the research design. For example, relatively "open-ended" or loosely structured field studies frequently yield various types of qualitative data such as observational accounts of events, incidents, and interactions, conversations with informants and historical and other types of documents. Such data cannot be easily analyzed through the use of conventional statistical and other quantitative techniques; they require novel techniques and methods for their analysis.

Based upon experience gathered from the sugar industry study and other organizational studies found in the literature, it is contended here that the problem of dealing with qualitative data is an essential ingredient of a methodology for the study of organizational effectiveness and functioning. This is so primarily for two main reasons. First, it is generally not possible to use experimental and other types of "tight" research designs in studying organizational effectiveness. Factors such as the large size of formal organizations, complexity of their operations and resistance of organizational members to outsiders invariably stand in the way of systematic experimentation under controlled conditions. A vast majority of organizational field studies have, therefore, been conducted by the use of observational and other types of relatively "loose" research designs.[40] Second, organizational studies frequently undergo changes and reconstructions in their original study designs due to factors such as discovery of alternative hypothesis, changes in the subject organization during the course of the investigation, and alterations in the relationships between the researcher and organizational leaders and members.[41] Reconstructions of research designs are frequently accompanied by the accumulation of qualitative materials and data.

Qualitative data have been viewed historically with scepticism and distrust by many social scientists. A common attitude has been to look upon such data as preliminary materials for more rigorous explorations based upon quantitative methods and techniques. This viewpoint, however, is now being challenged. Some social scientists have now begun to advance the argument that rather than being preliminary materials for more rigorous analysis, qualitative data should be looked upon as an end-product in certain situations. The main arguments favoring this viewpoint are summarized by Glaser and Strauss:

> To view qualitative research as merely preliminary to quantitative research neglects, hence underestimates, several important facts about qualitative analysis. First, it is more often than not the end product of research within a substantive area beyond which few, if any, researchers are motivated to move. Second, qualitative research is often the most "adequate" and "efficient" method for obtaining the type of information required and for contending with the difficulties of an empirical research situation. . . . Third, sociologists (and informed laymen) manage often to profit quite well in their everyday work life from analysis based on qualitative research.[42]

The emerging change in attitudes towards qualitative data has been accompanied by the advancement of newer conceptual schemes, tools, and techniques suitable for analysis of such data.[43] At the conceptual level, special mention needs to be made of the works of Glaser, and Barton and Anderson.[44] Based upon his experiences in conducting field investigations in hospital situations, Glaser has advanced a new approach for handling qualitative data, called the "Constant Comparative Method of Qualitative Analysis."[45] This method can be described in four stages: (1) comparing incidents applicable to each category—pertinent incidents in the data are coded into as many categories of analysis as possible; (2) integrating categories and their properties: as coding continues, the constant comparative units change from comparison of incident with incident to incident with properties of the category which resulted from initial comparison of incidents—this step forms the basis for integration, theory formulation and broad conceptualization; (3) delimiting the theory: paring down and reducing theory and categories; (4) writing the theory.[46] The Constant Comparative Method has been used successfully by Glaser and his colleagues in hospital studies dealing with awareness of dying by patients suffering from terminal diseases and related areas. It provides a means for reducing and quantifying qualitative data as well as generating theoretical propositions and ideas.

Another interesting and pathbreaking attempt at formalizing qualitative data is evident in a study by Barton and Anderson.[47] In this case, the authors used data provided by McCleery's study of prison management.[48] This monograph consisted of qualitative descriptions of changes in the relationships of various prison groups as a result of changes in policies over a period of time. By utilizing McCleery's qualitative descriptions of changes in prison relationships, Barton and Anderson show how qualitative data can be used to depict the system aspect of organizations in empirical research. Casual relationships were depicted in the form of input-output flow charts and other pictorial diagrams. Relevent variables were then "quantified" and used as basis for describing various networks of relationships and changes over a period of time.

Along with the formulation of conceptual approaches of the type described above, social scientists have recently been experimenting with a variety of techniques and tools for analysis of qualitative data. The most commonly used method for dealing with qualitative data is content analysis. This method enables objective, systematic and quantitative description of variety of qualitative materials such as verbal communications, documents, newspapers, and intelligence reports.[49] Content analysis relies upon a variety of mathematical and descriptive techniques for the analysis of qualitative materials; the range here is from elaborate statistical and factor analytic methods to simple descriptive flow charts and diagrams. The technology used ranges from manual card-sorting procedures to computerized programs for coding and sorting qualitative materials.

Content analysis was used originally in research dealing with mass media communication and military intelligence reports. It has recently been gaining acceptance in sociological research and has been used in studies dealing with the motivation to achieve, analysis of grand cultural changes over millennia, and transmission of knowledge and culture among ancient civilizations.[50] Content analysis has not as yet been used extensively in organizational research. One example of how content analysis can be used in organizational research for dealing with qualitative data is provided by a study done by Friedlander and Walton which dealt with motivation of scientists in a research agency of the U.S. Navy.[51] In this study, eighty-two scientists were interviewed in an open-ended fashion on their motivation for working within the research agency. The answers received from the scientists were transcribed verbatim and were analyzed in terms of categories developed after the survey was completed. The categories utilized permitted a test of two hypotheses derived from Herzberg's motivation-hygiene theory.

1.   J. V. Ghorpade, "Study of Relative Effectiveness of Joint Stock and Cooperative Sugar Factories located in Maharashtra, India," (Ph.D. diss., University of California, Los Angeles, 1968).

2.   Details about operationalization of these criteria and the techniques used in assessing effectiveness are presented in Ghorpade, ibid., pp. 107–213.

3.   Ghorpade, ibid., pp. 107–36.

4.   Discussion of major methodological problems encountered in conducting the sugar industry study is presented in Ghorpade, ibid., pp. 107–36.

5.   Joseph E. McGrath, "Toward a 'Theory of Method' for Research on Organizations," in *New Perspectives in Organization Research*, ed. W. W. Cooper, H. J. Leavitt, and W. M. Shelly (New York: John Wiley & Sons, 1964), pp. 533–56; David Mechanic, "Some Considerations in the Methodology of Organizational Studies," in *The Social Sciences of Organizations*, ed. H. J. Leavitt (Englewood Cliffs, N.J.: Prentice-Hall, 1963), pp. 137–82; C. West Churchman and F. E. Emory, "On Various Approaches to the Study of Organizations," in *Operational Research and the Social Sciences*, ed. J. R. Lawrence (London: Tavistock Publications, 1966), pp. 77–84; W. R. Scott, "Field Methods in the Study of an Organization," in *Handbook of Organizations*, ed. J. G. March (Skokie, Ill.: Rand McNally & Co., 1965), pp. 261–304; Stanley E. Seashore, "Field Experiments with Organizations," *Human Organization* 23(1962): 164–70; M. Zelditch, "Some Methodological Problems of Field Studies," *Amer. J. Sociol.* 67(1962): 566–76.

6.   Julius Gould and W. L. Kolb, eds., *A Dictionary of the Social Sciences* (New York: Free Press, 1964).

7.   Daniel Katz and Robert L. Kahn, *The Sociology of Organizations* (New York: John Wiley & Sons, 1966).

8.   Ghorpade, op. cit., pp. 120–22.

9. Ibid.

10. Severin T. Bruyn, *The Human Perspective in Sociology: The Methodology of Participant Observation* (Englewood Cliffs, N.J.: Prentice-Hall, 1966); Melville Dalton, "Preconceptions and Methods in Men Who Manage," in *Sociologists at Work,* ed. P. E. Hammond (New York: Basic Books, 1964), pp. 50–95; W. R. Scott, "Field Work in a Formal Organization," *Human Organization* 22(1963): pp. 162–68; W. F. Whyte, "Observational Field Work Methods," in Marie Jahoda et al., *Research Methods in Social Relation,* vol. 2 (New York: Holt, Rinehart & Winston, 1951), pp. 493–513.

11. William Delany, "Some Field Notes on the Problem of Access in Organizational Research," *Admin. Sci. Quart.* 5 (1960): 448–57.

12. Chris Argyris, "Diagnosing Defenses Against Outsiders," *J. Soc. Issues* 8(1952): 24–34.

13. Ghorpade, op. cit., pp. 120–22.

14. Theoretical rationale for the use of such criteria of effectiveness is provided in B. S. Georgopoulos and A. S. Tannenbaum, "A Study of Organizational Effectiveness," *Amer. Sociol. Rev.* 22 (1957): 534–40; and Stanley E. Seashore, "Criteria of Organizational Effectiveness," *Michigan Bus. Rev.* 17(1965): 26–30.

15. Ghorpade, op. cit., pp. 120–22.

16. Some alternative solutions for such problems are discussed in abstract terms by Churchman and Emery, op. cit., 1966.

17. The definition of data utilized here corresponds roughly to the definition of organizational "parts" provided by social systems theorists. See W. G. Scott, "Organization Theory: An Overview and an Appraisal," *J. Acad. Manage.* 4 (1961): 7–26.

18. Ghorpade, op. cit., pp. 107–13.

19. Ibid., pp. 120–22.

20. Alfred C. Krober, ed., *Anthropology Today: An Encyclopedic Inventory* (Chicago: University of Chicago Press, 1953), p. 443.

21. Peter M. Blau, *The Dynamics of Bureaucracy* (Chicago: University of Chicago Press, 1955); Melville Dalton, *Men Who Manage* (New York: John Wiley & Sons, 1959); Seymour M. Lipset, M. A. Trow, and James S. Coleman, *Union Democracy* (New York: Free Press, 1956); William F. Whyte, *Street Corner Society* (Chicago: University of Chicago Press, 1955).

22. William F. Whyte, "Interviewing in Field Research," in *Human Organization Research,* ed. R. N. Adams and J. J. Preiss (Homewood, Ill.: Dorsey Press, 1960), p. 358.

23. Melville Dalton, "Preconceptions and Methods in Men Who Manage," pp. 65–66.

24. Gideon Sjoberg, "The Interviewee as a Marginal Man," *Southwestern Soc. Sci. Quart.* 38(1957): 124–32.

25. K. W. Back, "The Well-Informed Informant," *Human Organization* 14(1956): 30–33.

26. This definition of a cosmopolitan has been provided by A. W. Gouldner, "Cosmopolitans and Locals," *Admin. Sci. Quart.* 2 (1957): 282–92. Of the three traits listed in this definition, that of loyalty has caused some confusion and debate. The phrase "low on loyalty to the employing organization" is sometimes interpreted as "disloyalty," which tends to offend the formal professional norms of managers and executives in Western nations. It needs to be noted that Gouldner used this term in a special sense to describe the conflict experienced by professionals in relation to commitment to their professions versus commitment to their employing organizations. In Gouldner's writings, the opposite of "loyalty" is not "disloyalty," but rather

"(1) a willingness to limit or relinquish the commitment to a specialized professional task and (2) a dominant career orientation to the employing organization as a reference group" (Ibid., p. 291). It is in this sense that the term "loyalty" is used in this paper. (For an empirical investigation of loyalty, see Lionel S. Lewis, "On Prestige and Loyalty of University Faculty," *Admin. Sci. Quart.* 11 (1967): 629–42.

27. Ghorpade, op. cit., pp. 107–36.

28. Robert L. Kahn and Charles F. Cannell, "Interviewing," *Encyclopedia of the Social Sciences* (New York: Macmillan Co., 1968), p. 149.

29. W. R. Scott, op. cit., 1965; Adams and Preiss, op. cit., pp. 41–123; Phillip E. Hammond, ed., *Sociologists at Work* (New York: Basic Books, 1964).

30. Kahn and Cannell, op. cit., pp. 154–55.

31. Martin Patchen, "Alternative Questionnaire Approaches to the Measurement of Influence in Organization," *Amer. J. Sociol.* 69(1964): 50–52; M. W. Klein, N. H. Berkowitz, and M. F. Malone, "Some Considerations in the Use of Qualitative Judgements as Measures of Organizational Performance," *Sociol. and Soc. Res.* 46(1961): 31–35.

32. In this regard, see F. Herzberg, B. Mausner, and B. Snyderman, *The Motivation to Work* (New York: John Wiley & Sons, 1959); and Hammond, op. cit., 1964.

33. Patchen, op. cit., 1964; Klein, Berkowitz, and Malone, op. cit., 1957; and Frank Friedlander and Hal Pickle, "Components of Effectiveness in Small Organizations," *Admin. Sci. Quart.* 9 (1964): 194–207.

34. Klein, Berkowitz, and Malone, op. cit., 1964.

35. Since the assumptions underlying parametric statistical tests could not be assured in this case, the nonparametric Mann Whitney U Test was utilized in testing for significance. This test required the use of relative ranks of factories within each group rather than their actual scores on the two measures used. The results of the Mann Whitney U Test are presented in summary form in Table 3. As can be seen, the test yielded a $U = 48$ for sugar losses, which is not significant at the .10 level, and $U = 40$ for work hour losses, which is barely significant at the .10 level.

36. Ghorpade, op. cit., pp. 210–12.

37. As the Indian caste system is extremely complex, it is not possible to present all the relevant background essential for fully understanding and interpreting the results of this study. The reader should carefully scrutinize Table 5, which summarizes pictorially the structure and hierarchy of traditional Indian village societies.

38. Some empirical investigations have revealed that ownership and control of the organized private sector is centralized in the hands of less than one hundred families originating primarily from the traditional business or merchant castes of India. See D. R. Gadgil, *Origins of the Modern Indian Business Class* (New York: Institute of Pacific Relations, 1959); Government of India, *Report of Monopolies Inquiry Commission*, vols. I and II (New Delhi: Government of India Press, 1965); R. L. Park and I. Tinker, eds., *Leadership and Political Institutions in India* (Princeton, N.J.: Princeton University Press, 1959); and Ghorpade, op. cit., pp. 7–9.

39. Op. cit., 1961.

40. W. R. Scott, op. cit., 1965.

41. Some extremely frank and enlightening discussions on this point are provided in Hammond, op. cit., 1964.

42. Barney G. Glaser and Anselm L. Strauss, "The Purpose and Credibility of Qualitative Research," *Nursing Res.* 15(1966): 56–61.

43. General discussions pertaining to the role of qualitative analysis in social research are provided in Allen H. Barton and Bo Anderson, "Change in an Organizational System," in Amitai Etzioni, ed., *A Sociological Reader on Complex Organiza-

tions (New York: Holt, Rinehart & Winston, 1969), pp. 540–58; D. P. Cartwright, "The Analysis of Qualitative Material," in *Research Methods in the Behavioral Sciences,* ed. Leon Festinger and D. Katz (New York: Holt, Rinehart & Winston, 1953), pp. 421–70; A. Vidich and J. B. Bensman, "The Validity of Field Data," *Human Organization* 13(1954): 20–27; and H. O. Hicks, "Advantages and Limitations of Quantitative Analysis," *Southwestern Soc. Sci. Quart.* 42(1962): 374–80.

44. Glaser, op. cit., Barton and Anderson, op. cit.

45. Glaser, op. cit., pp. 436–45.

46. Ibid, pp. 439–43.

47. Barton and Anderson, op. cit.

48. R. H. McCleery, "Policy Change in Prison Management," in *A Sociological Reader on Complex Organizations,* ed. Amitai Etzioni (New York: Holt, Rinehart & Winston, 1957), pp. 200–22.

49. R. E. Mitchell, "The Use of Content Analysis for Explanatory Studies," *Public Opinion Quart.* 31(1967): 230–41; Robert G. Murdick, *Business Research: Concept and Practice* (Scranton, Pa.: International Textbook Co., 1969); Bernard Berleson, *Content Analysis in Communications Research* (New York: Free Press, 1952).

50. Julian L. Simon, *Basic Research Methods in the Social Sciences* (New York: Random House, 1969).

51. Frank Friedlander and Eugene Walton, "Positive and Negative Motivations Toward Work, *Admin. Sci. Quart.* 9 (1964): 194–207.

ADDITIONAL READINGS

Additional readings for this part are divided into four sections. The first section contains books and monographs on research methodology. The works of Adams and Preiss, 1960, Cooper, Leavitt and Shelly, 1964, and Vroom, 1967, deal specifically with organizational research methods; the others are general reference sources on research methods in the social and behavioral sciences. The books by Agnew, 1969, and Webb et al., 1966, present some challenging and novel ideas about research methodology.

The second section contains sources which provide discussions of philosophical approaches, research designs, and general problems in social and organizational research. In the philosophical realm, the article by Smith, 1959, is particularly worth pursuing. In this writer's judgment, Smith provides one of the clearest and most insightful discussions on the differences in two major traditions of science: the inductive natural history approach, and the deductive social philosophy approach. French, 1953, Seashore, 1964, Weick, 1965, 1967, and Zelditch, 1961, discuss the role of experiments, while Scott, 1965, describes nonexperimental or field methods in organizational research.

The third section contains sources which deal with problems, methods, and techniques in field research. The work by Bruyn, 1966, is particularly worth pursuing; it presents a comprehensive and elaborate discussion of the methodology of participant observation.

The fourth section contains sources on qualitative analysis in organizational research. The works by Barton and Lazarsfeld, 1961, and Glaser, 1965, contain challenging discussions of the role of qualitative analysis in organizational and social research.

Books on Research Methodology

Adams, R. N., and Preiss, J. J., eds. 1960. *Human organization research: Field relations and techniques.* Homewood, Ill.: Dorsey Press.

Agnew, N. M. and Pyke, Sandra W. 1969. *The science game.* Englewood Cliffs, N.J.: Prentice-Hall.

Beveridge, W. I. B. 1957. *The art of scientific investigation.* New York: Vintage Books.

Blalock, H. M. 1964. *Casual inference in non-experimental research.* Chapel Hill, N.C.: University of North Carolina Press.

Blalock, H. M. and Blalock, Ann B., eds. 1968. *Methodology in social research.* New York: McGraw-Hill Book Co.

Braybrooke, D. 1965. *Philosophical problems of the social sciences.* New York: Macmillan Co.

Campbell, Donald T., and Stanley, Julian C. 1966. *Experimental and quasi-experimental designs for research.* Skokie, Ill: Rand McNally & Co.

Cooper, W. W., Leavitt, H. J., and Shelly, M. W. 1964. *New perspectives in organizational research.* New York: John Wiley & Sons.

Fallding, Harold. 1968. *The sociological task.* Englewood Cliffs, N.J.: Prentice-Hall.

Ferber, Robert, and Verdoorn, P. J. 1962. *Research methods in economics and business.* New York: Macmillan Co.

Festinger, Leon, and Katz, D., eds. 1953. *Research methods in the behavioral sciences.* New York: Holt, Rinehart & Winston.

Glock, C. Y., ed. 1967. *Survey research in the social sciences.* New York: Russell Sage Foundation.

Gould, Julius, and Kolb, W. L., eds. 1964. *A dictionary of the social sciences.* New York: Free Press.

Goode, W. J., and Hatt, P. K. 1952. *Methods in social research.* New York: McGraw-Hill Book Co.

Hammond, Phillip E., ed. 1964. *Sociologists at work.* New York: Basic Books.

Kaplan, Abraham. 1964. *The conduct of inquiry.* San Francisco: Chandler Publishing Co.

Kroeber, Alfred C., ed. 1953. *Anthropology today: An encyclopedia inventory.* Chicago: University of Chicago Press.

Lazarsfeld, P., and Rosenberg, M., eds. 1955. *The language of social research.* New York: Free Press.

Lerner, Daniel, ed. 1962. *The human meaning of the social sciences.* New York: World Publishing Co.

Merten, R. K., and Lazarsfeld, P. F., eds. 1950. *Continuities in social research.* New York: Basic Books.

Rappaport, S., and Wright, H. 1964. *Science: Method and meaning.* New York: Washington Square Press.

Selltiz, Claire, et al. 1959. *Research methods in social relations,* rev. ed. New York: Holt, Rinehart & Winston.

Shostak, A. B. 1966. *Sociology in action.* Homewood, Ill.: Downey Press.

Riley, M. W. 1963. *Sociological research,* vols. I and II. New York: Harcourt, Brace & World.

Vidich, A. J., ed. 1964. *Reflections on community studies.* New York: John Wiley & Sons.

Vroom, Victor H. 1967. *Methods of organizational research.* Pittsburgh: University of Pittsburgh Press.

Webb, Eugene J., Campbell, D. T., Schwartz, R. D., and Sechrest, L. 1966. *Unobtrusive measures: Non-reactive research in the social sciences.* Skokie, Ill.: Rand McNally & Co.

Wolf, H. ed. 1961. *Quantification: A history of the meaning of measurement in the natural and social sciences.* New York: Bobbs-Merrill Co.

Whyte, William Foote. 1955. *Street corner society.* 2d ed. Chicago: University of Chicago Press.

Zetterberg, Hans L. 1954. *On theory and verification in sociology.* New York: Tressler Press.

Philosophical and Conceptual Issues and Problems in Organizational Research

Arensberg, C. M. 1954. "The community study method." *Am. J. Sociol.* 60: 109–24.

Blau, Peter. 1965. "The comparative study of organizations." *Ind. Labor Relations Rev.* 18: 323–38.

Breedlove, J. L., and Krause, M. S. 1966. "Evaluative research design: A social casework illustration." In *Methods of research in psychotherapy,* ed. L. A. Gottschalk and A. H. Auerback, pp. 456-77. New York: Appleton-Century-Crofts.

Burns, Tom. 1967. "The comparative study of organizations." In *Methods of organizational research,* ed. Victor H. Vroom, pp. 113–70. Pittsburgh: University of Pittsburgh Press.

Caro, Francis G. 1969. "Approaches to evaluative research: A review." *Human Organ.* 28: 87–99.

Churchman, C. West, and Emery, F. E. 1966. "On various approaches to the study of organizations." In *Operational research and the social sciences,* ed. J. R. Lawrence, pp. 77–84. London: Tavistock Publications.

Dill, W. R. 1964. "Desegregation or integration? Comments about contemporary research on organizations." In *New perspective in organization research,* ed. W. W. Cooper, H. J. Leavitt, and M. W. Shelley, pp. 39–52. New York: John Wiley & Sons.

Duncan, O. D., and Schnore, L. F. 1959. "Cultural, behavioral and ecological perspectives in the study of social organization." *Am. J. Sociol.* 65: 132–46.

French, J. R. P. 1953. "Experiments in field settings." In *Research methods in the behavioral sciences,* ed. L. Festinger and D. Katz, pp. 98–135. New York: Holt, Rinehart & Winston.

Gardner, B. B., and Whyte, W. F. 1946. "Methods for the study of human relations in industry." *Am. Sociol. Rev.* 11: 506–12.

Jacobson, E., Kahn, R., Mann, F. C., and Morse, Nancy. 1951. "Research in functioning organizations." *J. Soc. Issues* 7: 64–71.

Heyns, R. W., and Lippitt, R. 1954. "Systematic observational techniques." In *Handbook of social psychology,* vol. 1, ed. G. Lindsay, pp. 370–404. Reading, Mass.: Addison-Wesley.

Katz, Daniel. 1953. "Field studies." In *Research methods in the behavioral sciences,* ed. L. Festinger and D. Katz, pp. 15–55. New York: Holt, Rinehart & Winston.

Kelly, Horace O., Jr., and Denney, H. Joe. 1969. "The purpose of pilot studies." *Personnel J.* 48: 48–51.

McGrath, Joseph E. 1964. "Toward a 'theory of method' for research on organizations." In *New perspectives in organization research,* ed. W. W. Cooper, H. J. Leavitt, and M. W. Shelly, pp. 533–56. New York: John Wiley & Sons.

Mechanic, David. 1963. "Some considerations in the methodology of organizational studies." In *The social science of organizations,* ed. H. J. Leavitt, pp. 137–82. Englewood Cliffs, N.J.: Prentice-Hall.

Phillip, D. L., and Thomas, T. P. 1967. "Applications of experimental design in survey settings." *Sociol. Inquiry* 37: 333–40.

Price, James L. 1964. "The use of new knowledge in organizations." *Human Organ.* 23: 224–34.

Scott, W. R. 1965. "Field methods in the study of organizations." In *Handbook of organizations,* ed. James G. March, pp. 261–303. Skokie, Ill.: Rand McNally & Co.

Seashore, Stanley E. 1964. "Field experiments with organizations." *Human Organization* 23: 164–70.

Smith, Marian W. 1959. "Boas' 'Natural History' approach to field method." In *The anthropology of Franz Boas,* ed. Walter Goldschmidt, pp. 46–60. San Francisco: Chandler Press.

Suchman, Edward A. 1967. *Evaluative research: Principles and practices in public service and social action programs.* New York: Russell Sage Foundation.

Weick, Karl E. 1965. "Laboratory experimentation with organizations." In *Handbook of organizations,* ed. James G. March, pp. 194–261. Skokie, Ill.: Rand McNally & Co.

_____. 1967. "Organizations in the laboratory." In *Methods of organizational research,* ed. Victor H. Vroom, pp. 1–56. Pittsburgh: University of Pittsburgh Press.

Whyte, W. F. 1951. "Observational and field work methods." In *Research methods in social relations,* vol. 2, ed. Marie Joheda et al., pp. 493–513. New York: Holt, Rinehart & Winston.

Zelditch, M., and Hopkins, T. K. 1961. "Laboratory experiments with organizations." In *Complex organizations,* ed. Amitai Etzioni, pp. 464–76. New York: Holt, Rinehart & Winston.

Zelditch, M. 1962. "Some methodological problems of field studies." *Am. J. Sociol.* 67: 556–76.

Field Relations Problems, Methods, and Techniques

Argyris, Chris. 1952. "Diagnosing defenses against outsiders." *J. Soc. Issues* 8: 24–34.

_____. 1958. "Creating effective relationships in organizations." *Human Organization* 17: 34–40.

_____. 1961. "Explorations in consulting-client relationships." *Human Organization* 20: 121–38.

Babchuk, N. 1962. "The role of the researcher as participant observer and participant-as-observer, in the field situation." *Human Organization* 21: 225–28.

Back, K. W. 1956. "The well-informed informant." *Human Organization* 14: 30–33.

Becker, H. S. 1957. "Participant observation and interviewing: A comparison." *Human Organization* 16: 28–32.

_____. 1958. "Problems of inference and proof in participant observation." *Am. Sociol. Rev.* 23: 652–60.

Blum, F. H. 1952. "Getting individuals to give information to the outsider." *J. Soc. Issues* 8: 35–42.

Bruyn, Severin T. 1963. "The methodology of participant observation." *Human Organization* 22: 224–35.

_____. 1966. *The human perspective in sociology: The methodology of participant observation*. Englewood Cliffs, N.J.: Prentice-Hall.

Campbell, D. T. 1955. "The informant in quantitative research." *Am. J. Sociol.* 60: 339–42.

Cannell, Charles F., and Kahn, R. L. 1953. "The collection of data by interviewing." In *Research methods in the behavioral sciences,* ed. Leon Festinger and Daniel Katz, pp. 327–80. New York: Holt, Rinehart & Winston.

Dalton, Melville. 1964. "Preconceptions and methods in 'men who manage.' " In *Sociologists at work,* ed. P. E. Hammond, pp. 50–95. New York: Basic Books.

Dean, L. R. 1958. "Interaction, reported and observed: The case of one local union." *Human Organization* 17: 36–47.

Dean, J. P., and Whyte, W. F. 1958. "How do you know if the informant is telling the truth?" *Human Organization* 17: 34–38.

Delany, William. 1960. "Some field notes on the problem of access in organizational research." *Admin. Sci. Quart.* 5: 448–57.

Demerath, N. J. 1952. "Initiating and maintaining research relations in a military organization." *J. Soc. Issues* 8: 11–23.

Dohrenwend, B. S. 1965. "Some effects of open and closed questions." *Human Organization* 24: 175–84.

Dohrenwend, B. S., and Richardson, S. A. 1964. "A use for leading questions in research interviewing." *Human Organization* 22: 76–77.

Enoch, Rex. 1963. "Role of the participant observer in social research." *Southwest Sociol. Ass.* 13: 105–14.

Erikson, Kai T. 1967. "A comment on disguised observation in sociology." *Soc. Problems* 14: 366–73.

Frankenberg, Ronald. 1963. "Participant observers." *New Society* 1: 22–23.

Gallin, B. 1959. "A case for intervention in the field." *Human Organization* 18: 140–47.

Gibb, J. R., and Lippitt, R., eds. 1959. "Consulting with groups and organizations." *J. Soc. Issues* 15: entire issue.

Gold, R. L. 1958. "Roles in sociological field observation." *Soc. Forces* 36: 217–23.

Goldstein, Rhoda L. 1966. "The participant as observer: Sociological gains from public roles." In *Sociology in action,* ed. A. B. Shostak, pp. 141–47. Homewood, Ill.: Dorsey Press.

Hill, R. J., and Hall, N. E. 1963. "A note on rapport and the quality of interview data. *Southwestern Soc. Sci. Quart.* 44: 247–55.

Holmberg, H. R. 1955. "Participant intervention in the field." *Human Organization* 14: 23–26.

Hyman, H. H. 1965. *Interviewing in social research.* Chicago: University of Chicago Press.

Junker, B. H. 1960. *Field work: An introduction to the social sciences.* Chicago: University of Chicago Press.

Kahn, R. L., and Mann, F. 1952. "Developing research relations." *J. Soc. Issues* 8: 4–10.

Mann, F. C. 1951. "Human relations skills in social research." *Human relations* 4: 341–54.

Mann, F. C., and Lippitt, R., eds. 1952. "Social relations skills in field research." *J. Soc. Issues* 8: entire issue.

Miller, S. M. 1952. "The participant observer and over-rapport." *Am. Sociol. Rev.* 17: 97–99.

Namias, J. 1966. "Measuring variation in interviewer performance." *J. Advertising Res.* 6: 8–12.

Olesen, V., and Whittaker, E. W. 1967. "Role making in participant observation: Processes in the researcher-actor relationship." *Human Organization* 26: 273–81.

Paul, B. D. 1953. "Interview techniques in field relations." In *Anthropology today,* ed. A. L. Kroeber, pp. 430–51. Chicago: University of Chicago Press.

Phillips, H. P. 1960. "Problems of translation and meaning in field work." *Human Organization* 18: 184–92.

Richardson, S. A. 1960. "The use of leading questions in non-schedule interviewing." *Human Organization* 19: 86–89.

Richardson, S. A., Dobrenwend, B. S., and Klein, D. 1965. *Interviewing: Its forms and functions.* New York: Basic Books.

Rodman, Hyman, and Kolodny, Ralph. 1964. "Organizational strains in the researcher-practitioner relationship." *Human Organization* 23: 171–82.

Roth, J. A. 1962. "Comments on 'secret observation' " *Soc. Problems* 9: 283–84.

Roy, D. F. 1965. "The role of the researcher in the study of social conflict." *Human Organization* 24: 262–75.

Scott, W. R. 1963. "Field work in a formal organization." *Human Organization* 22: 162–68.

Schman, Howard. 1966. "The random probe: A technique for evaluating the validity of closed questions." *Am. Sociol. Rev.* 31: 218–22.

Schwartz, M. S., and Schwartz, C. G. 1955. "Problems in participant observation." *Am. J. Sociol.* 60: 343–53.

Sjoberg, Gideon. 1957. "The interviewee as a marginal man." *Southwestern Soc. Sci. Quart.* 38: 124–32.

Sullivan, M. A., Queen, S. A., and Patrick, R. C. 1958. Participant observation as employed in the study of a military training program." *Am. Sociol. Rev.* 23: 660–67.

Trow, M. A. 1957. "Comment on participant observation and interviewing." *Human Organization* 16: 33–45.

Wax, Rosalie. 1952. "Reciprocity in field work." *Human Organization* 11: 34–41.

———. 1957. "Twelve years later: An analysis of field experience." *Am. J. Sociol.* 63: 133–42.

Whyte, William Foote. 1953. "Interviewing for organizational research." *Human Organization* 12: 15–22.

Qualitative Analysis

Angell, R. C., and Freedman, Ronald. 1953. "The uses of documents, records, census materials and indices." In *Research methods in the behavioral sciences,* ed. Leon Festinger and Daniel Katz, pp. 300–326. New York: Holt, Rinehart & Winston.

Barton, A. H., and Lazarsfeld, P. F. 1961. "Some functions of qualitative analysis in social research." In *Sociology: The progress of a decade,* ed. S. M. Lipset and Neil J. Smelser, pp. 50–67. Englewood Cliffs, N.J.: Prentice-Hall.

Barton, Allen H., and Anderson, Bo. 1968. "Change in an organizational system: Formalization of a qualitative study." In *A sociological reader on complex organizations,* 2d. ed., ed. Amitai Etzioni, pp. 540–58. New York: Holt, Rinehart & Winston.

Becker, H. S. 1958. "Problems in inference and proof in participant observation." *Am. Sociol. Rev.* 23: 652–60.

Becker, H. S., and Geer, B. 1960. "Participant observation: The analysis of qualitative data." In *Human organization research,* ed. R. N. Adams and J. J. Preiss, pp. 267–89. Homewood, Ill.: Dorsey Press.

Berelson, Bernard. 1952. *Content analysis in communications research.* New York: Free Press.

Blalock, H. M. 1967. "Casual inferences in natural experiments: Some complications and matching designs." *Sociometry* 30: 300–315.

Byers, Paul. 1964. "Still photography in the systematic recording and analysis of behavioral data." *Human Organization* 22: 78–84.

Capecchi, Vittorio, 1963. "Qualitative and quantitative analysis in sociology." *Sociol.* 12: 171–200.

Cartwright, D. P. 1953. "The analysis of qualitative material." In *Research methods in the behavioral sciences,* ed. Leon Festinger and D. Katz, pp. 421–70. New York: Holt, Rinehart & Winston.

Chapple, Eliot D. 1962. "Quantitative analysis of complex organizational systems." *Human Organization* 21: 67–87.

Coleman, J. S. 1958. "Relational analysis: The study of social structure with survey methods." *Human Organization* 17: 28–36.

Dibble, Vernon K. 1963. "Four types of inference from documents to events." *Hist. Theory* 3: 203–21.

Glaser, Barney G. 1962. "Secondary analysis: A strategy for the use of knowledge from research elsewhere." *Soc. Problems* 10: 70–74.

_____. 1965. "The constant comparative method of qualitative analysis." *Soc. Problems* 12: 436–45.

Glaser, B. G., and Strauss, A. L. 1966. "The purpose and credibility of qualitative rsearch." *Nursing Res.* 15: 56–61.

Hay, Robert D. 1969. "Use of modified semantic differentials to evaluate formal organizational structure." *Acad. Manage. J.* 12: 247–57.

Hicks, H. C. 1962. "Advantages and limitations of quantitative analysis." *Southwestern Soc. Sci. Quart.* 42: 374–80.

Leunbach, Gustav. 1961. "On quantitative models for qualitative data." *Acta Sociol.* 5: 144–56.

Melbin, Murray. 1954a. "An interaction recording device for participant observers." *Human Organization* 13: 29–33.

_____. 1954b. "The action interaction chart." *Human Organization* 13: 34–35.

Miller, F. B. 1958. "Situational interaction—a worthwhile concept." *Human Organization* 17: 37–47.

Mitchell, R. E. 1967. "The use of content analysis for explanatory studies." *Public Opinion Quart.* 31: 230–41.

Price, James L. 1968. "Design of proof in organizational research." *Admin. Sci. Quart.* 13: 121–66.

Psathas, George. 1966. "Problems and prospects in the use of a computer system of content analysis." *Sociol. Quart.* 7: 449–68.

Richardson, S. A. 1953. "A framework for reporting field relations experiences." *Human Organization.* 12: 31–37.

Schoenherr, R. A., and Fritz, Judith. 1967. "Some new techniques in organization research." *Public Personnel Rev.* 28: 151–61.

Seaman, M., Evans, J. W., and Rogers, L. E. 1960. "The measurement of stratification in formal organizations." *Human Organization* 19: 90–96.

Selvin, H. C. 1966. "Data dredging procedures in survey analysis." *Am. Statistician* 20: 20–22.

Smith, Keith. 1953. "Distribution-free statistical methods and the concept of power efficiency." In *Research methods in the behavioral sciences,* ed. Leon Festinger and Daniel Katz, pp. 536–77. New York: Holt, Rinehart & Winston.

Vidich, A., and Bensman, J. 1954. "The validity of field data." *Human Organization* 13: 20–27.

LIST OF REFERENCES CITED

Abegglen, James C. 1958. *The japanese factory.* New York: Free Press.

Adams, R. N., and Preiss, J. J. eds. 1960. *Human organization research: Field relations and techniques.* Homewood, Ill.: Dorsey Press.

Argyris, Chris. 1952. "Diagnosing defenses against outsiders." *J. Soc. Issues* 8: 24–34.

_____. 1958. "Creating effective relationships in organizations." *Human Organization* 17: 34–40.

_____. 1961. "Explorations in consulting-client relationships." *Human Organization* 20: 121–38.

_____. 1962. *Interpersonal competence and organizational effectiveness.* Homewood, Ill.: Dorsey Press.

_____. 1964. "T-groups for organizational effectiveness." *Harvard Bus. Rev.* (Mar.-Apr.): 60–74.

Back, K. W. 1956. "The well-informed informant." *Human Organization* 14: 30–33.

Barton, Allen H., and Anderson, Bo. 1969." Change in an organizational system: Formalization of a qualitative study." In *A sociological reader on complex organizations,* 2d. ed., Amitai Etzioni, pp. 540–58. New York: Holt, Rinehart & Winston.

Baum, Bernard, and Burack, Elmer. 1969. "Information technology, manpower development, and organizational performance." *Acad. Manage. J.* 12: 279–92.

Berelson, Bernard. 1952. *Content analysis in communications research.* New York: Free Press.

Berelson, Bernard, and Steiner, Gary A. 1964. *Human behavior: An inventory of scientific findings.* New York: Harcourt, Brace & World.

Berrien, F. Kenneth. 1968. *General and social systems.* New Brunswick, N.J.: Rutgers University Press.

Blau, Peter M. 1955. *The dynamics of bureaucracy.* Chicago: University of Chicago Press.

Blau, Peter M., and Scott, W. Richard. 1962. *Formal organizations.* San Francisco: Chandler Publishing Co.

Bruyn, Severin T. 1963. "The methodology of participant observation." *Human Organization* 22: 224–35.

_____. 1966. *The human perspective in sociology: The methodology of participant observation.* Englewood Cliffs, N.J.: Prentice-Hall.

Burns, Tom. 1966. "On the plurality of social systems." In *Operational research and the social sciences,* ed. J. R. Lawrence, pp. 165–77. London: Tavistock Publications.

Caplow, Theodore. 1953. "Criteria of organizational success." *Soc. Forces* 32: 1–9.

Caro, Francis G. 1969. "Approaches to evaluative research: A review." *Human Organization* 28: 87–99.

Cartwright, D. P. 1953. "The analysis of qualitative material." In *Research methods in the behavioral sciences,* ed. Leon Festinger and D. Katz, pp. 421–70. New York: Holt, Rinehart & Winston.

Christman, Luther. 1968. "The role of nursing in organizational effectiveness." *Hospital Admin.* 13: 40–47.

Churchman, C. West, and Emery, F. E. 1966. "On various approaches to the study of organizations. In *Operational research and the social sciences,* ed. J. R. Lawrence, pp. 77–84. London: Tavistock Publications.

Cressey, Donald R., ed. 1961. *The prison: Studies in institutional and organizational change.* New York: Holt, Rinehart & Winston.

Dalton, Melville. 1959. *Men who manage.* New York: John Wiley & Sons.

_____. 1964. "Preconceptions and methods in 'Men Who Manage.' " In *Sociologists at work,* ed. P. E. Hammond, pp. 50–95. New York: Basic Books.

Delany, William. 1960. "Some field notes on the problem of access in organizational research." *Admin. Sci. Quart.* 5: 448–57.

Educational Testing Service. 1968. "Managing organizational effectiveness," *Proc. Executive Study Conference.* Princeton, N.J.: Educational Testing Service.

Etzioni, Amitai. 1959. "Authority structure and organizational effectiveness." *Admin. Sci. Quart.* 4: 43–67.

_____. 1960. "Two approaches to organizational analysis: A critique and a suggestion." *Admin. Sci. Quart.* 5: 257–78.

_____. 1964. *Modern organizations.* Englewood Cliffs, N.J.: Prentice-Hall.

Friedlander, Frank, and Pickle, Hal. 1968. "Components of effectiveness in small organizations." *Admin. Sci. Quart.* 13: 257–78.

Friedlander, Frank, and Walton, Eugene. 1964. "Positive and negative motivations toward work." *Admin. Sci. Quart.* 9: 194–207.

Gadgil, D. R. 1959. *Origins of the modern Indian business class.* New York: Institute of Pacific Relations.

Georgopoulous, Basil S. 1965. "Normative structure variables and organizational behavior: A comparative study." *Human Relations* 18: 155–70.

Georgopoulous, Basil S., and Tannenbaum, Arnold S. 1957. "A study of organizational effectiveness." *Am. Sociol. Rev.* 22: 534–40.

Ghorpade, J. V. 1968. "Study of relative effectiveness of joint stock and cooperative sugar factories located in Maharashtra, India." Unpub. Ph.D. diss., University of California, Los Angeles.

_____. 1970. "Study of organizational effectiveness: Two prevailing viewpoints." *Pacific Sociol. Rev.* 13: 31–40.

Glaser, Barney G. 1965. "The constant comparative method of qualitative analysis." *Soc. Problems* 12: 436–45.

Glaser, Barney G., and Strauss, Anselm L. 1966. "The purpose and credibility of qualitative research." *Nursing Res.* 15: 56–61.

Gould, Julius, and Kolb, W. L., eds. 1964. *A dictionary of the social sciences.* New York: Free Press.

Gouldner, Alvin W. 1957. "Cosmopolitans and locals: Toward an analysis of latent social roles—I." *Admin. Sci. Quart.* 2: 282–92.

Grusky, O. 1963. "Managerial succession and organizational effectiveness." *Am. J. Sociol.* 69: 21–30.

Hammond, Phillip E., ed. 1964. *Sociologists at work.* New York: Basic Books.

Herzberg, F., Mausner, B., and Snyderman, B. 1959. *The motivation to work.* New York: John Wiley & Sons.

Hicks, H. C. 1962. "Advantages and limitations of quantitative analysis." *Southwestern Soc. Sci. Quart.* 42: 374–80.

India, Government of. 1965. *Report of monopolies inquiry commission,* vols. I and II. New Delhi, India: Government of India Press.

Jaques, Elliott. 1952. *The changing culture of the factory.* New York: Dryden.

_____. 1964. "Social analysis and the glacier project." *Human Relations* 17: 361–75.

Jones, Halsey R. 1969. "A study of organization performance for experimental structures of two, three and four levels." *Acad. Manage. J.* 12: 351–66.

Kaczka, Eugene, and Kirk, Roy V. 1967. "Managerial climate, work groups, and organizational performance." *Admin. Sci. Quart.* 12: 253–72.

Kahn, Robert L., and Cannell, Charles F. 1968. "Interviewing." *Encyclopedia of the social sciences,* pp. 149–61. New York: Macmillan Co.

Katz, Daniel, and Kahn, Robert L. 1966. *The social psychology of organizations.* New York: John Wiley & Sons.

Klein, M. W., Berkowitz, N. H., and Malone, M. F. 1961. "Some considerations in the use of qualitative judgments as measures of organizational performance." *Sociol. Soc. Res.* 46: 26–35.

Krech, D., Crutchfield, R. S., and Ballachy, E. L. 1962. *Individual in society.* New York: McGraw-Hill Book Co.

Kroeber, Alfred C. ed. 1953. *Anthropology today: An encyclopedic inventory.* Chicago: University of Chicago Press.

Leavitt, Harold J., ed. 1963. *The social science of organizations.* Englewood Cliffs, N.J.: Prentice-Hall.

Lewis Lionel S. 1967. "On prestige and loyalty of university faculty." *Admin. Sci. Quart.* 11: 629–42.

Lipset, Seymour M., Trow, M. A., and Coleman, James S. 1956. *Union democracy.* New York: Free Press.

McCleery, R. H. 1957. "Policy change in prison management." In *A sociological reader on complex organizations,* 2d ed., ed. Amitai Etzioni, pp. 200–222. New York: Holt, Rinehart & Winston.

McGrath, Joseph E. 1964. "Toward a 'theory of method' for research on organizations." In *New perspectives in organization research,* ed. W. W. Cooper, H. J. Leavitt, and M. W. Shelly, pp. 533–56. New York: John Wiley & Sons.

Mechanic, David. 1963. "Some considerations in the methodology of organizational studies." In *The social science of organizations,* ed. H. J. Leavitt, pp. 137–82. Englewood Cliffs, N.J.: Prentice-Hall.

Merton, Robert K. 1957. *Social theory and social structure.* New York: Free Press.

Michels, Robert. 1962. *Political parties.* New York: Crowell Collier & Macmillan.

Mitchell, R. E. 1967. "The use of content analysis for explanatory studies." *Public Opinion Quart.* 31: 230–41.

Morse, Nancy C., and Reimer, Everett. 1956. "The experimental change of a major organizational variable." *J. Abnormal Soc. Psychol.* 52: 120–29.

Murdick, Robert G. 1969. *Business research: Concept and practice.* Scranton, Pa.: International Textbook Company.

Park, R. L., and Tinker, I., eds. 1959. *Leadership and political institutions in India.* Princeton, N.J.: Princeton University Press.

Parsons, Talcott. 1959. "Suggestions for a sociological approach to the theory of organizations—I." *Admin. Sci. Quart.* 1: 63–85.

_____. 1960. "The analysis of formal organizations." In *Structure and process in modern societies,* pp. 16–96. New York: Free Press.

Patchen, Martin. 1964. "Alternative questionnaire approaches to the measurement of influence in organizations." *Am. J. Sociol.* 69: 41–52.

Perrow, Charles. 1961. "The analysis of goals in complex organizations." *Am. Social Rev.* 26: 854–66.

Price, James L. 1963. "The impact of governing boards on organizational effectiveness and morale." *Admin. Sci. Quart.* 8: 361–78.

_____. 1968. *Organizational effectiveness: An inventory of propositions.* Homewood, Ill.: Richard D. Irwin.

Rice, A. K. 1958. *Productivity and social organization: The ahmedabad experiment.* London: Tavistock Publications.

_____. 1963. *The enterprise and its environment.* London: Tavistock Publications.

Roberts, K., Miles, R. E., and Blankenship, L. V. 1968. "Organizational leadership, satisfaction and productivity: A comparative analysis." *Acad. Manage. J.* 11: 401–14.

Rushing, William A. 1968. "The effects of industry size and division of labor on administration." *Admin. Sci. Quart.* 12: 273–95.

Schein, Edgar H. 1965. *Organizational psychology.* Englewood Cliffs, N.J.: Prentice-Hall.

Scott, W. G. 1961. "Organization theory: An overview and an appraisal." *J. Acad. Manage.* 4: 7–26.

Scott, W. R. 1963. "Field work in a formal organization." *Human Organization* 22: 162–68.

_____. 1965. "Field methods in the study of organizations." In *Handbook of organizations,* ed. J. G. March, pp. 261–304. Skokie, Ill.: Rand McNally & Co.

Seashore, Stanley E. 1964. "Field experiments with organizations." *Human Organization* 23: 164–70.

_____. 1965. "Criteria of organizational effectiveness." *Mich. Bus. Rev.* 17: 26–30.

Selznick, Phillip. 1948a. "Foundations of the theory of organizations." *Am. Sociol. Rev.* 13: 25–35.

_____. 1948b. *TVA and the grass roots.* Berkeley, Calif.: University of California Press.

Siegel, Sidney. 1956. *Non-parametric statistics for the behavioral sciences.* New York: McGraw-Hill Book Co.

Simon, Julian L. 1969. *Basic research methods in social science.* New York: Random House.

Sjoberg, Gideon. 1957. "The interviewee as a marginal man." *Southwestern Soc. Sci. Quart.* 38: 124–32.

Thompson, James D. 1967. *Organizations in action.* New York: McGraw-Hill Book Co.

Thompson, J. D., and McEwen, W. J. 1958. "Organizational goals and environment: Goal-setting as an interaction process." *Am. Sociol. Rev.* 23: 23–31.

Tittle, Charles R., and Tittle, Drollene F. 1964. "Structural handicaps to organizational effectiveness. A case study." *Proc. Southwest Sociol. Ass.* 14: 118–27.

Vidich, A., and Bensman, J. 1954. "The validity of field data." *Human Organization* 13: 20–27.

Von Bertalanfty, Ludwig. 1950. "An outline of general system theory." *Brit. J. Phil. Sci.* 1: 134–65.

Vroom, Victor H. 1967. *Methods of organizational research.* Pittsburgh: University of Pittsburgh Press.

Webb, E. J., Campbell, D. T., Schwartz, R. D., and Sechrest, L. 1966. *Unobtrusive measures: Non-reactive research in the social sciences.* Skokie, Ill.: Rand McNally & Co.

Whyte, William Foote. 1951. "Observational field work methods." In Marie Jahoda et al., *Research methods in social relation,* vol. 2, pp. 493–513. New York: Holt, Rinehart, & Winston.

_____. 1955 *Street corner society: The social structure of an Italian slum,* 2d ed. Chicago: University of Chicago Press.

_____. 1960. "Interviewing in field research." In *Human organization research: Field relations and techniques,* ed. R. N. Adams and J. J. Preiss, pp. 352–74. Homewood, Ill.: Dorsey Press.

Yuchtman, Ephraim. 1966. "A study of organizational effectiveness." Unpubl. Ph.D. diss., University of Michigan, Ann Arbor.

Zald, Mayer N. 1967. "Urban differentiation, characteristics of boards of directors and organizational effectiveness." *Am. J. Sociol.* 73: 261–72.

Zelditch, M. 1962. "Some methodological problems of field studies." *Am. J. Sociol.* 67: 566–76.

25-401